american classics

*the discographies of
leonard bernstein
and eugene ormandy*

compiled by john hunt
dedicated to syd gray

American classics: an introduction

As far as recordings of classical music in North America are concerned, two figures dominated in the boom years of the fifties, sixties and seventies: Leonard Bernstein (1918-1990), the first American-born musician to achieve pre-eminence in the field both as composer and interpreter; and in complete contrast Eugene Ormandy (1899-1985), the European émigré who built his entire conducting career in the New World and who inherited the mantle of no less a figure than Leopold Stokowski.

A recent annotator for some of Bernstein's music films conveniently sums up his progress as a classical recording artist :- "The first phase precedes his appointment as sole music director of the New York Philharmonic in 1958 when, as a podium part-timer, he specialised in contemporary novelties before setting down his first established classics for American Decca in 1953. The maestro of the second phase made over 200 records for American Columbia, latterly CBS, galvanising his forces into enthusiastic accounts of esoterica and invigorating renditions of standard works. A third, European period, capitalising on his long-standing relationship with the Vienna Philharmonic, yielded weightier revivifications of mainstream repertoire, guaranteed worldwide distribution by Deutsche Grammophon………..
"equally crucial in the development of his music making was the contract Bernstein signed on 19 January 1971 with Munich-based Unitel to film Mahler and Brahms. Employing the Vienna Philharmonic whenever feasible, the films were made during concert performances, a departure for the company, as largely for the conductor himself. Live taping with the 35mm film magazines of the day posed logistical and technical problems, yet over the next 20 years Bernstein would create and perform in many such sessions, rarely returning to conventional studio work."

Ormandy's career pattern was more conventional if no less extensive. Coming to America from his native Hungary in the early twenties, his earliest work was on his chosen instrument, the violin, in various dance music combinations before gaining conducting work in New York and Minneapolis. With the orchestra of the latter city he entered into his first contract with RCA Victor as conductor, transferring to Columbia once he was established in Philadelphia as Stokowski's successor. Broadly speaking, the repertoire made for shellac (78rpm) records was remade for LP in the late forties and early fifties, remade for a third time for the stereo LP era, and then for yet a fourth time when orchestra and conductor returned to the RCA Victor stable around 1970. One Philadelphia tradition successfully carried on from the Stokowski era was the performance and recording of orchestral transcriptions, although Ormandy does not appear to have been personally involved in their preparation to the same extent that his predecessor was.

I have aimed to include as many North American and European catalogue numbers in the various formats as possible (78, 45, LP, CD and video) but in addition to commercially made recordings have embraced the increasing number of privately issued CDs of concert and radio broadcasts now being made available both in Europe and the USA by individuals such as Russ Oppenheim, Terry Ellsworth and the label Disco Archivia. In the case of the latter company, information available on the internet does not always make clear if a recording is taken from the live concert or copied from the commercial recording made around the same time. Even for some commercial recordings from the major companies it was not possible to give a precise date: as always, I am happy to hear from collectors who can fill in gaps in the available data.

In the case of Leonard Bernstein, I have not attempted to embrace fully his work as presenter and educator in the many talks and lectures given for television. However, at the end of his discography a supplement does list those of the famed Young Peoples' Concerts as have been commercially published both in VHS format and subsequently for DVD video.

The reader may find it useful to have a summary of the main recording venues which were available to our conductors when working for Columbia and RCA Victor :-

New York venues
Columbia recording studios
RCA Victor recording studios
NBC broadcasting studios
Carnegie Hall
Philharmonic Hall / *later known as Avery Fisher Hall*
Manhattan Centre
St George's Hotel Brooklyn
Metropolitan Opera / *both old and new houses*
Philadelphia venues
Academy of Music
Town Hall / *formerly known as Scottish Rite Temple*
Broadwood Hotel / *formerly known as Philadelphia Athletic Club*
Philadelphia Metropolitan Opera

For my initial research on Ormandy I was grateful to an internet discography compiled by Kenji Yokota. A number of other publications have provided useful background information on the discographies of both conductors, including :-

New York Philharmonic: discography of the authorised recordings by James H. North/*Scarecrow Press 2006*

Those Fabulous Philadelphians by Herbert Kupferberg/ *W.H. Allen 1970*

Bernstein by Paul Robinson/*Macdonald 1982*

Bernstein: the television work/*Museum of Broadcasting 1985*

Additional help has been forthcoming from John Baker, Dennis Davis, Michael H. Gray, the late Syd Gray, John Hancock, Roderick Krüsemann, Alan Lambert, Bob Matthew-Walker and James Simpson.

John Hunt 2009

American Classics
Published by John Hunt.
© 2009 John Hunt
reprinted 2009
ISBN 978-1-901395-24-2

Sole distributors:
Travis & Emery,
17 Cecil Court,
London, WC2N 4EZ,
United Kingdom.
(+44) 20 7 459 2129.
sales@travis-and-emery.com

The discographies of Leonard Bernstein and Eugene Ormandy

Contents
The discography of Leonard Bernstein/*page 7*
The discography of Eugene Ormandy/*page 181*

KENNETH ALFORD (1881-1945)
colonel bogey march
recorded on 20 october 1970 in philharmonic hall

new york philharmonic	lp: columbia M 30943/MG 35919 cd: MLK 44723/MDK 45734/ SMK 63154/SMK 64075/SBK 89305

THOMAS ARNE (1710-1778)
rule britannia!
recorded on 12 october 1970 in philharmonic hall

new york philharmonic	lp: columbia M 30943/MG 35919 cd: MDK 45734/SMK 63154/ SBK 89305

LARRY AUSTIN (born 1930)
improvisations for orchestra and jazz soloists
recorded on 13 january 1964 in philharmonic hall

new york philharmonic	lp: columbia ML 6133/MS 6733

JACOB AVSHALOMOV (born 1919)
sinfonietta
recorded on 11 march 1957 in the columbia studios new york city

columbia symphony	lp: columbia ML 5412 cd: russ oppenheim ROCD 0083

JOHANN SEBASTIAN BACH (1685-1750)
matthäus-passion
recorded on 23-24 april 1962 in the manhattan centre

new york
philharmonic
collegiate chorale
transfiguration
church choir
addison, allen, lloyd,
bressler, wildermann,
bell

lp: columbia M3L-292/M3S-692
cd: SM2K 60727
lp editions included a seven-inch disc with bernstein discussing musical and dramatic structure of the work

magnificat
recorded on 18 december 1959 in the columbia studios new york city

new york
philharmonic
schola cantorum
venora, tourel,
oberlin, farrow,
bressler

lp: columbia ML 5775/MS 6375/
BRG 72085/SBRG 72085/book of the
month club 61-7554
cd: SBK 60261

recorded in 1976 at a concert in symphony hall boston

boston symphony
orchestra and chorus
valente, killebrew,
riegel, cheek

cd: disco archivia 553

televised in march 1977 in saint augustine's church kilburn

english bach festival
orchestra and chorus
mory, parker,
mitchinson, hudson

unpublished video recording

brandenburg concerto no 3
recorded on 12 april 1957 in the columbia studios new york city

new york
philharmonic

columbia unpublished

bach/**brandenburg concerto no 5**
recorded on 5 december 1959 at a concert in carnegie hall
new york philharmonic
bernstein, harpsichord
wummer, flute
stern, violin

cd: new york philharmonic NYP 2003

piano concerto bwv 1052
recorded on 11 april 1957 in the columbia studios new york city
columbia symphony
gould

lp: columbia ML 5211/philips A01357L
cd: SMK 87760/SM2K 52591/
SX7K 52562/88697 148102
recording completed on 30 april 1957

violin concerto bwv 1042
recorded on 7 february 1966 in philharmonic hall
new york philharmonic
stern

lp: columbia ML 6349/MS 6949/
BRG 72531/SBRG 72531
cd: SMK 60211/SMK 66471/
SX11K 67193
recording completed on 16 february 1966

concerto for two violins bwv 1043
recorded on 18 may 1976 at a concert in carnegie hall
new york philharmonic
menuhin, stern
bernstein conducts
from the harpsichord

lp: columbia M2X 34256/79200
cd: SM2K 46743/SK 93017

concerto for violin and oboe bwv 1060
recorded on 16 february 1966 in philharmonic hall
new york philharmonic
stern, gomberg

lp: columbia ML 6349/MS 6949/
M2 42228/BRG 72531/SBRG 72531
cd: MK 42258/SMK 60211/SMK 66471/
SX11K 67193/SK 93017

EDWIN BAGLEY (1857-1922)
national emblem march
recorded on 12 october 1970 in philharmonic hall

new york	lp: columbia M 30943/MG 35919
philharmonic	cd: MDK 45734/SMK 63154/
	SBK 89305

SAMUEL BARBER (1910-1981)
violin concerto
recorded on 27 april 1964 in the manhattan centre

new york	lp: columbia ML 6113/MS 6713/
philharmonic	MP 39070/BRG 72345/
stern	SBRG 72345/61621
	cd: SMK 63088/SMK 64506/
	SX9K 67194/SK 90390

second essay for orchestra
recorded on 24 october 1959 at a concert in carnegie hall

new york	cd: new york philharmonic NYP 2003
philharmonic	

adagio for strings
recorded on 12 january 1971 in philharmonic hall

new york	lp: columbia M 30573/MG 31155/
philharmonic	MY 38484
	cd: MYK 38484/SFK 46715/SMK 47567/
	MLK 62617/SMK 63088/SK 90390/
	SK 92726/S3K 90578/tutti 2

recorded on 24 july 1982 at a concert in the davies symphony hall

los angeles	lp: deutsche grammophon 2532 083
philharmonic	cd: 413 3242/427 8062/439 5282/
	471 7372/477 6352

BELA BARTOK (1881-1945)
concerto for orchestra
recorded on 30 november 1959 in saint george's hotel brooklyn
new york	lp: columbia ML 5471/MS 6140/
philharmonic	BRG 72543/SBRG 72543
	cd: MK 44707/SMK 47510/SMK 60730

music for strings, percussion and celesta
recorded on 20 march 1961 in the manhattan centre
new york	lp: columbia ML 5979/ML 6356/
philharmonic	MS 6579/MS 6956/MP 38779/
	book of the month club 81-6407
	cd: MK 44707/SMK 47510/SMK 60730

recorded on 16 november 1983 at a concert in the erkel theatre budapest
sinfonie-orchester	cd: hungaroton HCD 12631
des bayerischen	*also unpublished video recording*
rundfunks	

piano concerto no 2
recorded on 19 january 1967 in philharmonic hall
new york	lp: columbia MS 7145
philharmonic	cd: SM2K 47511
entremont	

piano concerto no 3
recorded on 17 january 1967 in philharmonic hall
new york	lp: columbia MS 7145
philharmonic	cd: SM2K 47511
entremont	

bartok/**violin concerto no 2**
recorded on 26 january 1958 in the columbia studios new york city
new york lp: columbia ML 5283/MS 6002/
philharmonic MP 38886/book of the month club
stern 81-6407/philips fontana 698 020CL/
876 000CY
cd: SM2K 47511/SMK 64502/
SX9K 67194

the two rhapsodies for violin and orchestra
recorded on 16 april 1962 in the manhattan centre
new york lp: columbia ML 5773/MS 6373/
philharmonic MP 38886/BRG 72070/SBRG 72070
stern cd: SM2K 47511/SMK 64502/
SX9K 67194

concerto for two pianos and percussion
recorded on 14 may 1966 in philharmonic hall
members of new lp: columbia ML 6356/MS 6956/
york philharmonic BRG 72543/SBRG 72543
gold, fizdale cd: SM2K 47511

LUDWIG VAN BEETHOVEN (1770-1827)
symphony no 1
recorded on 20 january 1964 in the manhattan centre
new york lp: columbia MS 7084/D8S 815/
philharmonic MY 38469/61901
cd: MYK 38469/MK 42219/SMK 47514/
SMK 60967/SB6K 87885
recording completed on 27 january 1964

televised between 9-12 november 1978 at concerts in the musikverein vienna
wiener lp: deutsche grammophon 2531 308/
philharmoniker 2740 216/410 8361
cd: 419 4342/423 4812/447 9002/
447 9012/474 9242
vhs video: 072 1773
dvd video: 073 4497/073 4500

beethoven/**symphony no 2**
recorded on 6 january 1964 in the manhattan centre
new york philharmonic
lp: columbia MS 7084/D8S 815/61901
cd: MK 42219/SMK 47515/SMK 61835/SB6K 87885

televised between 4-6 february 1978 at concerts in the musikverein vienna
wiener philharmoniker
lp: deutsche grammophon 2531 309/2740 216/410 8361
cd: 423 4812/447 9002/447 9022/474 9242
vhs video: 072 1773
dvd video: 073 4498/073 4500

symphony no 3 "eroica"
recorded on 22 june 1953 in carnegie hall
new york philharmonic
lp: american decca DL 9697/musical appreciation society
cd: deutsche grammophon 477 0002/membran documents 222 370/andromeda ANDRCD 5115
orchestra described for this recording as stadium concerts orchestra; musical appreciation society and deutsche grammophon issues also include bernstein's spoken analysis

recorded on 27 january 1964 in the manhattan centre
new york philharmonic
lp: columbia ML 6174/MS 6774/D2L 349/D2S 749/D8S 815/M 31822/D3M 33273/BRG 72426/SBRG 72426/61902
cd: MYK 36719/MK 42220/SMK 47514/SMK 60692/SX10K 89750/SB6K 87885

televised between 4-6 february 1978 at concerts in the musikverein vienna
wiener philharmoniker
lp: deutsche grammophon 2531 310/2740 216
cd: 413 7782/423 4812/431 0242/431 0502/431 1972/447 9002/447 9032/474 9242
vhs video: 072 1113
dvd video: 073 4499/073 4500

televised in 1983 at a concert for pope john paul in the vatican city
santa cecilia orchestra
unpublished video recording

14
beethoven/**symphony no 4**
recorded on 7 may 1962 in the manhattan centre

new york philharmonic	lp: columbia MS 7412/D8S 815/61903 cd: MK 42221/SMK 47516/ SMK 63079/SB6K 87885

televised between 30 october-2 november 1978 at concerts in the musikverein vienna

wiener philharmoniker	lp: deutsche grammophon 2531 308/ 2740 216 cd: 423 0492/423 4812/447 9002/ 447 9042/463 4682/474 9242 vhs video: 072 1783 dvd video: 073 4499/073 4500

beethoven/**symphony no 5**
televised on 14 november 1954 in the columbia studios new york city
symphony of the air
unpublished video recording
included bernstein's spoken introduction

recorded on 25 september 1961 in the manhattan centre
new york philharmonic
lp: columbia ML 5868/MS 6468/
MSC 6468/D8S 815/M4X 821/
M 31810/D3M 32273/MY 36719/
MYX 39141/60106/61904
cd: MYK 36719/MK 42221/
SMK 47516/SXK 47645/SMK 63079/
SB6K 87885/82876 787402
most issues included bernstein's spoken analysis of the first movement

televised in 1970 in nagoya during a japanese tour
new york philharmonic
unpublished video recording

televised on 17 october 1976 at a concert in the herkulessaal munich
sinfonieorchester des bayerischen rundfunks
lp: deutsche grammophon 2721 153
cd: 477 6690
also unpublished video recording

televised on 8-9 september 1977 at concerts in the musikverein vienna
wiener philharmoniker
lp: deutsche grammophon 2531 311/
2740 216
cd: 419 4352/423 4812/
447 9022/474 9242
dvd video: 073 4499/073 4500

recorded on 22 october 1980 at a concert in the musikverein vienna
wiener philharmoniker
cd: live classics best (japan) LCB 105/
disco archivia 561
disco archivia edition is dated 1979

beethoven/**symphony no 6 "pastoral"**
recorded on 13 may 1963 in the manhattan centre
new york philharmonic   lp: columbia ML 5949/MS 6549/ D8S 815/M3X 33020/ D3M 33273/61905
cd: MK 42222/SMK 47517/ SMK 60557/SB6K 87885

televised in 1973 in the wgbh studios boston
boston symphony   unpublished video recording

televised between 9-12 november 1978 at concerts in the musikverein vienna
wiener philharmoniker   lp: deutsche grammophon 2531 312/2740 216
cd: 413 7792/423 4812/431 0252/ 431 0502/431 1972/447 9002/ 447 9012/463 4682/474 9242
vhs video: 072 1013
dvd video: 073 4498/073 4500

beethoven/**symphony no 7**
recorded on 26 april 1957 at a concert in symphony hall boston
boston   cd: living stage LS 1081/
symphony   dynamic IDI 6556
                      authenticity of this recording is in some doubt:
                      see entry under schubert symphony no 9
recorded on 6 october 1958 in the saint george's hotel brooklyn
new york   lp: columbia ML 5438/MS 6112/
philharmonic   78203/philips ABL 3325/SABL 139/
                      A01427L/835 527AY
                      cd: SMK 60967
recorded on 4 may 1964 in philharmonic hall
new york   lp: columbia MS 7414/D8S 815/
philharmonic   D3M 33273/61906
                      cd: MK 42223/SMK 47515/
                      SMK 61835/SB6K 87885
                      recording completed on 26 may 1964
televised between 30 october-2 november 1978 at concerts in the
musikverein vienna
wiener   lp: deutsche grammophon
philharmoniker   2531 313/2740 216
                      cd: 419 4342/423 4812/447 9002/
                      447 9042/474 9242
                      vhs video: 072 1113
                      dvd video: 073 4498/073 4500
recorded on 18 august 1990 at a concert in the tanglewood music centre
boston   cd: 431 7682/477 6690
symphony   *recorded at bernstein's final public*
                      conducting appearance

symphony no 8
recorded on 7 october 1963 in the manhattan centre
new york   lp: columbia MS 7412/D8S 815/61903
philharmonic   cd: MK 42223/SMK 47517/
                      SMK 60557/SB6K 87885
televised between 4-7 november 1978 at concerts in the musikverein vienna
wiener   lp: deutsche grammophon
philharmoniker   2707 074/2740 216
                      cd: 419 4352/423 4812/447 9002/
                      447 9012/474 9242
                      vhs video: 072 1783
                      dvd video: 073 4497/073 4500

beethoven/**symphony no 9 "choral"**
recorded on 18 may 1964 in the manhattan centre
new york　　　　　　　　lp: columbia M2S 794/D8S 815/61907
philharmonic　　　　　　cd: MK 42224/SMK 47518/SMK 63152/
juilliard choir　　　　　　SMK 64201/SB6K 87885
arroyo, sarfaty,
di virgilio, scott
televised on 4-5 april 1970 at concerts in the konzerthaus vienna
wiener　　　　　　　　　laserdisc: toshiba TOLW 3706
philharmoniker　　　　　dvd video: kultur 1525
chor der wiener
staatsoper
jones, verrett,
domingo, talvela
recorded on 21 august 1974 at a concert for the tanglewood festival
boston symphony　　　　cd: disco archivia 554
orchestra and chorus
meier, wilder,
simon, berberian
televised between 2-4 september 1978 at concerts in the musikverein vienna
wiener　　　　　　　　　lp: deutsche grammophon
philharmoniker　　　　　2707 124/2740 216
chor der wiener　　　　　cd: 410 8592/423 4812/431 0262/
staatsoper　　　　　　　431 0502/439 4952/447 9002/447 9052/
jones, schwarz,　　　　　457 9102/463 4682/474 9242
kollo, moll　　　　　　　vhs video: 072 1083/laserdisc: 072 1081
　　　　　　　　　　　　dvd video: 073 4497/073 4500
recorded on 22 august 1979 at a concert in the grosses festspielhaus salzburg
wiener　　　　　　　　　cd: drum can (japan) DM 60001/
philharmoniker　　　　　disco archivia 551
konzertvereingung
wiener staatsopernchor
jones, schwarz,
kollo, moll
televised on 25 december 1989 at a concert in the schauspielhaus berlin
sinfonieorchester　　　　lp: deutsche grammophon 429 8611
des bayerischen　　　　　cd: 429 8612/477 6690
rundfunks　　　　　　　vhs video: 072 1503
various choirs　　　　　　laserdisc: 072 2501
anderson, walker,　　　　dvd video: euroarts 207 2038/205 7068
könig, rootering　　　　　*orchestra augmented for this special german*
　　　　　　　　　　　　reunification concert by members of orchestras
　　　　　　　　　　　　from london, new york, dresden,
　　　　　　　　　　　　leningrad and paris

beethoven/**fantasy for piano, chorus and orchestra**
recorded on 1 may 1962 in the manhattan centre
new york philharmonic
westminster choir
serkin

lp: columbia ML 6016/MS 6616/D4L 340/
D4S 740/M2S 794/BRG 72346/
SBRG 72346/MY 38526
cd: MYK 38526/SM2K 47522/SB2K 63240

televised on 5 november 1985 at a concert in the musikverein vienna
wiener philharmoniker
wiener jeunesse choir
francesch

dvd video: deutsche grammophon
073 4500/073 4501

triple concerto
recorded on 17 october 1959 at a concert in carnegie hall
new york philharmonic
corigliano, violin
varga, cello
bernstein conducts
from the piano

lp: new york philharmonic NYP 85
cd: new york philharmonic NYP 2003

piano concerto no 1
recorded on 24 october 1960 in the manhattan centre
new york philharmonic
bernstein conducts
from the piano

lp: columbia ML 5807/MS 6407/
BRG 72108/SBRG 72108
cd: SMK 47519/SM3K 47166

recorded on 5 january 1968 at a concert in philharmonic hall
new york philharmonic
bernstein conducts
from the piano

cd: disco archivia 564

televised in 1970 at a concert in the musikverein vienna
wiener philharmoniker
bernstein conducts
from the piano

dvd video: kultur 1525

piano concerto no 2
recorded on 9-10 april 1957 in the columbia studios new york city
columbia symphony
gould

lp: columbia ML 5160/ML 5211/Y4 34640/
77409/philips A01357L/A01360L
cd: SM3K 52632/SX17K 52562

beethoven/**piano concerto no 3**
recorded on 4-5 may 1959 in the columbia studios new york city
columbia　　　　　　　　　lp:　columbia ML 5418/MS 6096/
symphony　　　　　　　　　Y4 34640/77409
gould　　　　　　　　　　　cd: SM3K 52632/SX17K 52562/
　　　　　　　　　　　　　　88697 147572

recorded on 20 january 1964 in the manhattan centre
new york　　　　　　　　　lp:　columbia ML 6016/MS 6616/D4L 340/
philharmonic　　　　　　　　D4S 740/MY 38526/BRG 72223/
serkin　　　　　　　　　　　SBRG 72223
　　　　　　　　　　　　　　cd: MYK 38526/MK 42259/SMK47520/
　　　　　　　　　　　　　　SMK 63080/SK 92738/SK 93448

recorded in april 1966 at a concert in the musikverein vienna
wiener　　　　　　　　　　　cd: madrigal (japan) MADR 202
philharmoniker
kempff

recorded on 29 october 1966 at a concert in philharmonic hall
new york　　　　　　　　　cd: new york philharmonic NYP 2003
philharmonic
kempff

televised on 12 september 1989 at a concert in the musikverein vienna
wiener　　　　　　　　　　　cd: deutsche grammophon 429 7492/
philharmoniker　　　　　　　435 4672
zimerman　　　　　　　　　dvd video: 073 4269/073 4500

beethoven/**piano concerto no 4**
recorded on 20 march 1961 in the manhattan centre
new york philharmonic gould
lp: columbia ML 5662/MS 6262/
Y4 34640/77409
cd: SM3K 52632/SX17K 52562/
88697 147572

televised on 17 october 1976 at a concert in the herkulessaal munich
sinfonieorchester des bayerischen rundfunks arrau
lp: deutsche grammophon 2721 153
cd: dg 477 6690
also unpublished video recording

televised on 12 september 1989 at a concert in the musikverein vienna
wiener philharmoniker zimerman
cd: deutsche grammophon 429 7492/
435 4673
dvd video: 073 4269/073 4500

piano concerto no 5 "emperor"
recorded on 1 may 1962 in the manhattan centre
new york philharmonic serkin
lp: columbia ML 5766/MS 6366/D4L 340/
D4S 740/M2X 788/M4X 821/M 31807/
MY 37223/BRG 72051/SBRG 72051
cd: MYK 37223/MK 42260/SMK 47520/
SMK 63080/SK 92738/SK 93448

televised on 12 september 1989 at a concert in the musikverein vienna
wiener philharmoniker zimerman
cd: deutsche grammophon 429 7942/
435 4673
dvd video: 073 4269/073 4500

violin concerto
recorded on 20 april 1959 in the saint george's hotel brooklyn
new york philharmonic stern
lp: columbia ML 5415/MS 6093/D3L 321/
D3S 721/MG 31418/M 31805/BRG 72092/
SBRG 72092/philips fontana 699 049CL/
876 001CY
cd: MYK 37224/SMK 47521/MYK 62799/
SB6K 87885/SX11K 67193

coriolan overture
televised between 20-23 february 1981 at concerts in the musikverein vienna
wiener philharmoniker
lp: deutsche grammophon 2531 347
cd: 423 4812/431 0252/431 0502/
431 1972/445 5052/477 6690
vhs video: 072 1773
dvd video: 073 4500/073 4502

beethoven/**egmont overture**
recorded on 12 february 1970 in philharmonic hall
new york philharmonic
lp: columbia M 30079
cd: MK 42220/SMK 47516/SMK 63079

televised between 20-23 february 1981 at concerts in the musikverein vienna
wiener philharmoniker
lp: deutsche grammophon 2531 347
cd: 413 7782/423 4812/423 9892/
445 5052/477 6690
vhs video: 072 1783
dvd video: 073 4500/073 4502

die geschöpfe des prometheus, overture
televised on 11-12 november 1978 at concerts in the musikverein vienna
wiener philharmoniker
lp: deutsche grammophon 2531 347/
2740 216
cd: 419 4392/423 4812/477 6690
vhs video: 072 1783
dvd video: 073 4500/073 4501

adagio-allegro, adagio-andante and finale/die geschöpfe des prometheus
televised on 11-12 november 1978 at concerts in the musikverein vienna
wiener philharmoniker
dvd video: deutsche grammophon
073 4500/073 4501

könig stephan, overture
recorded on 4 october 1966 in philharmonic hall
new york philharmonic
lp: columbia M 36079
cd: MK 42219/SMK 47517/
SMK 60557/SB6K 87885

televised between 4-7 november 1978 at concerts in the musikverein vienna
wiener philharmoniker
lp: deutsche grammophon 2531 347/
2740 216
cd: 419 4392/423 4812/431 0252/
431 0502/431 1972/477 6690
vhs video: 072 1773
dvd video: 073 4500/073 4501

fidelio

recorded on 17 march 1970 in the rai auditorium rome
rai roma orchestra and chorus
nilsson, donath, spiess, unger, crass, adam, vogel
cd: arkadia CDLSMH 34049

recorded on 9 june 1970 at a performance in the theater an der wien vienna
wiener philharmoniker
chor der wiener staatsoper
jones, popp, king, dallapozza, crass, nienstedt, berry
cd: private edition vienna/first classics (japan) FC 104-105
excerpts from rehearsal and performance
dvd video: kultur 1525

televised on 24 january 1978 at a performance in the staatsoper vienna
wiener philharmoniker
chor der wiener staatsoper
janowitz, popp, kollo, dallapozza, jungwirth, sotin, helm
vhs video: great performers (usa) 7
dvd video: deutsche grammophon 073 4159

recorded between 26 january-21 february 1978 in the musikverein vienna
wiener philharmoniker
chor der wiener staatsoper
janowitz, popp, kollo, dallapozza, jungwirth, sotin, fischer-dieskau
lp: deutsche grammophon 2709 082/ 2740 191/ 413 2881
cd: 419 4362/ 453 7002/ 453 7192/ 474 4202
excerpts
lp: 2531 347/ 2537 048
cd: 445 4612

fidelio overture

recorded on 31 january 1967 in philharmonic hall
new york philharmonic
lp: columbia M 30079
cd: MK 42220/ SMK 47518/ SMK 63152/ SB6K 87885

beethoven/**leonore no 3 overture**
recorded on 24 october 1960 in the manhattan centre
new york philharmonic
lp: columbia ML 5623/MS 6223/ M 30079/M 31071/M3X 31068
cd: MK 42222/SMK 47521/ SMK 63153/SB6K 87885

recorded on 18 may 1976 at a concert in carnegie hall
new york philharmonic
lp: columbia M2X 34256/79200
cd: SM2K 46742

recorded on 17 october 1976 at a concert in the herkulessaal munich
sinfonieorchester des bayerischen rundfunks
lp: deutsche grammophon 2721 153
cd: 477 6690
also unpublished video recording

televised on 11-12 november 1978 at concerts in the musikverein vienna
wiener philharmoniker
cd: deutsche grammophon 413 7792
dvd video: 073 4500/073 4502

recorded on 22 october 1983 at the centennial gala of the metropolitan opera house
metropolitan opera orchestra
cd: private edition vienna
also unpublished video recording

televised in 1983 at a concert in the vatican city for pope john paul
santa cecilia orchestra
unpublished video recording

recorded in 1988 at a concert in the musikverein vienna
wiener philharmoniker
cd: first classics (japan) FC 107

die weihe des hauses, overture
recorded on 9 october 1962 in philharmonic hall
new york philharmonic
lp: columbia M 30079
cd: MK 42222/SMK 47521/ SMK 63153/SB6K 87885

string quartet op 131, orchestral arrangement
televised between 8-14 september 1977 at concerts in the konzerthaus vienna
wiener philharmoniker
lp: deutsche grammophon 2531 077
cd: 419 4392/435 7792/477 6690
dvd video: 073 4500/073 4502

beethoven/**string quartet op 135, orchestral arrangement**
recorded in september 1989 at a concert in the musikverein vienna
wiener cd: deutsche grammophon 435 7792/
philharmoniker 477 6690/disco archivia 561
disco archivia edition is dated 1979

missa solemnis
recorded between 18-21 april 1960 in the manhattan centre
new york lp: columbia M2L 270/M2S 619/
philharmonic 77208
westminster choir cd: SM2K 47522
farrell, smith,
lewis, borg

recorded on 27 may 1969 at a concert in the musikverein vienna
wiener cd: private edition vienna
philharmoniker
chor der wiener
staatsoper
janowitz, ludwig,
kmentt, berry

recorded in 1971 at a concert in symphony hall boston
boston symphony cd: disco archivia 557
orchestra and chorus
curtin, forrester,
cochran, milnes

televised between 28 february-3 march 1978 at concerts in the concertgebouw amsterdam
concertgebouw lp: deutsche grammophon 2707 110
orkest cd: 413 7802/469 5462/477 6690
hilversum radio chorus dvd video: 073 4500/073 4501
moser, schwarz,
kollo, moll

gloria/missa solemnis
recorded on 23 september 1962 at the opening concert in philharmonic hall
new york lp: columbia L2L 1007/L2S 1008
philharmonic
schola cantorum
farrell, verrett,
vickers, bell

VINCENZO BELLINI (1801-1835)
la sonnambula
recorded on 5 march 1955 at a performance in teatro alla scala milan

la scala orchestra and chorus callas, ratti, valletti, modesti	lp: historical opera treasures ERR 108/ bjr records BJR 138/raritas OPR 3 cetra LO 32 cd: documents LV 955-956/myto MCD 89006/emi 567 9062/ dynamic CDS 552

excerpts
lp: limited edition records 100/historical recording enterprises HRE 219
cd: arkadia CD 517/fabbri GVS 03/ emi 331 4612

PAUL BEN-HAIM (1897-1974)
sweet psalmist of israel
recorded on 2 may 1959 in carnegie hall

new york philharmonic	lp: columbia ML 5451/MS 6123 cd: SM2K 47533

ALBAN BERG (1885-1935)
violin concerto
recorded on 6 december 1959 in the columbia studios new york city

new york philharmonic stern	lp: columbia ML 5773/MS 6373/M 42139/ BRG 72070/SBRG 72070 cd: MK 42139/SMK 64504/SX9K 67194

three orchestral pieces op 6
recorded on 3 march 1961 at a concert in carnegie hall

new york philharmonic	cd: new york philharmonic NYP 9701

HECTOR BERLIOZ (1803-1869)
symphonie fantastique
recorded on 27 may 1963 in the manhattan centre
new york philharmonic
lp: columbia ML 6007/MS 6607/BRG 72271/SBRG 72271/61910
cd: SMK 47525/SMK 60968
SMK 47525 was incorrectly dated 1968; SMK 60968 included bernstein's spoken analysis of the symphony

recorded on 5 march 1968 in philharmonic hall
new york philharmonic
lp: columbia MS 7278/M 31843/MY 38475
cd: MYK 38475
MS 7278 included bernstein's spoken analysis of the symphony as a bonus 45rpm disc

recorded on 17 july 1974 at a concert in the tanglewood music centre
jeunesse musicales orchestra
lp: private issue RC 1512

recorded on 4 november 1976 in the théatre des champs-élysées paris
orchestre national
lp: angel 37414/emi ASD 3397/1C065 02898/2C069 02898/3C065 02898
cd: emi 764 6302/769 0022/573 3382
also unpublished video recording

harold en italie
recorded on 23 october 1961 in the manhattan centre
new york philharmonic
lincer
lp: columbia ML 5758/MS 6358/BRG 72112/SBRG 72112
cd: SMK 60696

recorded on 3-4 november 1976 in the théatre des champs-élysées paris
orchestre national
macinnes
lp: angel 37413/emi ASD 3389/1C065 02893/2C069 02893/3C065 02893
cd: emi 764 7452/573 3382
also unpublished video recording

benvenuto cellini, overture
recorded on 31 october 1960 in the manhattan centre
new york philharmonic
lp: columbia ML 5623/MS 6253
cd: SMK 47525

berlioz/**le carnaval romain, overture**
recorded on 26 october 1959 in the columbia studios new york city
new york philharmonic
lp: columbia ML 5570/MS 6170/ M 30384
cd: SMK 47525

recorded on 6 january 1967 at a concert in the teatro communale florence
maggio musicale orchestra
cd: nuova era NE 2304

marche hongroise/la damnation de faust
recorded on 26 october 1967 in philharmonic hall
new york philharmonic
lp: columbia MS 7271/M 30384/ MG 35919
cd: SMK 47525/MDK 45734/ SMK 63154/SBK 89305

roméo et juliette, suite: roméo seul; fete chez capulet; scene d'amour; la reine mab
recorded on 26 october 1959 in the columbia studios new york city
new york philharmonic
lp: columbia ML 5570/MS 6170
cd: SM2K 47526

recorded on 6 january 1967 at a concert in the teatro communale florence
maggio musicale orchestra
cd: nuova era NE 2304

recorded on 11 march 1967 at a concert in philharmonic hall
new york philharmonic
cd: disco archivia 563

televised in 1973 in the wgbh television studios boston
boston symphony
cd: disco archivia 557
also unpublished video recording

grande messe des morts
televised between 28-30 september 1975 at concerts in the chapelle de saint louis des invalides paris
orchestre national
orchestre philharmonique
choeurs de radio france
burrows
lp: columbia MZ 34202/72905
cd: SMK 47526
dvd video: kultur 1525

berlioz/**la mort de cléopatre**
recorded on 9 october 1961 in the manhattan centre
new york   lp: columbia ML 5838/MS 6438/
philharmonic   CMS 6438
tourel   cd: SM2K 47526/SMK 60696

LEONARD BERNSTEIN (1918-1990)
symphony no 1 "jeremiah"
recorded on 1 december 1945 in saint louis
saint louis   78: victor M 1142/DM 1026
symphony   lp: CAL 196/SMA 7002
merriman   cd: membran 222 370/dutton CDBP 9758

recorded on 20 may 1961 in the manhattan centre
new york   lp: columbia ML 5703/MS 6303/
philharmonic   MG 32793/BRG 72399/SBRG 72399
tourel   cd: SM3K 47162/SMK 60697/
                     88697 279882

televised on 22-23 august 1977 at concerts in the philharmonie berlin
israel   lp: deutsche grammophon 2530 968
philharmonic   cd: 415 9642/445 2452/447 9532/
ludwig   447 9502/457 7572/469 8292
                     dvd video: kultur 1525

televised in 1983 at a concert for pope john paul in the vatican city
santa cecilia   unpublished video recording
orchestra
ludwig

bernstein/**symphony no 2 "the age of anxiety"**
recorded on 9 april 1949 at a concert in symphony hall boston
boston cd: boston symphony broadcast archives
symphony *this was the world premiere performance, and is*
koussevitzky, conductor *probably the sole recorded example of bernstein*
bernstein, piano *appearing as soloist under another conductor*

recorded on 27 february 1950 in the columbia studios new york city
new york 78: columbia M 946
philharmonic lp: ML 4325
foss, piano cd: SMK 60558/membran 222 370

recorded on 19 july 1965 in the manhattan centre
new york lp: columbia ML 6458/MS 7058/
philharmonic BRG 72503/SBRG 72503
entremont, piano cd: SM3K 47165/SMK 60697/
  88697 279882

recorded on 22-23 august 1977 at concerts in the philharmonie berlin
israel lp: deutsche grammophon 2530 969
philharmonic cd: 415 9642/445 2452/447 9532/
foss, piano 447 9502/457 7572/469 8292
  dvd video: kultur 1525

televised on 6 may 1986 at a concert in the barbican hall london
london symphony dvd video: deutsche grammophon
zimerman, piano 073 4514

bernstein/**symphony no 3 "kaddish"**
recorded between 15-17 september 1964 in the manhattan centre
new york philharmonic camerata and columbus choirs tourel
lp: columbia KL 6005/MS 6005/ MG 32793/BRG 72265/SBRG 72265
cd: SM3K 47162/SMK 60595/ 88697 279882/musical heritage society 516 3997

recorded on 25-26 august 1977 at concerts in the philharmonie berlin
israel philharmonic wiener jeunesses and sängerknaben caballé
lp: deutsche grammophon 2530 970
cd: 445 2452/447 9542/ 447 9502/469 8292

another performance with the same forces may have been recorded for television in the frederick mann auditorium tel aviv

divertimento
recorded on 4 july 1981 at a concert in the music centre tanglewood
boston symphony
cd: private edition vienna

recorded in 1981 at a concert in tel aviv
israel philharmonic
cd: deutsche grammophon 415 9662/ 447 9502/447 9552

televised on 13 november 1983 at a concert in the erkel theatre budapest
sinfonieorchester des bayerischen rundfunks
unpublished video recording

televised between 18-22 october 1984 at concerts in the musikverein vienna
wiener philharmoniker
cd: deutsche grammophon 437 1412/ 457 6912/469 8292
dvd video: 073 4514

recorded on 6 june 1989 at a concert in symphony hall boston
boston pops orchestra
cd: boston symphony orchestra CD 3
recorded at bernstein's fiftieth reunion concert

bernstein/**halil, nocturne for flute, strings and percussion**
recorded on 4 july 1981 at a concert in the music centre tanglewood
boston symphony   cd: private edition vienna
rampal

recorded in 1981 at a concert in tel aviv
israel philharmonic   cd: deutsche grammophon 415 9662/
rampal   447 9502/447 9552

jubilee games/ subsequently re-worked as concerto for orchestra
recorded on 29 november 1988 at a concert in avery fisher hall
new york   deutsche grammophon unpublished
philharmonic

recorded in 1989 at a concert in tel aviv
israel philharmonic   cd: deutsche grammophon
     447 9502/447 9562
     this recording is of the re-worked version

preludes, fugues and riffs
recorded on 6 may 1963 in the columbia studios new york city
columbia   lp: columbia ML 6077/ML 6205/
jazz combo   MS 6677/MS 6805/BRG 72406/
goodman, clarinet   SBRG 72406/61816
     cd: SMK 60559/SMK 61697/
     88697 279882

recorded on 22 september 1988 at a concert in the konzerthaus vienna
wiener   cd: deutsche grammophon 437 1412/
philharmoniker   445 4862/447 9502/447 9522
schmidl, clarinet

bernstein/**serenade for violin, strings and percussion**
recorded on 19 april 1956 in the columbia studios new york city
symphony   lp: columbia ML 5144
of the air   cd: SX9K 67194
stern

recorded on 22 july 1965 in the manhattan centre
new york   lp: columbia ML 6458/MS 7058/
philharmonic   BRG 72643/SBRG 72643
francescatti   cd: SM3K 47162/SMK 60559/
                             88697 279882

recorded between 6-14 october 1978 at concerts in tel aviv
israel   lp: deutsche grammophon 2531 196
philharmonic   cd: 445 1852/445 2452/447 9502/
kremer   447 9572/469 8292

televised on 6 may 1986 at a concert in the barbican hall london
london symphony   dvd video: deutsche grammophon
kremer   073 4514

anniversary no 1, for aaron copland
recorded on 17 september 1947 in the victor studios new york city
bernstein, piano   78: victor M 1278
                        lp: victor CAL 214
                        cd: symposium 1372

anniversary no 2, for my sister shirley
recorded on 23 november 1943 in new york
bernstein, piano   78: hargail (usa) MW 501

recorded on 17 september 1947 in the victor studios new york city
bernstein, piano   78: victor M 1278
                        lp: victor CAL 214
                        cd: symposium 1372

anniversary no 3, in memoriam alfred eisner
recorded on 17 september 1947 in the victor studios new york city
bernstein, piano   78: victor M 1278
                        lp: victor CAL 214
                        cd: pearl GEMMCD 9279/
                        symposium 1372

bernstein/**anniversary no 4, for paul bowles**
recorded on 17 september 1947 in the victor studios new york city
bernstein, piano   78: victor M 1209/V 15
                          lp: victor CAL 214
                          cd: symposium 1372

anniversary no 5, in memoriam nathalie koussevitzky
recorded on 23 november 1943 in new york
bernstein, piano   78: hargail (usa) MW 501
                          cd: pearl GEMMCD 9279

recorded on 17 september 1947 in the victor studios new york city
bernstein, piano   78: victor M 1209/V15
                          lp: victor CAL 214
                          cd: symposium 1372

anniversary no 7, for william schuman
recorded on 23 november 1943 in new york
bernstein, piano   78: hargail (usa) MW 501
                          cd: pearl GEMMCD 9279

sonata for clarinet and piano
recorded on 23 november 1943 in new york
oppenheim, clarinet   78: hargail (usa) MW 501
bernstein, piano

la bonne cuisine, 4 recipes for voice and piano
recorded on 18 november 1960 in the columbia studios new york city
tourel   cd: sony SMK 60697
bernstein, piano   *unpublished columbia lp recording*

i hate music, song cycle
recorded on 18 november 1960 in the columbia studios new york city
tourel   cd: sony SMK 60697
bernstein, piano   *unpublished columbia lp recording*

i hate music/individual song from the complete cycle
recorded on 24 december 1947 in the victor studios new york city
thebom   cd: bmg 09026 681012
bernstein, piano   *unpublished victor 78rpm recording*

bernstein/songfest, cycle of american poems for soloists and orchestra
recorded between 30 november-12 december 1977 at concerts in washington dc
national symphony
dale, elias, williams, rosenshein, gramm, reardon

lp: deutsche grammophon 2531 044
cd: 415 9652/447 9502/
447 9572/469 8292

televised on 24-25 november 1978 at concerts in the herkulessaal munich
sinfonieorchester des bayerischen rundfunks
dale, elias, williams, rosenshein, gramm, reardon

unpublished video recording

televised in 1979 at a concert in the théatre des champs-élysées paris
orchestre national
dale, elias, williams, rosenshein, luxon, howell

unpublished video recording

televised on 14 april 1982 at a concert in the royal festival hall london
bbc symphony
dale, walker, buchan, woollam, allen, hudson

unpublished video recording

mass, a theatre piece
recorded between august-october 1971
instrumentalists scribner and berkshire choirs titus

lp: columbia M2 31008/M2Q 31008/ 77256
cd: SM2K 63089/88697 279882
excerpts
lp: columbia QX 31403/MQ 31960/ MG 32174

bernstein/**three mediations from the mass, for cello and orchestra**
recorded in 1978 at a concert in tel aviv
israel　　　　　　　　　　cd: deutsche grammophon 415 9662/
philharmonic　　　　　　　447 9502/447 9552
rostropovich

chichester psalms
recorded on 26 july 1965 in the manhattan centre
new york　　　　　　　　lp: columbia ML 6192/MS 6792/
philharmonic　　　　　　　BRG 72374/SBRG 72374
camerata singers　　　　　cd: MK 47710/SFK 46701/SM3K 47162/
　　　　　　　　　　　　　SMK 60595/88697 279882/
　　　　　　　　　　　　　musical heritage society 516 3997

recorded on 22-23 august 1977 at concerts in the philharmonie berlin
israel　　　　　　　　　　lp: deutsche grammophon 2530 968
philharmonic　　　　　　　cd: 415 9652/447 9502/447 9542/
wiener jeunesse　　　　　　457 7572/469 8292
choir　　　　　　　　　　 dvd video: kultur 1525

televised on 6 may 1986 at a concert in the barbican hall london
london symphony　　　　　unpublished video recording
lso chorus

recorded on 28 april 1989 at a concert in the frederick mann auditorium tel aviv
israel　　　　　　　　　　cd: deutsche grammophon 429 2312
philharmonic
and chorus

bernstein/**candide, final version of the comic operetta**
televised on 12-13 december 1989 at concerts in the barbican hall london

london symphony
orchestra and chorus
anderson, d.jones,
ludwig, hadley,
gedda, green,
ollmann, treleaven

vhs video: deutsche grammophon
072 4233
laserdisc: 072 5231
dvd video: 073 4205
excerpts
vhs video: 072 1223

recorded between 14-18 december 1989 in the abbey road studios london

london symphony
orchestra and chorus
anderson, d.jones,
ludwig, hadley,
gedda, green,
ollmann, treleaven

lp: deutsche grammophon 429 7341
cd: 429 7342/447 9502/447 9582/
449 6562/474 4722/474 8572
excerpts
cd: 469 8292

candide, overture to the original version
recorded on 28 september 1960 in the manhattan centre

new york
philharmonic

lp: columbia ML 6077/ML 6388/MS 6677/
MS 6988/M2X 795/D3S 818/M 30304/
M3X 31068/MG 32174/M 39448/
GB 10/GS 10/BRG 72406/SBRG 72406/
60334/61816
cd: MLK 39448/MK 42263/MLK 44723/
SFK 46713/SM3K 47154/SMK 47529/
MLK 54058/SMK 63085/SMK 64075/
SBK 66493/SFK 89109/SK 92728/
SK 86859/88697 279882/
smithsonian RD 1-3-4
sacd: SS 89042
recording completed in may and june 1963

recorded on 8 june 1964 at a concert in symphony hall boston
boston pops
orchestra

cd: boston symphony orchestra CD 3
recorded at bernstein's twenty-fifth reunion concert

televised in 1976 at a concert in the royal albert hall london
new york
philharmonic

unpublished video recording

recorded on 4 july 1981 at a concert in the tanglewood music centre
boston
symphony

cd: private edition vienna

bernstein/candide, overture to the original version/concluded
recorded on 24 july 1982 at a concert in the davies symphony hall
los angeles philharmonic
lp: deutsche grammophon 2532 083
cd: 413 3242/423 1982/427 8062/ 447 9502/447 9552/471 7372

televised on 6 may 1986 in the barbican hall london
london symphony
unpublished video recording

dybbuk, complete ballet
recorded on 7 june 1974 in the columbia studios new york city
new york city ballet orchestra
johnson, ostendorf
lp: columbia M 33082/MQ 33082
cd: SMK 63090/SM3K 47158/ 88697 279882

dybbuk, first concert suite from the ballet
recorded on 9 april 1975 in the columbia studios new york city
new york philharmonic
sperry, fifer
lp: deutsche grammophon 2531 348
cd: 447 9502/447 9562/463 4622

dybbuk, second concert suite from the ballet
recorded on 14 april 1975 in the columbia studios new york city
new york philharmonic
lp: deutsche grammophon 2531 348
cd: 423 5822/447 9502/447 9562/ 463 4622/469 8292

bernstein/**facsimile, choreographic essay**
recorded on 24 january 1947 in the victor studios new york city
rca victor   78: victor M 1026/M 1142
orchestra   lp: victor CAL 196
                                   cd: rca 09026 616502/dutton CDBP 9758/
                                   membran 222 370

recorded on 18 june 1963 in philharmonic hall
new york   lp: columbia ML 6192/MS 6792/MG 32174/
philharmonic   BRG 72374/SBRG 72374
                                   cd: SM3K 47154/SMK 60969/
                                   88697 279882

recorded in 1981 at a concert in tel aviv
israel   cd: deutsche grammophon 447 9502/
philharmonic   447 9512

afterthought, study for the ballet facsimile
recorded on 24 january 1947 in the victor studios new york city
thebom   cd: rca 09026 681012
bernstein, piano   *unpublished victor 78rpm recording*

bernstein/**fancy free, ballet**
recorded on 2 june 1944 in new york city
ballet theatre   78: american decca DA 406
orchestra   lp: american decca DL 6023/
                            varese VC 81055
                            *this version includes prologue for soprano
                            performed by billie holiday (information in
                            world's encyclopedia of recorded music)*

recorded on 13 july 1956 in columbia studios new york city
columbia   lp: columbia CL 920
symphony

recorded on 11 june 1963 in philharmonic hall
new york   lp: columbia ML 6077/MS 6677/M 30304/
philharmonic   MG 32174/M 39448/BRG 72406/
                            SBRG 72406/61816
                            cd: MLK 39448/SM3K 47154/SMK 47530/
                            SMK 63085/SK 92728/88697 279882
                            sacd: SS 89042
                            excerpts
                            lp: columbia ML 6271/MS 6871

*recorded between 15-23 october 1978 at concerts in the frederick mann
auditorium new york city*
israel   lp: deutsche grammophon 2531 196
philharmonic   cd: 447 9502/447 9512/469 8292
                            *this version includes leonard bernstein
                            singing "big stuff"*

bernstein/**on the town, musical comedy**
recorded in may 1960 in the columbia studios new york city
orchestra	lp: columbia OL 5540/OS 2028/
walker, comden,	S 31005
green, reardon	cd: SK 60538

on the town, dance episodes
recorded between 3 february-2 march 1945 in the victor studios new york city
rca victor	78: victor M 995
orchestra	45: victor CAE 203
	lp: victor CAL 196
	cd: dutton CDBP 9758

recorded on 18 june 1963 in philharmonic hall
new york	lp: columbia ML 6077/MS 6677/M 30304/
philharmonic	MG 32174/M 39448/DMS 659/S2S 5462/
	BRG 72406/SBRG 72406/61816
	cd: MLK 39448/MK 42263/SM3K 47154/
	SMK 47530/SK 60538/SMK 60559/
	SBK 66493/88697 279882

recorded on 29 may 1981 at a concert in the frederick mann auditorium tel aviv
israel	lp: deutsche grammophon 2532 052
philharmonic	cd: 415 9662/427 8062/447 9502/
	447 9512/471 7372

on the waterfront, concert suite
recorded on 16 may 1960 in the manhattan centre
new york	lp: columbia ML 5651/MS 6251/61096
philharmonic	cd: SMK 47530/MK 42263/SM3K 47154/
	SMK 63085/SX10K 89750/SK 92728/
	88697 279882
	sacd: SS 89043

recorded on 4 july 1981 at a concert in the tanglewood music centre
boston	cd: private edition vienna
symphony

recorded in april 1985 at a concert in tel aviv
israel	cd: deutsche grammophon 415 2532/
philharmonic	447 9502/447 9522

bernstein/**a quiet place, opera in 3 acts**
recorded between 1-12 april 1986 at rehearsals and performance in the vienna studios of austrian radio
austrian radio
orchestra
ludgin, brandstetter,
morgan, kazaros,
kraft, uppman

cd: deutsche grammophon 447 9502/
447 9622

trouble in tahiti, opera in 7 scenes
recorded between 13-15 august 1973 in the cbs studios london
orchestra
williams, patrick,
butler, clarke

lp: columbia KM 32597/KMQ 32597

televised between 20-23 august 1973 in the studios of london weekend television
orchestra
williams, patrick,
butler, clarke

dvd video: kultur 1525

recorded between 1-12 april 1986 at rehearsals and performances in the vienna studios of austrian radio
austrian radio
orchestra
edeiken, white,
thomson, crafts,
ollman

cd: deutsche grammophon 459 0702
this version omits the first scene

west side story, a musical show in 2 acts
recorded between 4-8 september 1984 in the victor studios new york city
studio orchestra
and chorus
kanawa, troyanos,
horne, carreras,
ollman

lp: deutsche grammophon 415 2531
cd: 415 2532/447 9502/
447 9582/457 1992
excerpts
lp: deutsche grammophon 415 9631
cd: 415 9632/469 8292
rehearsal extracts (the making of west side story)
vhs video: 072 1063
laserdisc: 072 2061
dvd video: 477 7101

somewhere/west side story
recorded on 8 november 1987 at a concert in carnegie hall
orchestra
l.price

cd: deutsche grammophon 429 3922

bernstein/**west side story, symphonic dances**
recorded on 6 march 1961 in the manhattan centre
new york philharmonic
    lp: columbia ML 5651/MS 6251/
    MG 32174/M3X 31068/61096
    cd: MK 42263/SFK 46701/
    SM3K 47154/SK 60724/SMK 63085/
    SX10K 89750/SK 92728/
    88697 279882
    sacd: SS 89043

televised in 1976 at a concert in the jahrhunderthalle frankfurt-am-main
new york philharmonic   unpublished video recording

recorded on 4 july 1981 at a concert in the tanglewood music centre
boston symphony   cd: private edition vienna

recorded on 24 july 1982 at a concert in the davies symphony hall
los angeles philharmonic
    lp: deutsche grammophon 2532 082
    cd: 410 0252/427 8062/447 9502/
    447 9522/471 7372

take care of this home/ from the musical 1600 pennsylvania avenue
recorded in 1977 at a concert in washington dc
national symphony
von stade

slava !
recorded in 1978 at a concert in tel aviv
israel philharmonic
rostropovich
    cd: deutsche grammophon 447 9502/
    447 9552

a musical toast
recorded in 1981 at a concert in tel aviv
israel philharmonic
    cd: deutsche grammophon 447 9502/
    447 9552

GEORGES BIZET (1838-1875)
symphony in c
recorded on 27 may 1963 in the manhattan centre

new york philharmonic	lp: columbia MS 7159/MY 36725/ 61071 cd: MYK 36725/SMK 47532/ SMK 61830

carmen
recorded between 22 september-13 october 1972 in the manhattan centre

metropolitan opera orchestra and chorus	lp: deutsche grammophon 2709 043 cd: 427 4402/471 7502
	excerpts
horne, maliponte, mccracken, krause	lp: deutsche grammophon 2530 534

carmen, orchestral suite no 1
recorded on 15 may 1967 in philharmonic hall

new york philharmonic	lp: columbia M 31800/61350 cd: SMK 47531/SMK 63081 *excerpts* lp: MS 7271/MS 7517/MS 7415/ D3S 818/MG 30074

carmen, orchestral suite no 2
recorded between 15-20 may 1967 in philharmonic hall

new york philharmonic	lp: columbia M 31800 cd: SMK 47531/SMK 63081 *excerpts* lp: MS 7271/MS 7517/MS 7415/ D3S 818/MG 30074

1998: Mezzos and Contraltos: 5 Discographies: Janet Baker, Margarete Klose, Kathleen Ferrier, Giulietta Simionato, Elisabeth Höngen.

1999: The Furtwängler Sound Sixth Edition: Discography and Concert Listing.

1999: The Great Dictators: 3 Discographies: Evgeny Mravinsky, Artur Rodzinski, Sergiu Celibidache.

1999: Sviatoslav Richter: Pianist of the Century: Discography.

2000: Philharmonic Autocrat 1: Discography of: Herbert Von Karajan [Third Edition].

2000: Wiener Philharmoniker 1 - Vienna Philharmonic & Vienna State Opera Orchestras: Disc. Part 1 1905-1954.

2000: Wiener Philharmoniker 2 - Vienna Philharmonic & Vienna State Opera Orchestras: Disc. Part 2 1954-1989.

2001: Gramophone Stalwarts: 3 Separate Discographies: Bruno Walter, Erich Leinsdorf, Georg Solti.

2001: Singers of the Third Reich: 5 Discographies: Helge Roswaenge, Tiana Lemnitz, Franz Völker, Maria Müller, Max Lorenz.

2001: Philharmonic Autocrat 2: Concert Register of Herbert Von Karajan Second Edition.

2002: Sächsische Staatskapelle Dresden: Complete Discography.

2002: Carlo Maria Giulini: Discography and Concert Register.

2002: Pianists For The Connoisseur: 6 Discographies: Arturo Benedetti Michelangeli, Alfred Cortot, Alexis Weissenberg, Clifford Curzon, Solomon, Elly Ney.

2003: Singers on the Yellow Label: 7 Discographies: Maria Stader, Elfriede Trötschel, Annelies Kupper, Wolfgang Windgassen, Ernst Häfliger, Josef Greindl, Kim Borg.

2003: A Gallic Trio: 3 Discographies: Charles Münch, Paul Paray, Pierre Monteux.

2004: Antal Dorati 1906-1988: Discography and Concert Register.

2004: Columbia 33CX Label Discography.

2004: Great Violinists: 3 Discographies: David Oistrakh, Wolfgang Schneiderhan, Arthur Grumiaux.

2006: Leopold Stokowski: Second Edition of the Discography.

2006: Wagner Im Festspielhaus: Discography of the Bayreuth Festival.

2006: Her Master's Voice: Concert Register and Discography of Dame Elisabeth Schwarzkopf [Third Edition].

2007: Hans Knappertsbusch: Kna: Concert Register and Discography of Hans Knappertsbusch, 1888-1965. Second Edition.

2008: Philips Minigroove: Second Extended Version of the European Discography.

2009: American Classics: The Discographies of Leonard Bernstein and Eugene Ormandy.

Discography by Stephen J. Pettitt, edited by John Hunt:
1987: Philharmonia Orchestra: Complete Discography 1945-1987

Available from: Travis & Emery at 17 Cecil Court, London, UK.
(+44) 20 7 240 2129. email on sales@travis-and-emery.com .

© Travis & Emery 2009

bizet/l'arlésienne, suite no 1 from the incidental music
recorded on 25 january 1968 in philharmonic hall
new york lp: columbia M 31013
philharmonic cd: SMK 47531/SMK 63081
recording completed 2 february and 5 march 1968

l'arlésienne, suite no 2 from the incidental music
recorded on 25 january 1968 in philharmonic hall
new york lp: columbia M 31013
philharmonic cd: SMK 47531/SMK 63081
recording completed on 2 february 1968

l'arlésienne, intermezzo from the second suite
recorded on 2 february 1968 at a rehearsal in philharmonic hall
new york lp: columbia AS 493
philharmonic *this was a promtional lp for bernstein's sixtieth birthday*

MARC BLITZSTEIN (1905-1964)
airborne symphony for tenor, bass, narrator, chorus and orchestra
recorded on 27 may 1946 in the nbc studios new york city
nbc symphony unpublished radio broadcast

recorded on 30 october 1946 in the victor studios new york city
new york city 78: victor M 1117
symphony cd: rca 09026 625682/pearl GEMM 009
rca victor chorus
holland, scheff, shaw

recorded on 18 october 1966 in philharmonic hall
new york lp: columbia M 34136
philharmonic cd: SMK 61849
choral art society
velis, watson, welles

dusty, song
recorded on 27 october 1946 in the victor studios new york city
scheff 78: victor M 1117
bernstein, piano cd: rca 09026 625682

ERNEST BLOCH (1880-1959)
sacred service
recorded on 10 april 1960 in the manhattan centre
new york philharmonic metropolitan synagogue and community choirs merrill
lp: columbia ML 5621/MS 6221
cd: SM2K 47533

schelomo, for cello and orchestra
televised on 13 november 1976 at a concert in the théatre des champs-élysées paris
orchestre national rostropovich
lp: emi ASD 3334/1C065 02841/ 2C069 02841/3C065 02841/ angel 37256
cd: 749 3072
dvd video: 073 4381

recorded on 7 june 1988 at a concert in the frederick mann auditorium tel aviv
israel philharmonic maisky
cd: deutsche grammophon 427 3472

KARL-BIRGER BLOMDAHL (1916-1968)
forma ferritonans for orchestra
recorded on 11 march 1967 at a concert in philharmonic hall
new york philharmonic
cd: disco archivia 562

ARRIGO BOITO (1842-1918)
mefistofele, prologue to the opera
recorded on 12 april 1977 at a concert in the musikverein vienna
wiener philharmoniker chor der wiener staatsoper ghiaurov
lp: deutsche grammophon 2707 100
cd: 477 7112

ALEXANDER BORODIN (1833-1887)
in the steppes of central asia
recorded on 8 december 1969 in philharmonic hall
new york philharmonic
    lp: columbia M 34127/MY 37770
    cd: MYK 37770/SB2K 62406/
    SMK 47607/MLK 63076

nocturne from the second string quartet, orchestral arrangement by sargent
recorded on 19 march 1968 in philharmonic hall
new york philharmonic
    columbia unpublished

polovtsian dances / prince igor
recorded on 21 january 1963 in philharmonic hall
new york philharmonic
    lp: columbia ML 6414/MS 7014/M 31844/
    MY 37770/M3X 31068/BRG 72613/
    SBRG 72613
    cd: MYK 37770/SMK 47600
    excerpts
    lp: columbia MS 7246

dance of the polovtsian maidens / prince igor
recorded on 21 january 1963 in philharmonic hall
new york philharmonic
    lp: columbia M 34127/BRG 72613/
    SBRG 72613
    cd: SMK 47600

PIERRE BOULEZ (born 1926)
improvisations sur mallarmé I
recorded on 2 april 1960 at a concert in carnegie hall
new york philharmonic
    cd: new york philharmonic NYP 2003

48
JOHANNES BRAHMS (1833-1897)
symphony no 1
recorded between 21 april-2 may 1960 in the manhattan centre
new york   lp: columbia ML 5602/MS 6202/
philharmonic   D3M 32097
                            cd: SMK 47536/SMK 60970

recorded on 6 january 1967 at a concert in the teatro communale florence
maggio musicale   cd: nuova era NE 2304
orchestra

televised in 1973 at a concert in buyanet ha oumah jerusalem
israel   dvd video: euroarts 205 7068
philharmonic

televised between 1-12 october 1981 at concerts in the musikverein vienna
wiener   lp: deutsche grammophon 2741 023/
philharmoniker   410 0811
                            cd: 410 0812/415 5702/431 0292/
                            431 0502/431 1972/445 5052/
                            474 9302
                            dvd video: 073 4355/073 4331/
                            euroarts 207 2048

brahms/**symphony no 2**
recorded on 29 may 1962 in philharmonic hall
new york philharmonic
lp: columbia ML 5774/MS 6374/ D3M 32097
cd: SMK 47537/SMK 61829
first recording made in philharmonic hall

televised in august 1972 at a concert in the tanglewood music centre
boston symphony
dvd video: euroarts 207 2138

televised between 1-20 september 1982 at concerts in the musikverein vienna
wiener philharmoniker
lp: deutsche grammophon 2741 023/ 410 0821
cd: 410 0822/415 5702/445 5062/ 474 9302
dvd video: 073 4355/073 4331

recorded in 1988 at a concert in the musikverein vienna
wiener philharmoniker
cd: first classics (japan) FC 107

symphony no 3
recorded on 17 april 1964 in the manhattan centre
new york philharmonic
lp: columbia ML 6309/MS 6909/ D3M 32097/BRG 72525/ SBRG 72525
cd: SMK 47537/SMK 61829

televised in 1973 at a concert in buyanet ha oumah jerusalem
israel philharmonic
unpublished video recording

televised between 18-23 february 1981 at concerts in the musikverein vienna
wiener philharmoniker
lp: deutsche grammophon 2741 023/ 410 0831
cd: 410 0832/415 5702/445 5072/ 474 9302
dvd: 073 4353/073 4331/ euroarts 207 2048

brahms/**symphony no 4**
recorded on 29 june 1953 in carnegie hall

new york philharmonic	lp: american decca DL 9717/musical appreciation society/avm classics AVM 1001-1002
	cd: deutsche grammophon 477 0002/ andromeda ANDRCD 5115
	orchestra described for this recording as stadium concerts orchestra; musical appreciation society and deutsche grammophon also include bernstein's spoken analysis

recorded on 9 october 1962 in philharmonic hall

new york philharmonic	lp: columbia ML 5879/MS 6479/ D3M 32097
	cd: SMK 47538/SM6K 61846

televised in august 1972 at a concert in symphony hall boston

boston symphony	dvd video: euroarts 207 2138

televised between 1-12 october 1981 at concerts in the musikverein vienna

wiener philharmoniker	lp: deutsche grammophon 2741 023/ 410 0841
	cd: 410 0842/415 5702/ 445 5082/474 9302
	dvd video: 073 4355/073 4331

recorded in 1988 at a concert in the musikverein vienna

wiener philharmoniker	cd: first classics (japan) FC 107

brahms/**serenade no 2**
recorded on 1 february 1966 in philharmonic hall
new york philharmonic
lp: columbia MS 7132/61789
cd: SMK 47536/SMK 60970

televised in 1982 at concerts in the musikverein vienna
wiener philharmoniker
dvd video: deutsche grammophon 073 4355/073 4354

piano concerto no 1
televised in 1960 at a concert in the hochschule für musik berlin
new york philharmonic
bernstein conducts from the piano
unpublished video recording

recorded on 6 april 1962 at a concert in carnegie hall
new york philharmonic
gould
lp: new york philharmonic NYP 87
cd: melodram MEL 18002/sony SK 60675/82876 787532
melodram incorrectly dated 9 april 1962; bernstein introduces the performance

televised between 24-28 november 1983 at concerts in the musikverein vienna
wiener philharmoniker
zimerman
lp: deutsche grammophon 413 4721
cd: 413 4722/431 2072
vhs video: 072 1073
dvd video: 073 4332/073 4355

piano concerto no 2
recorded on 23 january 1968 in philharmonic hall
new york philharmonic
watts
lp: columbia MS 7134/78315
cd: SMK 47539

televised between 18-22 october 1984 at concerts in the musikverein vienna
wiener philharmoniker
zimerman
lp: deutsche grammophon 415 3591/ 415 5781
cd: 415 3592/431 0302/431 0502/ 431 2072/456 9972
vhs video: 072 1073
dvd video: 073 4332/073 4355

brahms/**violin concerto**
recorded on 15 april 1961 in the manhattan centre
new york philharmonic francescatti
lp: columbia ML 5871/MS 6471/
BRG 72130/SBRG 72130
cd: SMK 47540

televised between 1-20 september 1982 at concerts in the musikverein vienna
wiener philharmoniker kremer
lp: deutsche grammophon 2532 088/
410 0291
cd: 410 0292/431 0312/431 0502/
431 1972/431 2072/445 5952/
474 9302
vhs video: 072 1033
dvd video: 073 4333/073 4355

double concerto
televised between 1-20 september 1982 at concerts in the musikverein vienna
wiener philharmoniker kremer maisky
lp: deutsche grammophon 2532 090/
410 0311
cd: 410 0312/431 0312/431 0502/
431 1972/431 2072/445 5952/
474 9302
vhs video: 072 1033
dvd video: 073 4333/073 4355

haydn variations
recorded on 16 december 1971 in philharmonic hall
new york philharmonic
lp: columbia M 34572
cd: SMK 47539

recorded between 1-12 october 1981 at concerts in the musikverein vienna
wiener philharmoniker
lp: deutsche grammophon 2741 023/
410 0831
cd: 410 0832/415 5702/
445 5072/474 9302

brahms/**academic festival overture**
recorded on 7 october 1963 in the manhattan centre
new york philharmonic
    lp: columbia ML 6309/MS 6909/M 30307/
    M 34572/D2S 658/S2S 5462/
    BRG 72525/SBRG 72525
    cd: SMK 47538/MLK 39451/SMK 61846

recorded on 8 june 1964 at a concert in symphony hall boston
boston pops orchestra
    cd: boston symphony orchestra CD 3
    recorded at bernstein's twenty-fifth reunion concert

televised between 1-12 october 1981 at concerts in the musikverein vienna
wiener philharmoniker
    lp: deutsche grammophon 2741 023/
    410 0311/410 0821
    cd: 410 0312/410 0822/415 5702/
    423 9892/431 0292/431 0502/
    431 1972/445 5062/474 9302
    dvd video: 073 4355/073 4354

tragic overture
recorded on 1-2 may 1964 in the manhattan centre
new york philharmonic
    lp: columbia M 34572
    cd: SMK 47538/SMK 61846

televised between 1-12 october 1981 at concerts in the musikverein vienna
wiener philharmoniker
    lp: deutsche grammophon 2741 023/
    410 0841
    cd: 410 0842/415 5702/
    445 5082/474 9302
    dvd video: 073 4355/073 4354

hungarian dance no 5, arranged by parlow
recorded on 22 october 1970 in philharmonic hall
new york philharmonic
    lp: columbia M 30645
    cd: MLK 44724/SFK 46707/
    SMK 47572/SMK 64076

brahms/**hungarian dance no 6, arranged by parlow**
recorded on 12 october 1965 in the manhattan centre
new york philharmonic   lp: columbia ML 6271/MS 6871/
                         M 30307/M 30645/CSS 527
                         cd: MLK 44724.SFK 46707/
                         SMK 47572/MK 64076

recorded on 16 november 1983 at a concert in the erkel theatre budapest
sinfonieorchester   cd: hungaroton HCD 12631
des bayerischen
rundfunks

lieder recital: zigeunerlieder; immer leiser wird mein schlummer; feldeinsamkeit; ständchen; liebestreu; mädchenlied; sapphische ode; ruhe süssliebchen; die mainacht; von ewiger liebe
recorded on 2 may 1972 in the tel aviv museum
ludwig   lp: columbia M 34535/76379
bernstein, piano   *also unpublished video recording*

HENRY BRANT (1913-2008)
antiphony one
recorded on 2 april 1960 at a concert in carnegie hall
new york   cd: new york philharmonic NYP 2003
philharmonic   *bernstein conducts only the string section*
                   of the orchestra

BENJAMIN BRITTEN (1913-1976)
spring symphony
recorded on 4 may 1963 at a concert in philharmonic hall
new york   cd: new york philharmonic NYP 2003
philharmonic
collegiate chorale
and church choirs
vyvyan, sarfaty, lewis

suite on english folk tunes
recorded on 19 april 1976 in the columbia studios new york city
new york   lp: columbia M 34529/76640
philharmonic   cd: SMK 47541

variations and fugue on a theme of purcell/ young person's guide to the orchestra
recorded on 20 march 1961 in the manhattan centre
new york   lp: columbia ML 5768/ML 5998/MS 6368/
philharmonic   MS 6598/M 31808/D3S 785/CSS 1683/
chapin, narrator   BRG 72072/SBRG 72072/72393/72567
                                cd: SFK 46712/SMK 60175/SMK 47541
                                some versions had a narration dubbed in german, spanish or hebrew; SMK 47541 issued without narration

four sea interludes/ peter grimes
recorded on 8 march 1973 in the columbia studios new york city
new york   lp: columbia M 34529/76640
philharmonic   cd: SMK 47541
                           sacd: SS 87981

recorded on 19 august 1990 at a concert in the tanglewood music centre
boston   cd: deutsche grammophon 431 7682/
symphony   474 9362
                               recorded at bernstein's final conducting appearance

passacaglia/ peter grimes
recorded on 8 march 1973 in the columbia studios new york city
new york   lp: columbia M 34529/76640
philharmonic   cd: SMK 47541

HOWARD BRUBECK (born 1916)
dialogues for jazz combo and orchestra
recorded on 30 january 1960 in the columbia studios new york city

new york	lp: columbia CL 1466/CS 8257/
philharmonic	C 30522
brubeck quartet	cd: SMK 60566

ANTON BRUCKNER (1824-1896)
symphony no 6
recorded on 27 march 1976 at a concert in avery fisher hall

new york philharmonic	cd: new york philharmonic NYP 2003

symphony no 9
recorded on 4 february 1969 in philharmonic hall

new york	lp: columbia M 30828
philharmonic	cd: SMK 47542

televised on 2 march 1990 at a concert in the musikverein vienna

wiener	cd: deutsche grammophon 435 3502
philharmoniker	dvd video: euroarts 207 2018/
	205 7068

JOHN CAGE (1912-1992)
atlas eclipticalis
recorded on 9 february 1964 at a concert in philharmonic hall

new york philharmonic	cd: new york philharmonic NYP 2003

ELLIOTT CARTER (born 1908)
concerto for orchestra
recorded on 11 february 1970 in philharmonic hall

new york	lp: columbia M 30112/CRISD 469
philharmonic	cd: SMK 60203

EMANUEL CHABRIER (1841-1894)
espana
recorded on 21 january 1963 in philharmonic hall
new york philharmonic
lp: columbia ML 6186/ML 6388/
MS 6786/MS 6988/M3X 31068/
M 31816/MYK 37769/BRG 72423/
SBRG 72423/60334
cd: MYK 37769/SMK 42392/
SFK 46707/SMK 47613

GEORGE WHITEFIELD CHADWICK (1854-1931)
melpomene, dramatic overture
recorded on 25 october 1958 at a concert in carnegie hall
new york philharmonic
cd: new york philharmonic NYP 9904

ERNEST CHAUSSON (1855-1899)
poeme pour violon et orchestre
recorded on 6 january 1964 in the manhattan centre
new york philharmonic francescatti
lp: columbia ML 6017/MS 6617
cd: SMK 47548

CARLOS CHAVEZ (1899-1978)
sinfonia india
recorded on 15 april 1961 in the manhattan centre
new york philharmonic
lp: columbia ML 5914/MS 6514
cd: SMK 60571

LUIGI CHERUBINI (1760-1842)
medea
recorded on 10 december 1953 at a performance in the teatro alla scala milan
la scala orchestra and chorus
callas, barbieri, nache, penno, modesti
lp: unique opera recordings UORC 128/
bjr records BJR 129/mrf records MRF 102/morgan MOR 5301/melodram MEL 404/cetra LO 36
cd: cetra CDE 1019/melodram MEL 26022/verona 27088-27089/
emi 769 9092
excerpts
lp: historical recording enterprises HRE 219/dei della musica 12/laserlight 15096/fabbri GVS 03/hallmark 390362/311092/emi 331 4612

FREDERIC CHOPIN (1810-1849)
piano concerto no 1
recorded on 19-20 january 1963 at concerts in carnegie hall
new york   cd: disco archivia 564
philharmonic
lhevine

AARON COPLAND (1900-1990)
symphony no 3
recorded on 16-17 february 1966 in philharmonic hall
new york   lp: columbia ML 6354/MS 6954/
philharmonic   BRG 72559/SBRG 72559/61681
                    cd: SMK 63155

recorded on 10 december 1985 at a concert in avery fisher hall
new york   lp: deutsche grammophon 419 1701
philharmonic   cd: 419 1702/474 9402
                    finale only
                    cd: 445 4862

dance symphony
recorded on 31 january 1981 at a concert in avery fisher hall
new york   cd: new york philharmonic NYP 2003
philharmonic

organ symphony
recorded on 3 january 1967 in philharmonic hall
new york   lp: columbia ML 6458/MS 7058/
philharmonic   BRG 72643/SBRG 72643
power biggs   cd: SM2K 47232/SMK 63155

copland/**piano concerto**
recorded on 13 january 1964 in philharmonic hall
new york lp: columbia ML 6098/MS 6698/
philharmonic BRG 72352/SBRG 72352/61837
copland cd: SM2K 47232/SMK 60177

clarinet concerto
recorded on 24 october 1989 at a concert in avery fisher hall
new york cd: deutsche grammophon 431 6722/
philharmonic 474 9402
drucker

appalachian spring, ballet
recorded on 24 july 1982 at a concert in the davies symphony hall
los angeles lp: deutsche grammophon 2532 083
philharmonic cd: 413 3242/439 5282/477 6352

appalachian spring, concert suite from the ballet
recorded on 9 october 1961 in the manhattan centre
new york lp: columbia ML 5755/MS 6355/
philharmonic MS 7521/MG 30071/MY 37257/
  MG 31155/M 39443/BRG 72074/
  SBRG 72074
  cd: MYK 37257/MLK 39443/MK 42265/
  SMK 47543/SMK 63082/82876 787682/
  musical heritage society 516 5306
  sacd: SS 87327

billy the kid, concert suite
recorded on 21-23 june 1949 in the victor studios new york city
rca victor lp: victor LM 1031/SMA 7016
orchestra

recorded on 20 october 1959 in symphony hall boston
new york lp: columbia ML 5575/MS 6175/M 50155/
philharmonic M 31823/MY 36727/MG 30071/P 18865/
  BRG 72411/SBRG 72411/philips
  ABL 3357/SABL 192/A01481L/
  835 567AY
  cd: MYK 36727/MK 42265/SMK 63082/
  SX10K 89750/82876 787682
  sacd: SS 87327

copland/**connotations for orchestra**
recorded on 23 september 1962 at the opening concert in philharmonic hall
new york philharmonic
lp: columbia L2L 1007/L2S 1008/
MS 7431
cd: SM2K 47236/SMK 60177
world premiere performance

recorded on 24 october 1989 at a concert in avery fisher hall
new york philharmonic
cd: deutsche grammophon 431 6722/
474 9402

danzon cubano
recorded on 6 february 1963 in philharmonic hall
new york philharmonic
lp: columbia ML 5914/ML 6271/
MS 6514/MS 6871/MY 37257/61059
cd: MYK 37257/SMK 47544/
SMK 60571/musical heritage society
516 5306

fanfare for the common man
recorded on 16 february 1966 in philharmonic hall
new york philharmonic
lp: columbia MY 37257/CSS 1683
cd: MYK 37257/MK 42265/MLK 44723/
SFK 46715/SMK 47543/SMK 63082/
MLK 64059/SMK 64075/SK 90390/
82876 787682/musical heritage society
516 5306

in the beginning, for mezzo-soprano and chorus
recorded on 27 may 1953 in the columbia studios new york city
pro musica chorus
lipton
columbia unpublished

inscape for orchestra
recorded on 17 october 1967 in philharmonic hall
new york philharmonic
lp: columbia MS 7431
cd: SM2K 47236

copland/**a lincoln portrait**
televised on 3 june 1976 at a concert in the royal albert hall london
new york philharmonic lp: new york philharmonic NYP 86
warfield, narrator cd: new york philharmonic NYP 9904
also unpublished video recording

music for the theatre, suite
recorded on 15 december 1958 in saint george's hotel brooklyn
new york lp: columbia ML 5755/ML 6098/MS 6355/
philharmonic MS 6698/MG 30071
cd: SM2K 47232/SMK 60177/SMK 60989
excerpts
lp: columbia BRG 72074/SBRG 72074

recorded on 24 october 1989 at a concert in avery fisher hall
new york cd: deutsche grammophon 431 6722/
philharmonic 474 9402

seven old american songs
recorded on 6 february 1981 at a concert in avery fisher hall
new york cd: new york philharmonic NYP 9701
philharmonic
horne

orchestral variations
recorded on 6 december 1958 at a concert in carnegie hall
new york cd: new york philharmonic NYP 9904
philharmonic

an outdoor overture
televised on 12 november 1960 at a concert in carnegie hall
new york cd: new york philharmonic NYP 2003
philharmonic *also unpublished video recording*

recorded on 7 december 1976 in the manhattan centre
new york columbia unpublished
philharmonic

quiet city
recorded on 2 december 1985 in avery fisher hall
new york lp: deutsche grammophon 419 1701
philharmonic cd: 419 1702/474 9402

copland/**rodeo, 4 dance episodes**
recorded on 2 may 1960 in the manhattan centre
new york philharmonic

lp: columbia ML 5575/MS 6175/
MG 30071/MG 31823/MY 36727/
BRG 72411/SBRG 72411/philips
ABL 3357/SABL 192/A01481L/
835 567AY
cd: MK 36727/MK 42265/SMK 47543/
SMK 63082/SX10K 89750/82876
787682/smithsonian RD 103-4
sacd: SS 87327

el salon mexico
recorded between 22-30 march 1951 in the columbia studios new york city
columbia symphony

lp: columbia ML 2203/CL 920/
philips NBR 6019/N02600R

recorded on 20 may 1961 in the manhattan centre
new york philharmonic

lp: columbia ML 5575/ML 5841/
MS 6355/MS 6441/MS 7521/
MG 30071/MY 37257/MGP 13/
M 39443/BRG 72074/SBRG 72074
cd: MYK 37257/MLK 39443/
SMK 47544/SMK 60571/SFK 89274/
S3K 90578/musical heritage society
516 5306
sacd: SS 87327

recorded on 24 october 1989 at a concert in avery fisher hall
new york philharmonic

cd: deutsche grammophon 431 6722/
459 5522/474 9402

the second hurricane, play opera
recorded on 30 april 1960 in the columbia studios new york city and on 2 may 1960 in the manhattan centre
new york philharmonic and chorus

lp: columbia ML 5581/MS 6181/
AMS 6181/60339
cd: SMK 60560

copland/**sonata for piano**
recorded on 22 january 1947 in the victor studios new york city
bernstein, piano   78: victor M 1278
                               lp: victor SMA 7015
                               cd: symposium 1372

statements for orchestra
recorded on 23 june 1949 in the victor studios new york city
rca victor   78: victor M 1333
orchestra   cd: rca 09026 616502

the tender land, concert version of the opera
recorded on 31 july 1965 in the manhattan centre
new york   lp: columbia ML 6214/MS 6814
philharmonic   cd: S2K 89329
choral art society
clements, turner,
cassilly, fredericks,
treigle

JOHN CORIGLIANO (born 1938)
clarinet concerto
recorded on 9 december 1977 at a concert in avery fisher hall
new york   cd: new york philharmonic NYP 9701
philharmonic
drucker

LUIGI DALLAPICCOLA (1904-1975)
tartiniana for violin and orchestra
recorded on 27 april 1953 in the columbia studios new york city
columbia lp: columbia ML 4996
symphony cd: SMK 60725
posselt

CLAUDE DEBUSSY (1862-1918)
la mer
recorded on 16 october 1961 in the manhattan centre
new york   lp: columbia ML 6154/MS 6754/
philharmonic   BRG 72387/SBRG 72387
                 cd: SMK 47546/SMK 60972

recorded on 7 december 1976 in the manhattan centre
new york   columbia unpublished
philharmonic

recorded on 15 june 1989 at a concert in the santa cecilia auditorium rome
santa cecilia   cd: deutsche grammophon 429 7282/
orchestra   477 5014

nuages et fetes/nocturnes
recorded on 28 september 1960 in the manhattan centre
new york   lp: columbia ML 5671/MS 6271
philharmonic   cd: SMK 47546/SMK 60972

jeux
recorded on 2 may 1960 in the manhattan centre
new york   lp: columbia ML 5671/MS 6271/
philharmonic   D3M 32097
                 cd: SMK 47546/SMK 60972

debussy/**images pour orchestre**
recorded on 27 october 1958 in the saint george's hotel brooklyn
new york   lp: columbia ML 5419/MS 6097/philips
philharmonic   ABL 3328/SABL 171/A01507L/
                        835 577AY
                        cd: SMK 47545

recorded on 15 june 1989 at a concert in the santa cecilia auditorium rome
santa cecilia   cd: deutsche grammophon 429 7282/
orchestra   477 5014

prélude a l'apres-midi d'un faune
recorded on 28 september 1960 in the manhattan centre
new york   lp: columbia ML 5671/ML 5841/
philharmonic   ML 6154/MS 6271/MS 6441/MS 6754/
                        MS 7523/M3X 33024/M 35861/
                        M 39444/BRG 72387/SBRG 72387
                        cd: MLK 39444/SFK 46708/
                        SMK 47546/SMK 60972

televised in 1973 in wgbh studios boston
boston   cd: disco archivia 558
symphony   *also unpublished video recording*

recorded on 15 june 1989 at a concert in the santa cecilia auditorium rome
santa cecilia   cd: deutsche grammophon 429 7282/
orchestra   477 5014

first rhapsody for clarinet and orchestra
recorded on 16 october 1961 in the manhattan centre
new york   lp: columbia ML 6059/MS 6659/
philharmonic   BRG 72453/SBRG 72453
drucker   cd: SMK 60695

rhapsody for saxophone and orchestra, arranged by roger-ducasse
recorded on 16 october 1961 in the manhattan centre
new york   lp: columbia ML 6059/MS 6659/
philjarmonic   BRG 72453/SBRG 72453
rascher   cd: SMK 60695

debussy/**le martyre de saint sébastien**
recorded on 22 october 1962 in philharmonic hall
new york philharmonic
choral art society
addison, babikian, kleinman, simon
weara, narrator
montealagre, narrator

lp: columbia M2L 353/M2S 753
cd: SMK 60596

fantoches, song for voice and piano
recorded on 2 march 1969 in the columbia studios new york city
tourel
bernstein, piano

lp: columbia M 32231

DAVID DEL TREDICI (born 1937)
tattoo
recorded on 23 november 1988 at a concert in avery fisher hall
new york philharmonic

cd: deutsche grammophon 429 2312/
474 9402

EDISON DENISOV (1929-1996)
crescendo e diminuendo
recorded on 20 may 1967 in philharmonic hall
new york philharmonic

lp: columbia ML 6452/MS 7052
cd: SMK 61845

DAVID DIAMOND (born 1915)
symphony no 4
recorded on 13 january 1958 in the saint george's hotel brooklyn
new york philharmonic

lp: columbia ML 5412/MS 6089/
new world NW 258
cd: SMK 60594

GRIGORAS DINICU (1889-1949)
hora staccato
recorded on 22 october 1970 in philharmonic hall
new york philharmonic
lp: columbia M 30645
cd: MLK 44724/SFK 46707/SMK 64076

PAUL DUKAS (1865-1935)
l'apprenti sorcier
recorded on 16 february 1965 in the manhattan centre
new york philharmonic
lp: columbia ML 6343/MS 6943/MS 7165/
D3S 785/CC 23528/CC 25502/CR 21501/
MY 37769/DMS 659/S2S 5462/CRA 20401/
BRG 72740/SBRG 72740/61976
cd: MYK 37769/SFK 46706/
SMK 47596/SMK 60695

HENRI DUPARC (1843-1933)
la vie antérieure
recorded on 2 march 1969 in the columbia studios new york city
tourel
bernstein, piano
lp: columbia M 32231

ANTONIN DVORAK (1841-1904)
carnival overture
recorded on 1 february 1965 in the manhattan centre
new york philharmonic
lp: columbia ML 6279/MS 6879/MS 7524/
D3S 818/M 31817/BRG 72461/
SBRG 72461
cd: SFK 46713/SMK 47547/
SMK 60563/SK 92729

symphony no 7
recorded on 28 january 1963 in philharmonic hall
new york philharmonic
lp: columbia ML 6228/MS 6828/
BRG 72485/SBRG 72485
cd: SMK 60561

dvorak/**symphony no 9 "from the new world"**
recorded on 28 july 1953 in carnegie hall

new york philharmonic
lp: book of the month club MAR 37
cd: deutsche grammophon 477 0002/ andromeda ANDRCD 5015
orchestra described for this recording as stadium concerts orchestra; deutsche grammophon issue also includes bernstein's spoken analysis

recorded on 16 april 1962 in the manhattan centre

new york philharmonic
lp: columbia ML 5793/MS 6393/ D3L 337/D3S 737/M 31809
cd: SMK 47547/SMK 60563/SK 92729
sacd: SS 06393

recorded on 24 september 1986 at a concert in the salle pleyel paris

israel philharmonic
lp: deutsche grammophon 427 3461
cd: 427 3462

piano concerto
recorded on 14 april 1975 in the columbia studios new york city

new york philharmonic
frantz
lp: columbia M 33889/76480
cd: SMK 61828

cello concerto
recorded on 7 june 1988 at a concert in the frederick mann auditorium tel aviv

israel philharmonic
maisky
cd: deutsche grammophon 427 3472/ 445 5742

dvorak/**slavonic dance op 46 no 1**
recorded on 7 october 1963 in the manhattan centre
new york philharmonic
    lp: columbia ML 6271/ML 6279/
    MS 6871/MS 6879/M 30465/M 31817/
    BRG 72461/SBRG 72461
    cd: SFK 46707/SMK 47547/SMK 60563/
    SMK 61836/SK 92729

recorded on 7 june 1988 at a concert in the frederick mann auditorium tel aviv
israel philharmonic
    lp: deutsche grammophon 427 3461
    cd: 427 3462

slavonic dance op 46 no 3
recorded on 7 october 1963 in the manhattan centre
new york philharmonic
    lp: columbia ML 6279/MS 6879/
    M 31817/BRG 72461/SBRG 72461
    cd: SMK 47547/SMK 60563/
    SMK 61836/SK 92729

recorded on 7 june 1988 at a concert in the frederick mann auditorium tel aviv
israel philharmonic
    lp: deutsche grammophon 427 3461
    cd: 427 3462

slavonic dance op 46 no 8
recorded on 7 june 1988 at a concert in the frederick mann auditorium tel aviv
israel philharmonic
    lp: deutsche grammophon 427 3461
    cd: 427 3462

EDWARD ELGAR (1857-1934)
cockaigne overture
recorded on 9 february 1963 at a concert in philharmonic hall
new york philharmonic
    cd: new york philharmonic NYP 2003

march of the mogul emperors/crown of india
recorded on 15 april 1982 in the town hall watford
bbc symphony
    lp: deutsche grammophon 2532 067
    cd: 413 4902/431 0332

elgar/**enigma variations**
televised on 14 april 1982 at a concert in the royal festival hall london
bbc symphony   unpublished video recording

recorded on 15 april 1982 in the town hall watford
bbc symphony   lp: deutsche grammophon 2532 067
                       cd: 413 4902/431 0332/474 9362

pomp and circumstance, march no 1
recorded on 26 october 1967 in philharmonic hall
new york   lp: columbia MS 7271/MG 35919/
philharmonic   30055
                       cd: MDK 45734/SMK 47567/SFK 46709/
                       SMK 60989/SMK 63154/SBK 89305

recorded on 15 april 1982 in the town hall watford
bbc symphony   lp: deutsche grammophon 2532 067
                       cd: 413 4902/431 0332

pomp and circumstance, march no 2
recorded on 15 april 1982 in the town hall watford
bbc symphony   lp: deutsche grammophon 2532 067
                       cd: 413 4902/431 0332

GEORGES ENESCO (1881-1955)
rumanian rhapsody no 1
recorded on 16 december 1969 in philharmonic hall
new york   lp: columbia M 30645
philharmonic   cd: SMK 47572

MANUEL DE FALLA (1876-1946)
el amor brujo, ballet
recorded on 29 november 1976 in the columbia studios new york city
new york philharmonic horne
lp: columbia M 35102/76707
cd: MBK 44721/SMK 47613

danza del fuego/el amor brujo
recorded on 16 february 1965 in the manhattan centre
new york philharmonic
lp: columbia ML 6186/ML 6388/
MS 6786/MS 6988/M3X 31068/
M 31816/DMS 659/S2S 5462/
BRG 72423/SBRG 72423
cd: MLK 44725/SMK 64077

fanfare pour une fete
recorded on 29 november 1976 in the columbia studios new york city
new york philharmonic
lp: columbia M 35102/76707
cd: SMK 47613

el sombrero de 3 picos, suite no 1
recorded on 23 november 1964 in the manhattan centre
new york philharmonic
lp: columbia ML 6186/MS 6786/
M 31816/BRG 72423/SBRG 72423
cd: SMK 47613

el sombrero de 3 picos, suite no 2
recorded on 6 november 1961 in the manhattan centre
new york philharmonic
lp: columbia ML 6186/MS 6786/
M 31816/M3X 31068/BRG 72423/
SBRG 72423
cd: SMK 47613

interlude and dance/la vida breve
recorded on 11 february 1965 in the manhattan centre
new york philharmonic
lp: columbia ML 6186/ML 6388/
MS 6786/MS 6988/M 31816/
M3X 31068/BRG 72423/
SBRG 72423/60334
cd: SMK 47613

GABRIEL FAURE (1845-1924)
ballade pour piano et orchestre
recorded on 30 october 1961 in the manhattan centre
new york lp: columbia ML 5777/MS 6377/
philharmonic BRG 72105/SBRG 72105
casadesus cd: SMK 47548/SM2K 61725/
  503 3972

MORTON FELDMAN (1926-1987)
out of last pieces, for piano and orchestra
recorded on 11 february 1964 in the manhattan centre
new york lp: columbia ML 6133/MS 6733
philharmonic cd: SMK 61845
tudor

LORENZO FERNANDEZ (1897-1948)
batuque/reisado do pastorale
recorded on 6 february 1963 in philharmonic hall
new york lp: columbia ML 5914/ML 6271/
philharmonic MS 6514/MS 6871
  cd: SMK 47544/SMK 60571/
  S3K 90578

LUKAS FOSS (born 1922)
biblical cantata (song of songs)
recorded on 27 january 1958 in the saint heorge's hotel brooklyn

new york	lp: columbia ML 5451/MS 6123/
philharmonic	CRISD 284
tourel	cd: SM2K 47533/SMK 63164

introduction and goodbyes
recorded on 7 may 1960 at a concert in carnegie hall

new york	cd: new york philharmonic
philharmonic	NYP 9904/NYP 9915
choral art society	
reardon	

phorion
recorded on 2 may 1967 in philharmonic hall

new york	lp: columbia ML 6452/MS 7052
philharmonic	cd: SMK 63164

quintets for orchestra
recorded on 31 january 1981 at a concert in avery fisher hall

new york	cd: new york philharmonic NYP 2003
philharmonic	

time cycle
recorded on 22 november 1960 in the columbia studios new york city

columbia	lp: columbia ML 5680/MS 6280
symphony	cd: SMK 63164
addison	*recording completed on 26 january 1961*

CESAR FRANCK (1822-1890)
symphony in d minor
recorded on 2 february 1959 in the saint george's hotel brooklyn

new york philharmonic	lp: columbia ML 5391/MS 6072/D3L 337/ D3S 737/M 31803/philips ABL 3305/ SABL 146/A01429L/835 528AY cd: SMK 47548

televised on 22 november 1981 at a concert in the théâtre des champs-élysées paris

orchestre national	lp: deutsche grammophon 2532 051 cd: 400 0702/445 5122 dvd video: euroarts 205 7068

GEORGE GERSHWIN (1898-1937)
an american in paris
recorded on 6 december 1947 in the victor studios new york city

rca victor orchestra	78: victor M 1237/hmv C 3881-3882/ hmv (switzerland) FKX 220-221 lp: victor LM 1031/SMA 7016 cd: rca 09026 616502/dynamic IDI 6556

recorded on 15 december 1958 in the saint george's hotel brooklyn

new york philharmonic	lp: columbia ML 5413/MS 6091/ M 31804/MY 37242/MG 31155/ FM 42516/BRG 72080/SBRG 72080/ philips ABL 3232/SABL 160/ A01393L/G05654R cd: MYK 37242/MK 42264/MK 42516/ SFK 63086/SX10K 89750/SK 90393/ 82876 787682 sacd: SS 89033

televised in 1976 at a concert in the royal albert hall london

new york philharmonic	dvd video: deutsche grammophon 073 4513

gershwin/**rhapsody in blue**
recorded on 23 june 1959 in the columbia studios new york city
columbia   lp: columbia ML 5413/MS 6091/MS 7518/
symphony   MG 30074/MG 31804/BRG 72080/
bernstein conducts   SBRG 72080/philips ABL 3232/
from the piano   SABL 160/A01393L/G05654R
                     cd: 82876 787682

televised in 1976 at a concert in the royal albert hall london
new york   dvd video: deutsche grammophon
philharmonic   073 4513
bernstein conducts
from the piano

recorded on 24 july 1982 at a concert in the davies symphony hall
los angeles   lp: deutsche grammophon 2532 082
philharmonic   cd: 410 0252/427 8062/439 5282/
bernstein conducts   471 7372/477 6352/477 6677
from the piano

piano prelude no 2
recorded on 24 july 1982 at a concert in the davies symphony hall
bernstein, piano   lp: deutsche grammophon 2532 082
                     cd: 410 0252

DON GILLIS (1912-1978)
moto perpetuo
recorded on 2 june 1946 at a concert in the nbc studios new york city
nbc symphony   unpublished radio broadcast

REINHOLD GLIERE (1875-1956)
russian sailors' dance/the red poppy
recorded on 23 november 1964 in the manhattan centre
new york   lp: columbia ML 6271/MS 6871/
philharmonic   MS 7246/M3X 31068/M 34127/
                     MY 37770/DMS 659/S2S 5462
                     cd: MYK 37770/MLK 44725/
                     SMK 47607/SMK 64077

MIKHAIL GLINKA (1804-1857)
russlan and ludmilla, overture
recorded on 14 october 1963 in philharmonic hall

new york	lp: columbia ML 6414/MS 7014/
philharmonic	M2X 795/D3S 818/M 31844/
	MY 37770/BRG 72628/SBRG 72628
	cd: MYK 37770/SMK 47607

KARL GOLDMARK (1830-1915)
rustic wedding symphony
recorded on 21 march 1968 in philharmonic hall

| new york | lp: columbia MS 7261/60336 |
| philharmonic | cd: SMK 61836 |

CHARLES GOUNOD (1818-1893)
faust, ballet music
recorded on 20 may 1967 in philharmonic hall

| new york | lp: columbia MS 7415 |
| philharmonic | cd: SMK 47600 |

EDVARD GRIEG (1843-1907)
norwegian dance no 2
recorded on 12 october 1965 in the manhattan centre

new york	lp: columbia ML 6271/ML 6388/
philharmonic	MS 6871/MS 6988/MS 7505/
	M3X 31068/60334
	cd: MLK 44724/SFK 46707/
	SMK 47549/SMK 63156/
	SMK 64076/SFK 89109

march of the dwarves/lyric suite
recorded on 20 october 1970 in philharmonic hall

new york	lp: columbia MG 35919
philharmonic	cd: MLK 44724/MDK 45734/
	SMK 47549/SMK 63156/
	MLK 64064/SMK 64076

grieg/**peer gynt, first suite from the incidental music**
recorded on 10 january 1967 in philharmonic hall
new york philharmonic
lp: columbia M 31800/MY 36718/ MYX 39141/60105
cd: MYK 36718/SMK 47549/ SMK 63156
recording completed on 31 january 1967

peer gynt, second suite from the incidental music
recorded on 3 january 1967 in philharmonic hall
new york philharmonic
lp: columbia M 31800/MY 36718/ MYX 39141
cd: MYK 36718/SMK 47549/ SMK 63156
recording completed on 10 january 1967

FERDE GROFE (1892-1972)
grand canyon suite
recorded on 20 may 1963 in philharmonic hall
new york philharmonic
lp: columbia ML 6018/MS 6618/ M 31824/MY 37759/M3X 31068
cd: MYK 37759/MK 42264/ SMK 47544/SMK 63086/SK 90395
sacd: SS 89033
excerpts
lp: columbia 60334

CAMARGO GUARNIERI (1907-1993)
dansa brasileira
recorded on 6 february 1963 in philharmonic hall
new york philharmonic
lp: columbia ML 5914/ML 6271/ MS 6514/MS 6871
cd: SMK 47544/SMK 60571

GEORGE FRIDERIC HANDEL (1685-1759)
messiah/ abridged version
recorded on 31 december 1956 in the columbia studios new york city

new york philharmonic westminster choir addison, oberlin, lloyd, warfield	lp: columbia M2L 242/M2S 603/ philips ABL 3210-3211/ A01349-01350L/L09412-09413L cd: SM2K 60205

excerpts
45: philips ABE 10053/SBF 107/ 407 054AE
lp: columbia ML 5300/ML 5346/ ML 6328/MS 6020/MS 6041/ MS 6928/MY 38481/30115/philips ABL 3274/SABL 116/A01400L/ 835 519AY/G05625R

joy to the world/messiah
recorded on 3-4 september 1963 in the salt lake tabernacle salt lake city

new york philharmonic mormon tabernacle choir	lp: columbia ML 5899/MS 6499 cd: SFK 63303

bernstein also takes a vocal part in a rendition of the halleluja chorus at a 1976 carnegie hall anniversary concert issued on lp M2X 34256 and 79200 and on cd SM2K 46742

ode for saint cecilia's day
recorded on 2 may 1959 in the saint george's hotel brooklyn

new york philharmonic rutgers university choir addison, mccollum	lp: columbia ML 5606/MS 6206 cd: SMK 60731 *recording completed on 1 february 1960*

ROY HARRIS (1898-1979)
symphony no 3
recorded on 27 january 1957 at a concert in carnegie hall
new york philharmonic   cd: new york philharmonic NYP 9904

recorded on 28 september 1960 in the manhattan centre
new york philharmonic
lp: columbia ML 5703/MS 6303/ BRG 72399/SBRG 72399/61681
cd: SMK 60594

televised in 1976 at a concert in the royal albert hall london
new york philharmonic   unpublished video recording

recorded on 10 december 1985 at a concert in avery fisher hall
new york philharmonic
lp: deutsche grammophon 419 7801
cd: 419 7802/469 4602/474 9402

FRANZ JOSEF HAYDN (1732-1809)
symphony no 82 "the bear"
recorded on 7 may 1962 in the manhattan centre
new york philharmonic
lp: columbia ML 6009/MS 6609/D3L 369/ D3S 769/BRG 72240/SBRG 72240/77307
cd: SM2K 47550/SX10K 89750/ smithsonian RD 103-4

symphony no 83 "the hen"
recorded on 9 april 1962 in the manhattan centre
new york philharmonic
lp: columbia ML 6009/MS 6609/D3L 369/ D3S 769/BRG 72240/SBRG 72240/77307
cd: SM2K 47550/SX10K 89750

symphony no 84
recorded on 14 may 1966 in philharmonic hall
new york philharmonic
lp: columbia ML 6348/MS 6948/D3L 369/ D3S 769/BRG 72529/SBRG 72529/77307
cd: SM2K 47550
recording completed on 20 may 1966

haydn/**symphony no 85 "la reine"**
recorded on 20 may 1966 in philharmonic hall
new york philharmonic
lp: columbia ML 6348/MS 6948/D3L 369/
D3S 769/BRG 72529/SBRG 72529/77307
cd: SM2K 47550

symphony no 86
recorded on 7 march 1967 in philharmonic hall
new york philharmonic
lp: columbia ML 6465/MS 7065/D3L 369/
D3S 769/BRG 72641/SBRG 72641/77307
cd: SM2K 47550

symphony no 87
recorded on 21 march 1967 in philharmonic hall
new york philharmonic
lp: columbia ML 6465/MS 7065/D3L 369/
D3S 769/BRG 72641/SBRG 72641/77307
cd: SM2K 47550

symphony no 88
recorded on 7 january 1963 in philharmonic hall
new york philharmonic
lp: columbia MS 7259
cd: SM2K 47563

recorded on 11 march 1967 at a concert in philharmonic hall
new york philharmonic
cd: disco archivia 562

televised between 24-28 november 1983 at concerts in the musikverein vienna
wiener philharmoniker
lp: deutsche grammophon 413 7771
cd: 413 7772/445 5542/474 9192
also unpublished video recording

symphony no 92 "oxford"
televised between 2-5 february 1984 at concerts in the musikverein vienna
wiener philharmoniker
lp: deutsche grammophon 413 7771
cd: 413 7772/431 0342/431 0502/
431 1972/445 5542/474 9192
also unpublished video recording

haydn/**symphony no 93**
recorded on 7 december 1971 in philharmonic hall
new york philharmonic
lp: columbia M 32101/MQ 32101
cd: SM3K 47553/SM5K 87984/502 3152

symphony no 94 "surprise"
recorded on 14-16 december 1971 in philharmonic hall
new york philharmonic
lp: columbia M 32101/MQ 32101/ MP 39025
cd: SM3K 47553/SM5K 87984/502 3152

recorded on 22 october 1985 in the musikverein vienna
wiener philharmoniker
lp: deutsche grammophon 419 2331
cd: 419 2332/431 0342/431 0502/ 431 1972/445 5542/474 9192

symphony no 95
recorded on 12 february 1973 in the columbia studios new york city
new york philharmonic
lp: columbia M 35928/MQ 35928
cd: SM3K 47553/SM5K 87984/502 3152

symphony no 96 "miracle"
recorded between 5-8 march 1973 in the columbia studios new york city
new york philharmonic
lp: columbia M 35928/MQ 35928
cd: SM3K 47553/SM5K 87984/502 3152

symphony no 97
televised on 9 april 1975 in the columbia studios new york city
new york philharmonic
lp: columbia M 35844
cd: SM3K 47553/SM5K 87984/502 3152
also unpublished video recording

symphony no 98
televised on 10 april 1975 in the columbia studios new york city
new york philharmonic
lp: columbia M 35844
cd: SM3K 47553/SM5K 87984/502 3152
also unpublished video recording

haydn/**symphony no 99**
recorded on 19-20 october 1970 in philharmonic hall
new york philharmonic
lp: columbia M 34126
cd: SM3K 47553/SM5K 87984/502 3152

recorded on 4 july 1975 at a concert in symphony hall boston
boston symphony
cd: disco archivia 556

symphony no 100 "military"
recorded on 12 october 1970 in philharmonic hall
new york philharmonic
lp: columbia M 34126
cd: SM2K 47557/SM5K 87984/502 3152

symphony no 101 "the clock"
recorded on 12 february 1970 in philharmonic hall
new york philharmonic
lp: columbia M 33531/MP 39025
cd: SM2K 47557/SM5K 87984/502 3152

symphony no 102
recorded on 2 june 1946 in the nbc studios new york city
nbc symphony
unpublished radio broadcast

recorded on 31 october 1962 in philharmonic hall
new york philharmonic
lp: columbia MS 7259
cd: SM2K 47557/SM5K 87984/502 3152

recorded on 21 february 1971 at a concert in the musikverein vienna
wiener philharmoniker
cd: deutsche grammophon 435 3212/ 435 3222/live classics best (japan) LCB 147

recorded on 3 april 1976 in the columbia studios new york city
new york philharmonic
columbia unpublished

symphony no 103 "drum roll"
recorded between 10-12 february 1970 in philharmonic hall
new york philharmonic
lp: columbia M 33531
cd: SM2K 47557/SM5K 87984/502 3152

haydn/**symphony no 104 "london"**
recorded on 27 january 1958 in the saint george's hotel brooklyn
new york philharmonic
lp: columbia ML 5349/MS 6050/philips ABL 3265/SABL 138/A01402L/ 835 523AY
cd: SM2K 47557/SM5K 87984/502 3152

recorded on 6 july 1979 at a concert in the nhk hall tokyo
new york philharmonic
columbia unpublished

sinfonia concertante for wind and orchestra
recorded on 22 october 1985 in the musikverein vienna
wiener philharmoniker
lp: deutsche grammophon 419 2331
cd: 419 2332/474 9192

die schöpfung
recorded between 17-20 may 1966 in philharmonic hall
new york philharmonic
camerata singers
raskin, young, reardon
lp: columbia M2S 773
cd: SM2K 47560/AMS 015-016

recorded on 26-27 june 1986 at concerts in the herkulessaal munich
sinfonieorchester und chor des bayerischen rundfunks
blegen, popp, moser, ollman, moll
cd: deutsche grammophon 419 7652/ 453 0312/474 9192

mass no 10 "paukenmesse"
recorded on 20 january 1973 in the kennedy centre washington dc
national symphony
scribner chorus
wells, killebrew, titus, devlin
lp: columbia M 32196/MQ 32196

recorded in 1976 at a concert in symphony hall boston
boston symphony and chorus
valente, killebrew, riegel, cheek
cd: disco archivia 553

recorded on 28 september 1984 at a concert in the herkulessaal munich
sinfonieorchester und chor des bayerischen rundfunks
blegen, fassbänder, ahnsjö, sotin
cd: philips 412 7342/deutsche grammophon 474 9192

haydn/**mass no 12 "theresienmesse"**
televised between 12-15 may 1979 in the henry wood hall london
london symphony   lp: columbia M 35839
lso chorus   cd: SM2K 47522
popp, elias,   *also unpublished video recording*
tear, hudson

recorded on 27 may 1979 at a concert in the musikverein vienna
wiener   cd: sardana (japan) SACD 158/
philharmoniker   disco archivia 559/private
chor der wiener   edition vienna
staatsoper
blegen, elias,
rendall, holl

mass no 14 "harmoniemesse"
recorded on 19 february 1973 in the manhattan centre
new york   lp: columbia M 33267/MQ 33267
philharmonic   cd: SM2K 47560
westminster choir
blegen, von stade,
riegel, estes

HANS WERNER HENZE (born 1926)
symphony no 5
recorded on 18 may 1963 at a concert in philharmonic hall
new york   cd: new york philharmonic NYP 2003
philharmonic   *world premiere performance*

FERDINAND HEROLD (1791-1833)
zampa, overture
recorded on 21 january 1963 in philharmonic hall
new york   lp: columbia ML 6143/ML 6388/
philharmonic   MS 6743/MS 6988/D3S 818/
               M3X 31068/MY 37240/M 31815/
               BRG 72389/SBRG 72389/60334
               cd: MYK 37240/SFK 46713

ALFRED HILL (1870-1960)
prelude for orchestra
recorded on 27 may 1953 in the columbia studios new york city
columbia lp: columbia ML 4996
symphony cd: SMK 60725/SMK 61849

PAUL HINDEMITH (1895-1963)
symphony in e flat
recorded on 7 march 1967 in philharmonic hall
new york lp: columbia MS 7426/MP 38754
philharmonic cd: SMK 47566

mathis der maler, symphony
recorded on 23 december 1956 at a concert in carnegie hall
new york cd: new york philharmonic NYP 2003
philharmonic

violin concerto
recorded on 25 april 1964 in the manhattan centre
new york lp: columbia ML 6133/MS 6713/
philharmonic BRG 72345/SBRG 72345
stern cd: SMK 47599/SMK 64507/
 SX9K 67194

concert music for brass and strings
recorded on 13 march 1961 in the manhattan centre
new york lp: columbia ML 5979/MS 6579
philharmonic cd: SMK 47566

recorded on 30 april 1989 at a concert in the frederick mann auditorium
israel cd: deutsche grammophon
philharmonic 429 4042

symphonic metamorphoses on themes of weber
recorded on 16 january 1968 in philharmonic hall
new york lp: columbia MS 7246/MP 38754
philharmonic cd: SMK 47566

recorded on 30 april 1989 at a concert in the frederick mann auditorium
israel cd: deutsche grammophon
philharmonic 429 4042

GUSTAV HOLST (1874-1934)
the planets
recorded between 30 november-7 december 1971 in philharmonic hall

new york philharmonic
camerata singers

lp: columbia M 31125/MQ 31125/
MY 37226/73001
cd: MYK 37226/SMK 47567/
SBK 62400/SBK 63087
sacd: SS 87981

lullaby my liking/5 partsongs
recorded on 3-4 september 1963 in the salt lake tabernacle

new york philharmonic
mormon tabernacle choir

lp: columbia ML 5849/MS 6499
cd: SFK 63303

ARTHUR HONEGGER (1892-1955)
pacific 231
recorded on 31 october 1962 in philharmonic hall

new york philharmonic

lp: columbia ML 6059/MS 6659
cd: SMK 60695/MHK 62352

pastorale d'été
recorded on 31 october 1962 in philharmonic hall

new york philharmonic

lp: columbia ML 6059/MS 6659
cd: SMK 60695

rugby
recorded on 31 october 1962 in philharmonic hall

new york philharmonic

lp: columbia ML 6059/MS 6659
cd: SMK 60695/MHK 62352

JULIA HOWE (1819-1910)
battle hymn of the republic
recorded on 20 october 1970 in philharmonic hall

new york philharmonic

lp: columbia M 30943/MG 35919/
cd: MDK 45734/SFK 46709/
SMK 63154/SBK 89305

ENGELBERT HUMPERDINCK (1854-1921)
evening prayer/hänsek und gretel, arrangement
recorded on 22 october 1970 in philharmonic hall
new york philharmonic
lp: columbia M 30573
cd: MLK 44723/SFK 46714/
SMK 61836/MLK 62617/SFK 63303/
SMK 64075/SFK 89109

MIKHAIL IPPOLITOV-IVANOV (1859-1935)
in the village/caucasian sketches
recorded on 1 february 1965 in the manhattan centre
new york philharmonic
lp: columbia ML 6414/MS 7014/
M 31844/BRG 72628/SBRG 72628
cd: SMK 47607

procession of the sardar/caucasian sketches
recorded on 1 february 1965 in the manhattan centre
new york philharmonic
lp: columbia ML 6414/MS 7014/
MS 7271/M3X 31068/M 31844/
M 34127/MY 37770/MG 35919/
BRG 72628/SBRG 72628
cd: MYK 37770/MLK 44725/
MDK 45734/SMK 47607/SMK 63154/
SMK 64077/SBK 89305

CHARLES IVES (1874-1954)
symphony no 2
recorded on 25 february 1951 at a concert in carnegie hall
new york philharmonic
cd: new york philharmonic NYP 2003

recorded on 6 october 1958 in the saint george's hotel brooklyn
new york philharmonic
lp: columbia KL 5489/KS 6155/
ML 6289/MS 6889/D3S 783/77424
cd: MK 42407/SMK 47568/SMK 60202/
SK 94731/516 0232/82796 947312
ML 6289, MS 6889, SMK 60202 and 516 0232 also contained bernstein's introductory talk

televised on 14 april 1987 at a concert in avery fisher hall
new york philharmonic
cd: deutsche grammophon
429 2202/474 9402
dvd video: 073 4513

ives/**symphony no 3 "camp meeting"**
recorded on 15 december 1965 in philharmonic hall
new york philharmonic   lp: columbia ML 6243/MS 6843/ D3S 783/MP 38777/BRG 72458/ SBRG 72458/77424
cd: MK 42407/SMK 47568/ SMK 60202/516 0232

washington's birthday/holidays symphony
recorded on 31 january 1967 in philharmonic hall
new york philharmonic   lp: columbia ML 6415/MS 7015/ MS 7147/MG 31155/MP 39556/ 77424
cd: SMK 60203/516 0232

decoration day/holidays symphony
recorded on 27 may 1963 in the manhattan centre
new york philharmonic   lp: columbia ML 6243/MS 6843/ MS 7147/MP 38777/MP 39556/ BRG 72458/SBRG 72458/77424
cd: SMK 60203/516 0232

the fourth of july/holidays symphony
recorded on 23 november 1964 in the manhattan centre
new york philharmonic   lp: columbia ML 6289/MS 6889/ MS 7147/MG 31155/M4 32504/ MP 39556/BRG 72451/ SBRG 72451/77424
cd: SMK 60203/516 0232

thanksgiving day/holidays symphony
recorded on 5 march 1968 in philharmonic hall
new york philharmonic camerata singers   lp: columbia MS 7147/MP 39556/ BRG 72646/SBRG 72646/77424
cd: SMK 60203/516 0232

ives/**central park in the dark**
recorded on 23 november 1988 at a concert in avery fisher hall
new york philharmonic   cd: deutsche grammophon 429 2202/ 469 2772/ 474 9402

circus band march
recorded on 31 january 1967 in philharmonic hall
new york philharmonic   cd: columbia M3X 31068
unpublished columbia lp recording

the gong on the hook and ladder
recorded on 31 january 1967 in philharmonic hall
new york philharmonic   cd: columbia M3X 31068
unpublished columbia lp recording

recorded on 23 november 1988 at a concert in avery fisher hall
new york philharmonic   cd: deutsche grammophon 429 2202/ 474 9402

halloween
recorded on 23 november 1988 at a concert in avery fisher hall
new york philharmonic   cd: deutsche grammophon 429 2202/ 474 9402

largo cantabile
recorded on 23 november 1988 at a concert in avery fisher hall
new york philharmonic   cd: deutsche grammophon 429 2202/ 474 9402

tone roads
recorded on 23 november 1988 at a concert in avery fisher hall
new york philharmonic   cd: deutsche grammophon 429 2202/ 474 9402

ives/**the unanswered question**
recorded on 17 april 1964 in the manhattan centre
new york philharmonic lp: columbia ML 6243/MS 6843/
M4 32504/M3X 33028/MP 38777/
BRG 72458/SBRG 72458/77424
cd: MK 42407/SFK 46701/
SMK 60203/SK 90390/S3K 90578/
SK 94731/82796 947312

televised in 1976 at a concert in the royal albert hall london
new york philharmonic unpublished video recording

recorded on 23 november 1988 at a concert in avery fisher hall
new york philharmonic cd: deutsche grammophon 429 2202/
463 4652/469 2772/474 9402

LEOS JANACEK (1854-1928)
glagolithic mass
recorded on 28 january 1963 in philharmonic hall
new york philharmonic
westminster choir
pilarczyk, martin,
gedda, gaynes
lp: columbia ML 6137/MS 6737
cd: SMK 47569

GYORGY LIGETI (born 1923)
atmospheres
recorded on 6 january 1964 in the manhattan centre
new york philharmonic lp: columbia ML 6133/MS 6733/MS 7176
  cd: SMK 61845

FRANZ LISZT (1811-1886)
a faust symphony
recorded on 7 november 1960 in the manhattan centre
new york
philharmonic
chorale art society
bressler
  lp: columbia M2L 299/M2S 699
  cd: SMK 47570

televised on 26-27 july 1976 at concerts in symphony hall boston
boston
symphony
tanglewood festival chorus
riegel
  lp: deutsche grammophon 2707 100
  cd: 447 4492/disco archivia 555
  also unpublished video recording

piano concerto no 1
recorded on 3 february 1963 in philharmonic hall
new york
philharmonic
watts
  lp: columbia ML 5858/ML 6355/
  MS 6458/BRG 72570/SBRG 72570/
  78315
  cd: SMK 47571

liszt/**les préludes**
recorded on 3 february 1963 in philharmonic hall
new york philharmonic
lp: columbia ML 5858/MS 6458/
M2L 299/M2S 699/M 30306/
MY 37772/M 39450
cd: MYK 37772/MLK 39450/SFK 46706/
SMK 47572/MLK 64596

hungarian rhapsody no 1, arranged by doppler
recorded on 16 december 1969 in philharmonic hall
new york philharmonic
lp: columbia M 30645/MY 37772
cd: MYK 37772/SMK 47572

hungarian rhapsody no 4, arranged by doppler
recorded on 12 january 1971 in philharmonic hall
new york philharmonic
lp: columbia M 30645
cd: SMK 47572/SBK 60265

o quand je dors !
recorded on 2 march 1969 in the columbia studios new york city
tourel
bernstein, piano
lp: columbia M 32231

NIKOLAI LOPATNIKOFF (1903-1976)
concertino for orchestra
recorded on 27 may 1953 in the columbia studios new york city
columbia symphony
lp: columbia ML 4996
cd: SMK 60725

EDWARD MACDOWELL (1860-1908)
three movements from the indian suite
recorded on 11 october 1958 at a concert in carnegie hall
new york philharmonic
cd: new york philharmonic NYP 9904

GUSTAV MAHLER (1860-1911)
symphony no 1
recorded on 4 october 1966 in philharmonic hall

new york philharmonic	lp: columbia MS 7069/GMS 765/GM 15/ M4X 31427/M 31834/BRG 72649 SBRG 72649 cd: MK 42194/SM2K 47573/ SMK 60732/SX12K 89499/ SX12K 64204 sacd: SS 07069 *recording completed on 20 october 1966*

televised between 2-10 october 1974 at concerts in the konzerthaus vienna

wiener philharmoniker	cd: disco archivia 561 vhs video: deutsche grammophon 072 1233 dvd video: 073 4088/073 4089

recorded between 8-10 october 1987 at concerts in the concertgebouw amsterdam

concertgebouw orkest	cd: deutsche grammophon 427 3032/ 435 1622/459 0802/477 5174

symphony no 2 "resurrection"
recorded on 29-30 september 1963 in the manhattan centre

new york philharmonic collegiate chorale venora, tourel	lp: columbia M2L 295/M2S 695/ GMS 765/GM 15/M4X 31432/ BRG 72283-72284/SBRG 72283-72284 cd: SM2K 63159/SX12K 89499/ SX12K 64204

televised between 31 august-2 september 1963 at concerts in ely cathedral

london symphony edinburgh festival chorus armstrong, baker	lp: columbia M2 32681/M2Q 32681/ GM 2-3/78249 cd: M2K 42195/SM2K 47573/ 517 4943 vhs video: 072 1003 laserdisc: 072 1001 dvd video: 073 4088/073 4089

recorded in 1970 at a concert in symphony hall boston

boston symphony orchestra and chorus haywood, ludwig	cd: disco archivia 566

recorded on 21 april 1987 at a concert in avery fisher hall

new york philharmonic westminster choir hendriks, ludwig	lp: deutsche grammophon 423 3951 cd: 423 3952/435 1622/459 0802/ 477 5174/532 2022

mahler/**symphony no 2, final movement**
recorded in july 1967 at a concert in tel aviv
israel   lp: columbia ML 6453/MS 7053
philharmonic
orchestra and chorus
davrath, tourel

symphony no 3
recorded on 3 april 1961 in the manhattan centre
new york   lp: columbia M2L 275/M2S 675/
philharmonic   GMS 765/M4X 31432/GM 15/
schola cantorum   BRG 72065/SBRG 72065/77206
lipton   cd: M2K 42196/SM2K 47576/
                       SM2K 61831/SX12K 89499/
                       SX12K 64204

televised between 20-26 april 1972 at concerts in the musikverein vienna
wiener   cd: disco archivia 559
philharmoniker   vhs video: deutsche grammophon
konzertvereingung   072 1513
wiener staatsopernchor   dvd video: 073 4088/073 4089
ludwig   *disco archivia edition is dated 1974*

recorded on 28 november 1987 at a concert in avery fisher hall
new york   lp: deutsche grammophon 427 3281
philharmonic   cd: 427 3282/435 1622/459 0802/
choral artists choir   477 5174/532 2022/musical heritage
ludwig   society MHS 525 138Y

mahler/**symphony no 4**
recorded on 1 february 1960 in the saint george's hotel brooklyn
new york philharmonic grist

lp: columbia ML 5485/MS 6152/
GMS 765/M3X 31437/GM 15
cd: MK 42197/SMK 47579/
SMK 60733/SX12K 89499/
SX12K 64204

televised between 5-9 may 1972 at concerts in the musikverein vienna
wiener
philharmoniker
mathis

vhs video: deutsche grammophon
072 1233
dvd video: 073 4088/073 4090

televised on 23 june 1984 at a concert in the teatro alla scala milan
filharmonica
della scala
eiwanger

unpublished video recording

recorded in 1984 at a concert in the musikverein vienna
wiener
philharmoniker
bergius

cd: first classics (japan) FC 108/
sardana (japan) SACD 151

recorded on 24-26 june 1987 at concerts in the concertgebouw amsterdam
concertgebouw
orkest
wittek

lp: deutsche grammophon 423 6071
cd: 423 6072/459 0802/477 5174

mahler/**symphony no 5**
recorded on 7 january 1963 in philharmonic hall

new york philharmonic
lp: columbia M2L 298/M2S 698/
GMS 765/M3X 31437/GM 15/
BRG 72183-72184/SBRG 72183-72184
cd: MK 42198/SMK 47580/
SMK 63084/SX12K 89499/
SX12K 64204
adagietto
lp: columbia MY 38484
cd: MYK 38484/SFK 46701/SK 92726

televised on 17 april 1972 at a concert in the musikverein vienna

wiener philharmoniker
cd: disco archivia 552
vhs video: deutsche grammophon 072 1253
dvd video: 073 4088/073 4090
rehearsal extract
dvd video: kultur 1525
disco archivia edition is dated may 1972

recorded on 30 august 1987 at a concert in the grosses festspielhaus salzburg

wiener philharmoniker
cd: live classics best (japan) LCB 108/
halloo (japan) HAL 32

recorded between 6-8 september 1987 at concerts in the alte oper frankfurt

wiener philharmoniker
cd: deutsche grammophon 423 6082/
435 1622/459 0802/
477 5181/477 6334

recorded on 10 september 1987 at a concert in the royal albert hall london

wiener philharmoniker
cd: sardana (japan) SACD 150

mahler/**symphony no 5, adagietto**
recorded on 8 june 1968 at a memorial concert for john f kennedy in saint patrick's cathedral
new york philharmonic
lp: columbia D2S 792
cd: SM2K 63159/SX12K 89499

recorded on 8 november 1987 at a concert in carnegie hall
new york orchestra members
cd: deutsche grammophon 429 3922

symphony no 6
recorded between 2-6 may 1967 in philharmonic hall
new york philharmonic
lp: columbia M3S 776/M4X 31427/
GMS 765/GM 15/77215
cd: M3K 42199/SM3K 47581/
SMK 50208/SX12K 89499/
SX12K 64204
most issues include bernstein's spoken analysis

televised on 22-23 october 1976 at concerts in the musikverein vienna
wiener philharmoniker
cd: private edition vienna
vhs video: deutsche grammophon 072 1263
dvd video: 073 4088/073 4090

recorded in september 1988 at concerts in the musikverein vienna
wiener philharmoniker
cd: deutsche grammophon 427 6972/459 0802/477 5181

mahler/**symphony no 7**
recorded on 12 december 1965 at a concert in philharmonic hall
new york cd: private edition usa
philharmonic

recorded on 14-15 december 1965 in philharmonic hall
new york lp: columbia M2L 339/M2S 739/
philharmonic M4X 31441/GMS 765/GM 15/
BRG 72427-72428/SBRG 72427-72428
cd: M3K 42200/SM3K 47585/
SMK 60564/SX12K 89499/
SX10K 89750/SX12K 64204

recorded between 2-10 october 1974 in the musikverein vienna
wiener cd: private edition vienna
philharmoniker vhs video: deutsche grammophon
072 1273
dvd video: 073 4088/073 4091

recorded on 3 december 1985 at a concert in avery fisher hall
new york lp: deutsche grammophon 419 2111
philharmonic cd: 419 2112/435 1622/459 0802/
477 5181/musical heritage society
532 1022/disco archivia 565
disco archivia edition is dated 1986

symphony no 8 "symphony of a thousand"
recorded between 18-20 april 1966 in the town hall walthamstow
london symphony lp: columbia M2L 351/M2S 751/
lso chorus M4X 31441/GMS 765/GM 15/
leeds festival chorus MET 2013/BRG 72491-72492/
childrens' choirs SBRG 72491-72492/77507/77234
spoorenberg, jones, cd: M3K 42199/SM3K 47581/
annear, reynolds, SM2K 61837/SX12K 89499/
proctor, mitchinson, 517 4932/SX12K 64204
ruzdjak, mcintyre

mahler/symphony no 8/concluded
recorded on 30 august 1975 at a concert in the grosses festspielhaus salzburg
wiener　　　　　　　　cd: deutsche grammophon 435 1022/
philharmoniker　　　　　435 1622/459 0802/477 5187
chor der wiener
staatsoper
wiener singverein
m.price, blegen,
zeumer, schmidt,
baltsa, riegel,
prey, van dam

televised on 1-2 september 1975 at concerts in the konzerthaus vienna
wiener　　　　　　　　vhd video: deutsche grammophon
philharmoniker　　　　　072 1163
chor der wiener　　　　dvd video: 073 4088/073 4091
staatsoper
wiener singverein
moser, blegen,
zeumer, mayr,
baltsa, riegel,
prey, van dam

veni creator spiritus/symphony no 8
recorded on 23 september 1962 at the opening concert in philharmonic hall
new york　　　　　　　lp: columbia L2L 1007/L2S 1008
philharmonic　　　　　　cd: SM2K 63159/SX12K 89499
schola cantorum
juilliard and columbus
choirs
addison, amara,
chookasian, tourel,
tucker, flagello,
london

mahler/**symphony no 9**
recorded on 16 december 1965 in philharmonic hall
new york philharmonic
lp: columbia M3S 776/M4X 31427/ GMS 765/GM 15/77224
cd: M3K 42200/SM3K 47585/ SMK 60597/SX12K 89499/ SX12K 64204

televised in march 1971 at a concert in the philharmonie berlin
wiener philharmoniker
cd: disco archivia 560
vhs video: deutsche grammophon 072 1293
dvd video: 073 4088/073 4092
rehearsal extract
dvd video: kultur 1525

recorded on 29 july 1979 at a concert in symphony hall boston
boston symphony
cd: disco archivia 556

recorded on 4 october 1979 at a concert in the philharmonie berlin
berliner philharmonisches orchester
cd: deutsche grammophon 435 3782/ pandora's box (japan) CDBP 232/ sardana (japan)

recorded on 1-3 june 1985 at concerts in the concertgebouw amsterdam
concertgebouw orkest
lp: deutsche grammophon 419 2081
cd: 419 2082/459 0802/477 5187

adagio/symphony no 10, arranged by ratz
televised between 2-10 october 1974 at concerts in the musikverein vienna
wiener philharmoniker
cd: deutsche grammophon 435 1022/ 435 1622/459 0802/477 5187/ disco archivia 558
vhs video: 072 4153
dvd video: 073 4088/073 4092

recorded on 8 april 1975 in the columbia studios new york city
new york philharmonic
lp: columbia M 33532/MQ 33532/ GM 15/76475
cd: M3K 42200/SM3K 47585/ SMK 60732/SX12K 89499/ SX12K 64204
smithsonian RD 103-4

mahler/**das lied von der erde**
recorded between 4-6 april 1966 in the sofiensaal vienna
wiener　　　　　　　　　　lp: decca MET 331/SET 331/JB 13/
philharmoniker　　　　　　london OM 36005/OS 36005/
king　　　　　　　　　　　OSA 2233/STS 15499
fischer-dieskau　　　　　　cd: 452 3012/459 0942/459 0802/
　　　　　　　　　　　　　466 3812/477 5187

televised in may 1972 at concerts in the frederick mann auditorium
israel　　　　　　　　　　lp: columbia KM 31919/76105/
philharmonic　　　　　　　61884
ludwig, kollo　　　　　　　cd: SMK 47589
　　　　　　　　　　　　　vhs video: deutsche grammophon
　　　　　　　　　　　　　072 1283
　　　　　　　　　　　　　laserdisc: 072 1281
　　　　　　　　　　　　　dvd video: 073 4088/073 4092

des knaben wunderhorn
recorded on 17 october 1967 in philharmonic hall
new york　　　　　　　　　lp: columbia KS 7395/M3X 37892/
philharmonic　　　　　　　61825
ludwig, berry　　　　　　　cd: MK 42202/SMK 48590
　　　　　　　　　　　　　recording completed in february 1969

recorded on 24 april 1968 at a concert in the konzerthaus vienna
ludwig, berry　　　　　　　lp: columbia KS 7395/BS 19
bernstein, piano　　　　　　cd: SM2K 47170

televised on 23-24 may 1984 at concerts in the frederick mann auditorium
israel philharmonic　　　　dvd video: deutsche grammophon
popp, gronroos　　　　　　073 4167

recorded between 14-16 october 1987 at concerts in the concertgebouw amsterdam
concertgebouw　　　　　　cd: deutsche grammophon 427 3032/
orkest　　　　　　　　　　459 0802/477 5174
popp, a.schmidt

das irdische leben/des knaben wunderhorn
recorded on 8 february 1960 in the saint george's hotel brooklyn
new york　　　　　　　　　lp: columbia ML 5597/MS 6197
philharmonic　　　　　　　cd: SM2K 47576/SM2K 61831
tourel

mahler/**lieder eines fahrenden gesellen**
recorded on 4 november 1968 in the columbia studios new york city
fischer-dieskau   lp: columbia M 30942/KM 30942
bernstein, piano   cd: SM2K 47170/SM2K 61847
                         SM2K 47170 incorrectly described this
                         as a first release

recorded on 8 november 1968 at a concert in philharmonic hall
fischer-dieskau   cd: myto MCD 89008
bernstein, piano

recorded on 24 february 1990 at a concert in the musikverein vienna
wiener   cd: deutsche grammophon 431 6822/
philharmoniker   459 0802/477 5174
hampson   vhs video: 072 1803
                         dvd video: 073 4167

lieder und gesänge aus der jugendzeit
recorded on 5-6 november 1968 in the columbia studios new york city
fischer-dieskau   lp: columbia M 30492/KM 30492
bernstein, piano   cd: SM2K 47170

kindertotenlieder
recorded on 16 february 1960 in the saint george's hotel brooklyn
new york   lp: columbia ML 5597/MS 6197/
philharmonic   M2L 298/M2S 698/BRG 72182-
tourel   72183/SBRG 72182-72183
                         cd: SM2K 47576/SM2K 61831/
                         SX12K 89499/SX12K 64204

recorded in october 1974 at a concert in the frederick mann auditorium
israel philharmonic   lp: columbia M 33532/M2 32681/
baker   M2Q 32361/76475
                         cd: M2K 42195

recorded on 3 october 1988 at a concert in the musikverein vienna
wiener   cd: deutsche grammophon 427 6972/
philharmoniker   431 6822/459 0802/459 0882/
hampson   477 5181
                         vhs video: 072 1803
                         dvd video: 073 4167

mahler/**blicke mir nicht in die lieder!**/**rückert-lieder**
recorded on 6 november 1968 in the columbia studios new york city
fischer-dieskau   lp: columbia M 30942/KM 30942
bernstein, piano   cd: SM2K 47170
                               SM2K 47170 incorrectly described this
                               as a first release

recorded on 8 november 1968 at a concert in philharmonic hall
fischer-dieskau   cd: myto MCD 89008
bernstein, piano

recorded on 24 february 1990 at a concert in the musikverein vienna
wiener   cd: deutsche grammophon
philharmoniker   431 6822/459 0802/477 5181
hampson   vhs video: 072 1803
                               dvd video: 073 4167

ich atmet' einen linden duft/**rückert-lieder**
recorded on 8 february 1960 in the saint george's hotel brooklyn
new york   lp: columbia ML 5597/MS 6197
philharmonic   cd: SM2K 47576/SM2K 61831/
tourel   SX12K 89499/SX12K 64204

recorded on 6 november 1968 in the columbia studios new york city
fischer-dieskau   lp: columbia M 30942/KM 30942
bernstein, piano   cd: SM2K 47170
                               SM2K 47170 incorrectly described this
                               as a first release

recorded on 8 november 1968 at a concert in philharmonic hall
fischer-dieskau   cd: myto MCD 89008
bernstein, piano

recorded on 24 february 1990 at a concert in the musikverein vienna
wiener   cd: deutsche grammophon
philharmoniker   431 6822/459 0802/477 5181
hampson   vhs video: 072 1803
                               dvd video: 073 4167

mahler/**ich bin der welt abhanden gekommen/rückert-lieder**
recorded on 8 february 1960 in the saint george's hotel brooklyn
new york philharmonic tourel
lp: columbia ML 5597/MS 6197
cd: SM2K 47576/SM2K 61831/
SX12K 89499/SX12K 64204

recorded on 6 november 1968 in the columbia studios new york city
fischer-dieskau
bernstein, piano
lp: columbia M 30942/KM 30942
cd: SM2K 47170
SM2K incorrectly described this as a first release

recorded on 8 november 1968 at a concert in philharmonic hall
fischer-dieskau
bernstein, piano
cd: myto MCD 89008

recorded on 24 february 1990 at a concert in the musikverein vienna
wiener philharmoniker hampson
cd: deutsche grammophon
431 6822/459 0802/477 5181
vhs video: 072 1803
dvd video: 073 4167

liebst du um schönheit/rückert-lieder
recorded on 24 february 1990 at a concert in the musikverein vienna
wiener philharmoniker hampson
cd: deutsche grammophon
431 6822/459 0802/477 5181
vhs video: 072 1803
dvd video: 073 4167

mahler/**um mitternacht/rückert-lieder**
recorded on 8 february 1960 in the saint george's hotel brooklyn
new york philharmonic tourel
lp: columbia ML 5597/MS 6197
cd: SM2K 47576/SM2K 61831/
SX12K 89499/SX12K 64204

recorded on 6 november 1968 in the columbia studios new york city
fischer-dieskau
bernstein, piano
lp: columbia M 30942/KM 30942
cd: SM2K 47170
SM2K 47170 incorrectly described this as a first release

recorded on 8 november 1968 at a concert in philharmonic hall
fischer-dieskau
bernstein, piano
cd: myto MCD 89008

recorded on 24 february 1990 at a concert in the musikverein vienna
wiener philharmoniker hampson
cd: deutsche grammophon
431 6822/459 0802/477 5181
vhs video: 072 1803
dvd video: 073 4167

IGOR MARKEVITCH (1912-1983)
icare
recorded on 13 april 1958 at a concert in carnegie hall
new york philharmonic
cd: new york philharmonic NYP 2003

PIETRO MASCAGNI (1863-1945)
cavalleria rusticana
recorded on 7 february 1970 at a performance in the metropolitan opera house
met orchestra and chorus
bumbry, ordassy, corelli, cassel
unpublished met broadcast

FELIX MENDELSSOHN-BARTHOLDY (1809-1847)
symphony no 3 "scotch"
recorded on 13 january 1964 in philharmonic hall
new york philharmonic
lp: columbia ML 6376/MS 6976/ MG 32982/BRG 725272/ SBRG 72572
cd: SMK 47591

recorded on 20 august 1979 at a concert in the grosses festspielhaus salzburg
israel philharmonic
cd: disco archivia 558

recorded on 26 august 1979 at a concert in the deutsches museum munich
israel philharmonic
lp: deutsche grammophon 2531 256
cd: 431 0382/439 9802/477 5167

symphony no 4 "italian"
recorded on 13 january 1958 in the saint george's hotel brooklyn
new york philharmonic
lp: columbia ML 5349/MS 6218/ MS 6050/MS 6818/MS 7057/ D3L 337/D3S 737/M 31819/BM 13/ MG 32982/philips ABL 3265/ SABL 138/A01402L/835 523AY
cd: SMK 47592/SMK 61843

recorded on 23 october 1978 at a concert in the frederick mann auditorium
israel philharmonic
lp: deutsche grammophon 2531 097
cd: 431 0382/439 9802/477 5167/ helicon (israel) 02-9614

symphony no 5 "reformation"
recorded on 29 december 1966 in philharmonic hall
new york philharmonic
lp: columbia MS 7295/MG 32982
cd: SMK 47591

recorded between 6-23 october 1978 at concerts in the frederick mann auditorium
israel philharmonic
lp: deutsche grammophon 2531 097
cd: 431 0382/477 5167

mendelssohn/**violin concerto**
recorded on 9 july 1967 at an open air concert on mount scopus
israel lp: columbia ML 6453/MS 7053
philharmonic *recording featured in the film journey*
stern *to jerusalem*

recorded on 6 february 1969 in philharmonic hall
new york lp: columbia MS 7313/72768
philharmonic cd: SMK 47592/SMK 61843
zukerman

the hebrides, overture
recorded on 16 february 1966 in philharmonic hall
new york lp: columbia ML 6376/MS 6976/
philharmonic MG 32982/BRG 72572/
 SBRG 72572
 cd: SMK 47592/SMK 61843

recorded between 24-26 august 1979 at concerts in the deutsches museum munich
israel lp: deutsche grammophon 2531 256
philharmonic cd: 477 5167/helicon (israel) 02-9614

ruy blas, overture
recorded on 24 october 1960 in the manhattan centre
new york lp: columbia ML 5623/MS 6223
philharmonic cd: SMK 47591

war march of the priests/athalie
recorded on 26 october 1967 in philharmonic hall
new york lp: columbia MS 7271/MG 35919
philharmonic cd: MDK 45734/SMK 47592/
 SMK 61843/SMK 63154/
 SBK 89305

PETER MENNIN (1923-1983)
concertato for orchestra "moby dick"
recorded on 19 january 1963 at a concert in philharmonic hall
new york cd: new york philharmonic
philharmonic NYP 9904/NYP 9915/
 disco archivia 564

OLIVIER MESSIAEN (1908-1992)
turangalila symphony
recorded on 28 november 1949 at a concert in symphony hall boston
boston symphony cd: boston symphony broadcast archives

trois petites liturgies de la présence divine
recorded on 6 november 1961 in the manhattan centre
new york philharmonic
choral arts society
jacobs, canarina
lp: columbia ML 5982/MS 6582/ BRG 72281/SBRG 72281
cd: SMK 61845

GIACOMO MEYERBEER (1791-1864)
marche du couronnement/le prophete
recorded on 26 october 1967 in philharmonic hall
new york philharmonic
lp: columbia MS 7271/MG 35919
cd: MLK 44723/MDK 45734/ SMK 63154/SMK 64075/SBK 89305

DARIUS MILHAUD (1892-1974)
le boeuf sur le toit, ballet
televised on 12-13 november 1976 at concerts in the théatre des champs-élysées
orchestre national
lp: angel 37442/emi ASD 3444/ 1C063 29452/2C069 29452/ 3C065 29452
cd: 747 8452
dvd video: euroarts 205 7068

les choréphores, incidental music
recorded on 16 october 1961 in the manhattan centre
new york philharmonic
schola cantorum
jordan, babikian, boatwright, zorina
lp: columbia ML 5796/MS 6396/ AMS 6396/CMS 6396
cd: MHK 62352

milhaud/**la création du monde, ballet**
recorded on 21 november 1945 in the victor studios new york city
rca victor cd: rca 09026 681012
orchestra *unpublished victor 78rpm recording*

recorded between 22-30 march 1951 in the columbia studios new york city
columbia lp: columbia ML 2203/CL 920/
symphony philips NBR 6019/N02600R
  cd: membran 222 370

televised on 12-13 november 1976 at concerts in the théatre des champs-élysées
orchestre lp: angel 37442/emi ASD 3444/
national 1C063 29452/2C069 29452/
  3C065 29452
  cd: 747 8452
  dvd video: euroarts 205 7068

saudades do brasil, selection from the dance suite
recorded on 12-13 november 1976 at concerts in the théatre des champs-élysées paris
orchestre lp: angel 37442/emi ASD 3444/
national 1C063 29452/2C069 29452/
  3C065 29452
  cd: 747 8452
  also unpublished video recording

WOLFGANG AMADEUS MOZART (1756-1791)
symphony no 25
televised in october 1988 at concerts in the musikverein vienna

wiener
philharmoniker
    cd: deutsche grammophon 429 2212/
    474 3492/477 6697
    vhs video: 072 1813
    dvd video: euroarts 207 2088

symphony no 29
recorded between 6-8 september 1987 at concerts in the alte oper frankfurt

wiener
philharmoniker
    cd: deutsche grammophon 429 2212/
    474 3492/477 6697/halloo (japan)
    HAL 23-24

symphony no 35 "haffner"
recorded between 8-14 october 1984 at concerts in the musikverein vienna

wiener
philharmoniker
    lp: deutsche grammophon 415 3051/
    419 4271
    cd: 415 3052/419 4272/431 0392/
    431 0502/431 1972/460 6152/
    474 3492/477 6697/477 5745

symphony no 36 "linz"
recorded on 6 march 1961 in the manhattan centre

new york
philharmonic
    lp: columbia M 30444
    cd: SMK 47593

recorded between 21-26 march 1966 in the sofiensaal vienna

wiener
philharmoniker
    lp: decca MET 332/SET 332/JB 95/
    london CM 9499/CS 6499/JL 41025
    cd: 433 3302/433 3362/448 5702

recorded between 8-24 october 1984 at concerts in the musikverein vienna

wiener
philharmoniker
    lp: deutsche grammophon 415 4271
    cd: 415 4272/415 9622/474 3492/
    477 5745/477 6697

mozart/**symphony no 38 "prague"**
recorded on 22 october 1985 in the musikverein vienna
wiener   lp: deutsche grammophon 415 9621
philharmoniker   cd: 415 9622/ 419 4272/ 431 0392/
                                431 0502/ 431 1972/ 474 3492/
                                477 6697

symphony no 39
recorded on 27 march 1961 in the manhattan centre
new york   lp: columbia ML 6429/MS 7029
philharmonic   cd: SMK 47594/SMK 60973

televised on 10 april 1981 at a concert in the musikverein vienna
wiener   dvd video: euroarts 207 2098/
philharmoniker   205 7068

recorded between 1-12 october 1981 at concerts in the musikverein vienna
wiener   lp: deutsche grammophon 413 7761
philharmoniker   cd: 413 7762/ 419 4272/
                                474 3492/ 477 6697

symphony no 40
recorded on 20 may 1963 in philharmonic hall
new york   lp: columbia ML 6429/MS 7029/
philharmonic   M 31825/M2X 33014
                                cd: SMK 47593

televised in 1973 in the wgbh studios boston
boston   unpublished video recording
symphony

recorded on 30-31 january 1984 at concerts in the musikverein vienna
wiener   lp: deutsche grammophon 413 7761
philharmoniker   cd: 413 7762/ 419 4272/ 431 0402/
                                431 0502/ 431 1972/ 474 3492/
                                477 5745/ 477 6697

recorded on 12 february 1984 at a concert in the musikverein vienna
wiener   cd: first classics (japan) FC 116/
philharmoniker   halloo (japan) HAL 24

televised on 23 june 1984 at a concert in the teatro alla scala milan
filharmonica   unpublished video recording
della scala

mozart/**symphony no 41 "jupiter"**
recorded between 23-25 january 1968 in philharmonic hall
new york　　　　　　lp: columbia M 30444/M 31825
philharmonic　　　　cd: SMK 47594/SMK 60973

recorded on 30-31 january 1984 at concerts in the musikverein vienna
wiener　　　　　　　lp: deutsche grammophon 415 3051
philharmoniker　　　cd: 415 3052/419 4272/431 0402/
　　　　　　　　　　431 0502/431 1972/460 6152/
　　　　　　　　　　474 3492/477 6697

serenade no 13 "eine kleine nachtmusik"
recorded on 12 march 1973 in the columbia studios new york city
new york　　　　　　lp: columbia M 34574/61896
philharmonic　　　　cd: SMK 47593

german dance k605 no 3 "sleigh ride"
recorded on 12 october 1965 in the manhattan centre
new york　　　　　　lp: columbia ML 6271/MS 6871
philharmonic　　　　cd: MLK 44724/MDK 46267/
　　　　　　　　　　SFK 46707/SMK 62957/SMK 64078

clarinet concerto
recorded on 30 august 1987 at a concert in the grosses festspielhaus salzburg
wiener　　　　　　　cd: live classics best (japan) LCB 104/
philharmoniker　　　halloo (japan) HAL 23
schmidl

televised on 1-2 september 1987 at concerts in the musikverein vienna
wiener　　　　　　　cd: deutsche grammophon 429 2212/
philharmoniker　　　477 6697
schmidl　　　　　　　vhs video: 072 1813
　　　　　　　　　　dvd video: euroarts 207 2088

mozart/**piano concerto no 15 k450**
recorded between 4-7 may 1956 in the columbia studios new york city
columbia　　　　　　　　lp: columbia ML 5145
symphony　　　　　　　　cd: SMK 60734
bernstein conducts
from the piano

recorded between 21-26 march 1966 in the sofiensaal vienna
wiener　　　　　　　　　lp: decca MET 332/SET 332/JB 95/
philharmoniker　　　　　　london CM 9499/CS 6499/JL 41025
bernstein conducts　　　　cd: 433 3302/433 3362/
from the piano　　　　　　448 5702/477 6697

recorded on 6 may 1967 at a concert in philharmonic hall
new york　　　　　　　　cd: disco archivia 564
philharmonic
p.serkin

piano concerto no 17 k453
recorded between 4-7 may 1956 in the columbia studios new york city
columbia　　　　　　　　lp: columbia ML 5145
symphony
bernstein conducts
from the piano

televised in 1959 at a concert in the teatro la fenice venice
fenice orchestra　　　　　unpublished video recording
bernstein conducts
from the piano

televised on 10 april 1981 at a concert in the musikverein vienna
wiener　　　　　　　　　dvd video: euroarts 207 2098/
philharmoniker　　　　　　205 7068
bernstein conducts
from the piano

piano concerto no 23 k488
recorded on 30 january 1960 at a concert in carnegie hall
new york　　　　　　　　cd: new york philharmonic NYP 2003
philharmonic
janis

mozart/**piano concerto no 25 k503**
recorded in november 1974 at a concert in tel aviv
israel philharmonic   lp: columbia M 34574/61896
bernstein conducts
from the piano

concerto for two pianos
recorded on 7 february 1970 in philharmonic hall
new york   lp: columbia M 32173
philharmonic   cd: SMK 60598
gold, fizdale

concerto for three pianos
recorded on 21 march 1968 in philharmonic hall
new york   lp: columbia M 32173
philharmonic   cd: SMK 60598
gold, fizdale
bernstein conducts
from the piano

andante from the sonata for two pianos k448
recorded on 8 november 1987 at a concert in carnegie hall
levine and   cd: deutsche grammophon 429 3922
bernstein, pianos

piano quartet no 1
recorded on 4 april 1965 in the columbia studios new york city
members of the   lp: columbia ML 6329/MS 6929
juilliard quartet   cd: SMK 60596
bernstein, piano

ave verum corpus
televised between 4-8 april 1990 in the basilika waldsassen and the herkulessaal nunich
sinfonieorchester   cd: deutsche grammophon
und chor des   431 7912/477 6697
bayerischen   dvd video: 073 4240
rundfunks

mozart/**ch'io mi scordi di te?, concert aria for soprano and piano obbligato**
recorded on 18 may 1976 at a concert in carnegie hall
new york   columbia unpublished
philharmonic
arroyo
bernstein conducts
from the piano

exsultate jubilate, motet for soprano and orchestra
televised between 4-8 april 1990 in the basilika waldsassen and herkulessaal munich
sinfonieorchester   cd: deutsche grammophon
des bayerischen   431 7912/ 477 6697
rundfunks   dvd video: 073 4240
auger

mass in c minor "great"
televised between 4-8 april 1990 in the basilika waldsassen and herkulessaal munich
sinfonieorchester   cd: deutsche grammophon
und chor des   431 7912/ 477 6697
bayerischen   dvd video: 073 4240
rundfunks
auger, von stade,
lopardo, hauptmann

le nozze di figaro, overture
recorded on 5 march 1968 in philharmonic hall
new york   lp: columbia M3X 31068/MQ 32057
philharmonic   cd: MLK 44724/MDK 46267/
                               SFK 46714/SMK 47601/SMK 60973/
                               SMK 64076/SFK 89109

mozart/**requiem in d minor**
televised on 4-5 july 1988 at unicef benefit concerts in the klosterpfarrkirche maria himmelfahrt in diessen am ammersee

sinfonieorchester	cd: deutsche grammophon 427 3532/
und chor des	474 1702/477 6697
bayerischen	vhs video: 072 1433
rundfunks	laserdisc: 072 2431
mclaughlin, ewing,	dvd video: 073 4135
hadley, hauptmann	

die zauberflöte, overture
recorded on 29 october 1966 at a concert in philharmonic hall

new york   cd: new york philharmonic NYP 2003/
philharmonic   disco archivia 566

MODEST MUSSORGSKY (1839-1881)
pictures at an exhibition, arranged by ravel
recorded on 14 october 1958 in the saint george's hotel brooklyn

new york   lp: columbia ML 5401/MS 6081/
philharmonic   MY 36726/60113/philips A01428L/
               835 527AY/610 301VR/836 401VZ
               cd: MYK 36726/SMK 47595/
               SMK 60693/SK 92727

night on bare mountain, arranged by rimsky-korsakov
recorded on 16 february 1965 in the manhattan centre

new york   lp: columbia ML 6343/ML 6414/
philharmonic   MS 6943/MS 7014/MS 7165/
               D3S 785/M 31844/MY 36726/
               60113/61976
               cd: MYK 36726/SFK 46706/SMK 47596/
               SMK 60693/SK 92727

mussorgsky/**khovantschina, prelude arranged by rimsky-korsakov**
recorded on 2 december 1963 in the manhattan centre
new york philharmonic
lp: columbia ML 6414/MS 7014/
M 31844/MY 37770/BRG 72628/
SBRG 72628
cd: MYK 37770/MFK 46356/
SMK 47607

songs and dances of death
recorded between 21-25 january 1950 in the columbia studios new york city
tourel
bernstein, piano
lp: columbia ML 4289/Y2 32880/
english columbia 33CX 1029
cd: SMK 60695

NEW YORK PHILHARMONIC ORCHESTRA MEMBERS
four improvisations by the orchestra
recorded on 11 february 1964 in the manhattan centre
new york philharmonic
lp: columbia ML 6133/MS 6733
cd: SMK 61845

OTTO NICOLAI (1810-1849)
die lustigen weiber von windsor, overture
recorded on 20 may 1967 in philharmonic hall
new york philharmonic
lp: columbia MS 7085/M2X 795/
D3S 818/61349
cd: SMK 47601

CARL NIELSEN (1865-1931)
symphony no 2 "the four temperaments"
recorded on 12 february 1973 in the columbia studios new york city
new york philharmonic
lp: columbia M 32779/MQ 32779/
M3P 39639/73299
cd: S4K 45989/SMK 47597

symphony no 3 "sinfonia espansiva"
recorded on 16 may 1965 at a concert in the odd fellow palace copenhagen
royal danish orchestra
guldbaek, moeller
lp: columbia ML 6169/MS 6769
cd: SMK 47598

nielsen/**symphony no 4 "inextinguishable"**
recorded on 9 february 1970 in philharmonic hall
new york philharmonic
lp: columbia M 30293/M3P 39639
cd: S4K 45989/SMK 47597

symphony no 5
recorded on 9 april 1962 in the manhattan centre
new york philharmonic
lp: columbia ML 5814/MS 6414
cd: MK 44708/S4K 45989/SMK 47598

clarinet concerto
recorded on 11 march 1967 at a concert in philharmonic hall
new york philharmonic drucker
cd: disco archivia 562

recorded on 21 march 1967 in philharmonic hall
new york philharmonic drucker
lp: columbia ML 6428/MS 7028
cd: S4K 45989/SMK 47599

flute concerto
recorded on 15 february 1966 in philharmonic hall
new york philharmonic baker
lp: columbia ML 6428/MS 7028/73299
cd: S4K 45989/SMK 47599

JACQUES OFFENBACH (1819-1880)
gaite parisienne, ballet arranged by rosenthal
recorded on 16 december 1969 in philharmonic hall
new york　　　　　　　lp: columbia M 31013
philharmonic　　　　　cd: SMK 47532/SMK 61830

orfee aux enfers, overture
recorded on 21 march 1967 in philharmonic hall
new york　　　　　　　lp: columbia MS 7085/M2X 795/
philharmonic　　　　　D3S 818/MY 37769/M3X 31068/
　　　　　　　　　　　61349
　　　　　　　　　　　cd: MYK 37769/SFK 46713/
　　　　　　　　　　　SMK 47532/SMK 61830

2 arias from la perichole: o mon cher amant!; ah quel diner!
recorded on 2 march 1969 in the columbia studios new york city
tourel　　　　　　　　lp: columbia M 32231
bernstein, piano

WALTER PISTON (1894-1976)
the incredible flautist, suite
recorded on 2 december 1963 in the manhattan centre
new york　　　　　　　lp: columbia ML 6343/MS 6943/
philharmonic　　　　　MG 31155
　　　　　　　　　　　cd: SMK 61849

AMILCARE PONCHIELLI (1834-1886)
dance of the hours/la gioconda
recorded on 24 january 1968 in philharmonic hall

new york philharmonic	lp: columbia MS 7415/DMS 659/ S2S 5462
	cd: SFK 46714/SMK 47600

FRANCIS POULENC (1889-1963)
concerto for two pianos and orchestra
recorded on 23 october 1961 in the manhattan centre

new york philharmonic gold, fizdale	lp: columbia ML 5792/MS 6392/ MP 39069
	cd: SMK 47618

gloria
recorded on 20-21 december 1976 in the manhattan centre

new york philharmonic westminster choir blegen	lp: columbia M 34551/MP 39069/ 76670/book of the month club 61-7554
	cd: MK 44710/SMK 47569

3 melodies: voyage a paris; hotel; c
recorded on 6 may 1963 in the columbia studios new york city

tourel bernstein, piano	lp: columbia ML 5918/MS 6518

SERGEI PROKOFIEV (1891-1953)
symphony no 1 "classical"
recorded on 5 march 1968 in philharmonic hall
new york philharmonic
    lp: columbia MS 7159/MS 7528/
    MY 36725/MP 39755/61071
    cd: MYK 36725/MLK 39446/
    SMK 47602
    recording completed on 19 march 1968

symphony no 5
recorded on 7 february 1966 in philharmonic hall
new york philharmonic
    lp: columbia ML 6405/MS 7005/
    BRG 72607/SBRG 72607
    cd: SMK 47602
    recording completed on 15 february 1966

recorded on 20 august 1979 at a concert in the grosses festspielhaus salzburg
israel philharmonic
    cd: disco archivia 558

recorded on 25-26 august 1979 at concerts in the deutsches museum munich
israel philharmonic
    lp: columbia M 35877

piano concerto no 2
recorded on 29 november 1958 at a concert in carnegie hall
new york philharmonic
ashkenazy
    cd: new york philharmonic NYP 2003

violin concerto no 1
televised in 1982 at a concert in the teatro juarez guanajuato mexico
israel philharmonic
breuer
    unpublished video recording

violin concerto no 2
recorded on 21 january 1957 in the columbia studios new york city
new york philharmonic
stern
    lp: columbia ML 5243/M4 42003/
    philips fontana 698 014CL
    cd: M4K 42003/M3K 45956

prokofiev/**scythian suite**
recorded on 2 may 1964 in the manhattan centre
new york philharmonic
lp: columbia MS 7221
cd: SMK 47607/SK 93080

wedding of kije and troika/lieutenant kije
recorded on 12 january 1971 in philharmonic hall
new york philharmonic
lp: columbia M 34127/MY 36725
cd: MLK 39446/MLK 44725/ SFK 46707/SMK 47607/ SMK 64077
MY 36725 contained troika only

march/the love of three oranges
recorded on 12 january 1971 in philharmonic hall
new york philharmonic
lp: columbia M 34127/MG 35919/ MY 36725
cd: MYK 36725/MLK 44724/ MDK 45734/SMK 47607/ SMK 63154/SMK 64076/ SBK 89305

peter and the wolf
recorded on 16 february 1960 in the saint george's hotel brooklyn
new york philharmonic
bernstein conducts and narrates
lp: columbia ML 5593/MS 6193/ MS 7528/D3S 785/CC 25501/ CC 32527/M 31806/MY 37765/ 9059/61814
cd: MYK 37765/SFK 46712/ MLK 69249/MLK 39446/ SMK 60175/SMK 47596
bernstein's narration recorded on 25 may 1960; MS 7528, 9059, MLK 39446 and SMK 47596 contained a narration in portuguese by paulos santos

GIACOMO PUCCINI (1858-1924)
la boheme
recorded between 28 may-7 june 1987 at rehearsals and performance in the auditorium of santa cecilia rome
santa cecilia orchestra and chorus
reaux, daniels, hadley, hampson, plishka
cd: deutsche grammophon 453 1092

SERGEI RACHMANINOV (1873-1943)
piano concerto no 2
recorded on 3 february 1960 in the saint george's hotel brooklyn

new york	lp: columbia ML 5481/MS 6148/
philharmonic	D3L 315/D3S 715/MG 32050/
entremont	philips GBL 5579/G03563L
	cd: MBK 46271/SBK 53512

recorded on 26 may 1964 in philharmonic hall

new york	lp: columbia ML 6034/MS 6634/
philharmonic	MS 7508/M 31813/MY 36722/
graffman	MYX 39141/BRG 72275/
	SBRG 72275/60109/61802
	cd: MYK 36722/SMK 47630/
	SFK 63032

piano concerto no 3
recorded on 2 march 1977 at a concert in avery fisher hall

new york	cd: new york philharmonic NYP 2003
philharmonic	
berman	

recorded on 14 september 1979 at a concert in the theatre des champs-elysees

orchestre	lp: angel 37722/emi 1C065 03764/
national	2C069 03764
weissenberg	

rhapsody on a theme of paganini
recorded on 2 may 1964 in the manhattan centre

new york	lp: columbia ML 6034/MS 6634/
philharmonic	M 31813/MY 36722/MYX 39141/
graffman	BRG 72275/SBRG 72275/
	60109/61802
	cd: MYK 36722/SMK 47571

o cease thy singing, maiden fair!
recorded on 2 march 1969 in the columbia studios new york city

tourel	lp: columbia M 32231
bernstein, piano	

MAURICE RAVEL (1875-1937)
piano concerto in g

recorded on 2 june 1946 at a concert in the nbc studios new york city
nbc symphony   unpublished radio broadcast
bernstein conducts
from the piano

recorded on 1 july 1946 in the abbey road studios london
philharmonia   78: victor M 1209/V 15
bernstein conducts   lp: victor CAL 214
from the piano   cd: rca 09026 618502/dutton CDBP 9750/
                             symposium 1372/membran 222 370/
                             dynamic historical IDI 6538/
                             pearl GEMM 0066

recorded on 7 april 1958 in the columbia studios new york city
columbia symphony   lp: columbia ML 5337/MS 6043/
bernstein conducts   BRG 72170/SBRG 72170/60338/
from the piano   philips ABL 3330/SABL 134/
                             A01420L/A01507L/835 525AY/
                             835 577AY

recorded on 21 february 1971 at a concert in the musikverein vienna
wiener   cd: deutsche grammophon
philharmoniker   435 3212/435 3222
bernstein conducts
from the piano

televised in 1975 at a concert in the theatre des champs-elysees paris
orchestre national   dvd video: kultur 1525
bernstein conducts
from the piano

ravel/**tzigane pour violon et orchestre**
recorded on 6 january 1964 in the manhattan centre
new york philharmonic francescatti
lp: columbia ML 6017/MS 6617/
philips fontana 698 020CL/
876 000CY
cd: SMK 47548

recorded on 28 april 1975 in the manhattan centre
new york philharmonic belkin
columbia unpublished

televised in 1975 at a concert in the theatre des champs-elysees paris
orchestre national belkin
dvd video: kultur 1525

alborada del gracioso
recorded on 29 september 1963 in the manhattan centre
new york philharmonic
lp: columbia ML 6816/MS 6786/
MS 7512/M2X 795/M 31816/
MYX 39141/BRG 72423/
SBRG 72423
cd: MYK 36714/MLK 39439

televised on 21 october 1975 at a concert in the theatre des champs-elysees
orchestre national
lp: columbia M 35103
dvd video: kultur 1525

bolero
recorded on 27 january 1958 in the saint george's hotel brooklyn
new york philharmonic
lp: columbia ML 5293/MS 6011/
MS 7512/M 31847/61027/
philips GBL 5513/G03522L
cd: MLK 39439/SFK 46706/
SMK 60505

televised on 21 october 1975 at a concert in the theatre des champs-elysees
orchestre national
lp: columbia M 35103
dvd video: kultur 1525

ravel/**daphnis et chloe, complete ballet**
recorded on 13 march 1961 in the manhattan centre
new york philharmonic schola cantorum
lp: columbia ML 5660/MS 6260
cd: SMK 47604
second suite only
lp: columbia ML 6154/MS 6754/
M 31847/MY 36714/MYX 39141/
BRG 72387/SBRG 72387
cd: MYK 36714/SMK 47603/
SBK 64111/SMK 60565

ma mere l'oye, suite from the ballet
recorded on 1 february 1965 in the manhattan centre
new york philharmonic
lp: columbia M 32873
cd: SMK 47545
recording completed on 16 february 1965

pavane pour une infante defunte
recorded on 2 february 1968 in philharmonic hall
new york philharmonic
lp: columbia M 30573/MY 37769
cd: MYK 37769/SFK 46707/
SMK 47545/MLK 62617
recording completed on 5 march 1968

rapsodie espagnole
recorded on 27 january 1958 in the saint george's hotel brooklyn
new york philharmonic
lp: columbia ML 5293/MS 6011/
philips GBL 5513/G03522L
cd: SMK 60505

recorded on 6 march 1973 in the columbia studios new york city
new york philharmonic
lp: columbia M 32873
cd: SMK 47603

televised in 1973 in the wgbh studios boston
boston symphony
cd: disco archivia 558
also unpublished video recording

ravel/**scheherazade, song cycle**
recorded between 21-25 january 1950 in the columbia studios new york city
columbia symphony   78: columbia M 337
tourel   lp: columbia ML 4289/english
                    columbia 33CX 1029
                    cd: SMK 60695/membran 222 370
                    membran incorrectly dated march 1950

recorded on 20 may 1961 in the manhattan centre
new york   lp: columbia ML 5838/MS 6438/
philharmonic   CMS 6438
tourel

televised on 17 september 1975 at a concert in the theatre des champs-elysees
orchestre national lp: columbia M 35102/76707
horne   dvd video: kultur 1525

la valse, poeme choreographique
recorded on 6 january 1958 in the saint george's hotel brooklyn
new york   lp: columbia ML 5293/MS 6011/
philharmonic   M 31847/MY 36714/MYX 39141/
                    philips GBL 5513/G03522L
                    cd: MYK 36714/SMK 60505

recorded on 19 january 1963 at a concert in philharmonic hall
new york   cd: disco archivia 564
philharmonic

recorded on 21 january 1963 in philharmonic hall
new york   lp: columbia M 32873/61027
philharmonic

televised on 21 october 1975 at a concert in the theatre des champs-elysees
orchestre national lp: columbia M 35103
                    dvd video: kultur 1525

OTTORINO RESPIGHI (1879-1936)
feste romane
recorded on 19 march 1968 in philharmonic hall
new york philharmonic
lp: columbia MS 7448/KS 7448
cd: SMK 60174

pini di roma
recorded on 17 february 1970 in philharmonic hall
new york philharmonic
lp: columbia MS 7448/KS 7448
cd: SMK 60174/SK 92727

SILVESTRE REVUELTAS (1899-1940)
sensemaya
recorded on 6 february 1963 in philharmonic hall
new york philharmonic
lp: columbia ML 5914/MS 6514
cd: SMK 47544/SMK 60571

EMIL VON REZNICEK (1860-1945)
donna diana, overture
recorded on 10 january 1967 in philharmonic hall
new york philharmonic
lp: columbia MS 7085/D3S 818/61349
cd: SMK 47601

NIKOLAI RIMSKY-KORSAKOV (1844-1908)
capriccio espagnol
recorded on 2 may 1959 in carnegie hall
new york philharmonic
lp: columbia ML 5401/MS 6080/
MY 36728/SGM 1/SGS 1/60115/
A01428L/835 527AY
cd: MYK 36728/SMK 47595/
SMK 60737/MLK 69250

scheherazade, symphonic suite
recorded on 16 february 1959 in the saint george's hotel brooklyn
new york philharmonic
lp: columbia ML 5387/MS 6089/
M 31802/MY 38476/philips
ABL 3266/SABL 140/A01403L/
835 521AY
cd: MYK 38476/SMK 47605/
SMK 60737

dance of the tumblers/the snow maiden
recorded on 21 march 1967 in philharmonic hall
new york philharmonic
lp: columbia M 34127/MY 36728/
MY 37770/60115
cd: SFK 46714/SMK 47600/SMK 64075/
MLK 69250/SFK 89109

NED ROREM (born 1923)
symphony no 3
recorded on 18 april 1959 at a concert in carnegie hall
new york philharmonic
cd: new york philharmonic NYP 9904

violin concerto
recorded on 29 november 1988 at a concert in avery fisher hall
new york philharmonic
kremer
cd: deutsche grammophon
429 2312/445 1852/474 9402

GIOACHINO ROSSINI (1792-1868)
il barbiere di siviglia, overture
recorded on 27 march 1963 in philharmonic hall

new york philharmonic	lp: columbia ML 5933/MS 6533/ MS 7085/D3S 818/M 30305/ MG 35187/30108 cd: MLK 39449/SMK 47606

recorded on 8 june 1964 at a concert in symphony hall boston

boston pops orchestra	cd: boston symphony orchestra CD 3 *recorded at bernstein's twenty-fifth reunion concert*

la gazza ladra, overture
recorded on 8 february 1960 in the saint george's hotel brooklyn

new york philharmonic	lp: columbia ML 5933/MS 6533/ GB 6/GS 6/30108 cd: SFK 46713/SMK 47606

guillaume tell, overture
recorded on 2 december 1963 in the manhattan centre

new york philharmonic	lp: columbia ML 6143/MS 6743/ D3S 818/M 30305/M 31815/ MG 35187/MY 37240/M3X 31068/ BRG 72389/SBRG 72389 cd: MYK 37240/MLK 39449/ SFK 46713/SMK 47606

l'italiana in algeri, overture
recorded on 10 april 1960 in the manhattan centre

new york philharmonic	lp: columbia ML 5933/MS 6533/ GB 8/GS 8 cd: SMK 47606

rossini/**la scala di seta, overture**
recorded on 15 january 1963 in philharmonic hall
new york philharmonic
lp: columbia ML 5933/MS 6533
cd: SMK 47606

semiramide, overture
recorded on 28 september 1960 in the manhattan centre
new york philharmonic
lp: columbia ML 5623/ML 5933/
MS 6223/MS 6533/MG 35187/
30108
cd: SMK 47606/SBK 62653/
MLK 64598

MIKLOS ROSZA (1907-1995)
theme, variations and finale
recorded on 14 november 1943 at a concert in carnegie hall
new york philharmonic
lp: new york philharmonic NYP 83
cd: NYP 19054-1196
recorded at bernstein's public conducting debut

CLAUDE-JOSEPH ROUGET DE LISLE (1760-1836)
la marseillaise
recorded on 20 october 1970 in philharmonic hall
new york philharmonic
lp: columbia M 30943/MG 35919
cd: MDK 45734/SFK 46709/
SMK 63154/SBK 89305

ALBERT ROUSSEL (1869-1937)
symphony no 3
recorded on 25 september 1961 in the manhattan centre
new york philharmonic
lp: columbia ML 5982/MS 6582/
BRG 72281/SBRG 72281
cd: MHK 62352

recorded on 22 november 1981 at a concert in the theatre des champs-elysees
orchestre national
cd: deutsche grammophon 445 5122

CARL RUGGLES (1876-1971)
men and mountains
recorded on 18 october 1958 at a concert in carnegie hall
new york philharmonic   cd: new york philharmonic NYP 2003

WILLIAM RUSSO (born 1928)
symphony no 2 "titans"
recorded on 18 april 1959 at a concert in carnegie hall
new york philharmonic   cd: new york philharmonic NYP 2003

CAMILLE SAINT-SAENS (1835-1921)
symphony no 3 "organ"
recorded on 13 december 1976 in the manhattan centre
new york philharmonic
raver
lp: columbia M 34573/MY 37255
cd: MYK 37255/SMK 47608

piano concerto no 4
recorded on 30 october 1961 in the manhattan centre
new york philharmonic
casadesus
lp: columbia ML 5777/MS 6377/ BRG 72105/SBRG 72105
cd: SMK 47608/503 3972/ SM2K 61725

introdution and rondo capriccioso
recorded on 6 january 1964 in the manhattan centre
new york philharmonic
francescatti
lp: columbia ML 6017/MS 6617
cd: SMK 47608/MLK 66701

danse macabre
recorded on 3 january 1967 in philharmonic hall
new york philharmonic
lp: columbia MS 7165/MS 7246/ MS 7522/D3S 785/M3X 31068/ MY 37769/BRG 72740/ BRG 72740/61976
cd: MYK 37769/SFK 46707/ SMK 47596

saint-saens/**le carnaval des animaux**
recorded on 9 april 1962 in the manhattan centre
new york philharmonic
r.segal, n.segal
bernstein conducts and narrates

lp: columbia ML 5768/ML 5998/
MS 6368/MS 6598/D3S 785/M31808/
MY 37765/BRG 72393/BRG 72567/
SBRG 72393/SBRG 72567/61814
cd: MYK 37765/SFK 46712/
SMK 60175/SMK 47596
ML 5998 and MS 6598 contained a version with narration in spanish, BRG 72393 and SBRG 72393 in hebrew and BRG 72567 and SBRG 72567 in german; SMK 47596 is a version without narration

le rouet d'omphale
televised in 1981 at a concert in the theatre des champs-elysees paris
orchestre national
unpublished video recording

bacchanale/samson et dalila
recorded on 15 may 1967 in philharmonic hall
new york philharmonic
lp: columbia MS 7415/MY 37769/
DMS 659/S2S 5462
cd: MYK 37769/SFK 46714/
SMK 47600

ERIK SATIE (1866-1925)
le chapelier
recorded on 10 january 1967 in the columbia studios new york city
tourel
bernstein, piano
columbia unpublished

FRANZ SCHUBERT (1797-1828)
symphony no 5
recorded on 6 february 1963 in philharmonic hall
new york philharmonic   lp: columbia MS 7295
                          cd: SMK 47609

recorded between 24-26 june 1987 at concerts in the concertgebouw amsterdam
concertgebouw   cd: deutsche grammophon
orkest   427 6452/477 5167

symphony no 8 "unfinished"
recorded on 27 march 1963 in philharmonic hall
new york   lp: columbia ML 6218/MS 6818/
philharmonic   MS 7057/MS 7526/D3L 337/D3S 737/
                 M 31819/BM 13/MY 36719/
                 MYX 39141/60106
                 cd: MYK 36719/MLK 39445/
                 SMK 47610/SMK 61842

recorded between 8-10 october 1987 at concerts in the concertgebouw amsterdam
concertgebouw   cd: deutsche grammophon
orkest   427 6452/477 5167

schubert/**symphony no 9 "great"**
recorded on 11 october 1957 at a concert in symphony hall boston
boston symphony lp: paragon GM 1005
                 cd: living stage LS 1081/dynamic
                 historical IDI 6538
                 *in his discography of schubert symphony no 9
                 jerome weber questions the authenticity of this
                 recording, stating that bernstein did not appear
                 with the boston symphony in 1957*

recorded between 17-19 january 1967 in philharmonic hall
new york   lp: columbia M 31012
philharmonic   cd: SMK 47610/SMK 61842/
                 SK 48180

televised on 13-14 june 1987 at concerts in the deutsches museum munich
sinfonieorchester   dvd video: euroarts 207 2168
des bayerschen
rundfunks

recorded between 14-16 october 1987 at concerts in the concertgebouw amsterdam
concertgebouw   cd: deutsche grammophon
orkest   427 6462/477 5167

des teufels lustschloss, overture
recorded on 10 january 1967 in philharmonic hall
new york   cd: SMK 47609
philharmonic   *unpublished columbia lp recording*

GUNTHER SCHULLER (born 1925)
triplum
recorded on 1 july 1967 in philharmonic hall
new york   lp: columbia ML 6452/MS 7052
philharmonic   cd: SMK 61845

WILLIAM SCHUMAN (1910-1992)
symphony no 3
recorded on 17 october 1960 in the manhattan centre

new york philharmonic	lp: columbia ML 5645/MS 6245/ MS 7442
	cd: SMK 63163

recorded on 10 december 1985 at a concert in avery fisher hall

new york philharmonic	lp: deutsche grammophon 419 7801
	cd: 419 7802/474 9402

symphony no 5
recorded on 20 october 1966 in philharmonic hall

new york philharmonic	lp: columbia MS 7442
	cd: SMK 63163

symphony no 6
recorded on 20 april 1958 at a concert in carnegie hall

new york philharmonic	cd: new york philharmonic NYP 9904

symphony no 8
recorded on 9 october 1962 in philharmonic hall

new york philharmonic	lp: columbia ML 5912/MS 6512/ Y 34140
	cd: SMK 63163

american festival overture
recorded on 24 july 1982 at a concert in the davies symphony hall

los angeles philharmonic	lp: deutsche grammophon 2532 083
	cd: 413 3242

william schuman/**concerto on old english rounds**
recorded between 17-19 april 1976 in the columbia studios new york city
new york lp: columbia M 35101
philharmonic cd: russ oppenheim ROCD 0083
camerata singers
mcinnes, violin

to thee old cause
recorded on 22 october 1968 in philharmonic hall
new york lp: columbia MS 7392
philharmonic cd: SMK 63088/SK 90390

canticle for orchestra "in memory of shahn"
recorded on 12 february 1970 in philharmonic hall
new york lp: columbia M 30112
philharmonic cd: SMK 63088/SK 90390

ROBERT SCHUMANN (1810-1856)
symphony no 1 "spring"
recorded on 31 october 1960 in the manhattan centre
new york lp: columbia ML 5981/MS 6581/
philharmonic D3L 325/D3S 725
  cd: SMK 47611/SX2K 64205

televised on 2-3 july 1979 at concerts in the bunka kaikan hall tokyo
new york vhs video: kultur 1355
philharmonic dvd video: kultur 1355/1525

televised between 8-14 october 1984 at concerts in the musikverein vienna
wiener lp: deutsche grammophon
philharmoniker 415 2741/423 0991
  cd: 415 2742/423 0992/431 0502/
  431 1972/453 0492/
  460 6152/477 5167
  dvd video: 073 4512

schumann/**symphony no 2**
recorded in 1946 at a concert in symphony hall boston
boston   lp: melodram MEL 206
symphony

recorded between 24-26 june 1953 in carnegie hall
new york   lp: american decca DL 9715/musical
philharmonic   appreciation society
                              cd: deutsche grammophon 477 0002/
                              andromeda ANDRCD 5115
                              orchestra described for this recording as stadium
                              concerts orchestra; musical appreciation society
                              and deutsche grammophon issues also include
                              bernstein's spoken analysis

recorded on 10 october 1960 in the manhattan centre
new york   lp: columbia ML 5848/MS 6448/
philharmonic   D3L 325/D3S 725
                              cd: SMK 47611/SX2K 64205

televised on 13 november 1983 at a concert in the erkel theatre budapest
sinfonieorchester   unpublished video recording
des bayerischen
rundfunks

televised between 29 october-6 november 1985 at concerts in the musikverein vienna
wiener   lp: deutsche grammophon
philharmoniker   419 1901/423 0991
                              cd: 419 1902/423 0992/
                              453 0492/477 5167
                              dvd video: 073 4512

schumann/**symphony no 3 "rhenish"**
recorded on 17 october 1960 in the manhattan centre
new york philharmonic
lp: columbia ML 5694/MS 6294/
D3L 325/D3S 725
cd: SMK 47612/SX2K 64205

televised between 18-22 october 1984 at concerts in the musikverein vienna
wiener philharmoniker
lp: deutsche grammophon
415 3581/423 0991
cd: 415 3582/423 0992/431 0422/
431 0502/453 0492/477 5167
dvd video: 073 4512

symphony no 4
recorded on 10 october 1960 in the manhattan centre
new york philharmonic
lp: columbia ML 5656/MS 6256/
D3L 325/D3S 725
cd: SMK 47612/SX2K 64205

recorded on 21 february 1971 at a concert in the musikverein vienna
wiener philharmoniker
cd: live classics best (japan)
LCB 147

televised on 15 march 1971 at a concert in the royal albert hall london
wiener philharmoniker
unpublished unitel video recording

televised between 2-5 february 1984 at concerts in the musikverein vienna
wiener philharmoniker
lp: deutsche grammophon
415 2741/423 0991
cd: 415 2742/423 0992/
453 0492/477 5167
dvd video: 073 4512

schumann/**piano concerto**
recorded on 19 april 1976 in the columbia studios new york city
new york   columbia unpublished
philharmonic
perahia

televised between 2-5 february 1984 at concerts in the musikverein vienna
wiener   lp: deutsche grammophon
philharmoniker   415 3581/423 0991
frantz   cd: 415 3582/423 0992/423 9892/
                        431 0432/431 0502/477 5167
                        vhs video: 072 1813

cello concerto
recorded on 24 october 1960 in the manhattan centre
new york   lp: columbia ML 5623/MS 6253/
philharmonic   BRG 72580/SBRG 72580
rose   cd: SMK 47609

recorded on 3 marh 1967 at a concert in philharmonic hall
new york   cd: new york philharmonic NYP 2003
philharmonic
du pre

recorded on 13 november 1976 at a concert in the theatre des champs-elysees
orchestre   lp: angel 37256/emi ASD 3334/
national   1C065 02841/2C069 02841/
rostropovich   3C065 02841

televised between 2-5 february 1984 at concerts in the musikverein vienna
wiener   lp: deutsche grammophon
philharmoniker   415 3581/423 0991
maisky   cd: 415 3582/423 0992/
                        445 5742/477 5167
                        dvd video: 073 4351

schumann/**manfred overture**
recorded on 14 november 1943 at a concert in carnegie hall
new york philharmonic
    lp: new york philharmonic NYP 83
    cd: new york philharmonic 19054-1196
    recorded at bernstein's public conducting debut

recorded on 6 january 1958 in the saint george's hotel brooklyn
new york philharmonic
    lp: columbia ML 5656/MS 6256/ D3L 325/D3S 725
    cd: SMK 47612

televised in 1985 at a concert in the herkulessaal munich
sinfonieorchester des bayerischen rundfunks
    dvd video: euroarts 207 2168

televised between 29 october-6 november 1985 at concerts in the musikverein vienna
wiener philharmoniker
    vhs video: deutsche grammophon 072 1813

piano quintet
recorded on 19 april 1963 at a concert in the library of congress washington dc
juilliard string quartet
bernstein, piano
    cd: doremi DHR 5707-5708

recorded on 28 april 1964 in the columbia studios new york city
juilliard string quartet
bernstein, piano
    lp: columbia ML 6329/MS 6929/ D3S 806
    cd: SMK 62709

HAROLD SHAPERO (born 1920)
symphony for classical orchestra
recorded on 27 may 1953 in the columbia studios new york city
columbia   lp: columbia ML 4889
symphony   cd: SMK 60725

adagio for orchestra
recorded on 29 october 1966 at a concert in philharmonic hall
new york   cd: disco archivia 566
philharmonic

RODION SHCHEDRIN (born 1932)
mischievous folk ditties
recorded on 20 may 1967 at a concert in philharmonic hall
new york   cd: new york philharmonic
philharmonic   NYP 2003/NYP 2014

DIMITRI SHOSTAKOVICH (1906-1975)
symphony no 1
recorded on 14 december 1971 in philharmonic hall
new york   lp: columbia M 31307/MP 38750
philharmonic   cd: SMK 47614/SX4K 64206

recorded on 23 june 1988 at a concerrt in orchestra hall chicago
chicago   cd: deutsche grammophon
symphony   427 6322/477 5193

televised on 16 july 1988 at a concert in the holstenhalle neumünster and at rehearsals in salzau
schleswig-holstein   dvd video: euroarts 207 2158
festival orchestra

shostakovich/**symphony no 5**
recorded in september 1959 in the philharmonic hall leningrad
new york philharmonic
lp: melodiya
concert given in the composer's presence

recorded on 20 october 1959 in the saint george's hall brooklyn
new york
philharmonic
lp: columbia ML 5445/MS 6115/
MY 37218/BRG 72172/SBRG 72172/
philips A01448L/835 548AY
cd: MYK 37218/MK 44711/SMK 47615/
SX4K 64206/SMK 61841/SX10K 89950

televised on 7-8 december 1966 at concerts in the bbc television centre and royal festival hall london
london symphony
unpublished video recording
extracts from rehearsal and performance
vhs video: warner classics 4509 950383
laserdisc: warner classics 4509 950386
dvd video: warner classics 0927 426672

recorded on 27-28 april 1979 at concerts in the musikverein vienna
wiener
philharmoniker
cd: sardana (japan) SACD 145/
live classics best (japan) LCB 114/
first classics (japan) FC 103/
disco archivia 560
sardana incorrectly dated may 1979

televised on 2-3 july 1979 at concerts in the bunka kaikan hall tokyo
new york
philharmonic
lp: columbia M 35854
cd: MK 35854/MDK 44903/SK 94733
vhs video: kultur 1355
dvd video: kultur 1355/1525

shostakovich/**symphony no 6**
recorded on 14 october 1963 in philharmonic hall
new york philharmonic
lp: columbia MS 7221
cd: SMK 47614/SX4K 64206

televised on 6 october 1986 at a concert in the musikverein vienna
wiener philharmoniker
lp: deutsche grammophon 419 7711
cd: 419 7712/477 5193
dvd video: 073 4170
video edition includes bernstein's spoken introduction

symphony no 7 "leningrad"
recorded on 22-23 october 1962 in philharmonic hall
new york philharmonic
lp: columbia M2L 322/M2S 722/
BRG 72349-72350/
SBRG 72349-72350
cd: MK 44855/SMK 47616/
SX4K 64206

recorded on 23 june 1988 at a concert in orchestra hall chicago
chicago symphony
cd: deutsche grammophon 427 6322/
477 5193/477 7587

symphony no 9
recorded on 19 october 1965 in philharmonic hall
new york philharmonic
lp: columbia M 31307
cd: MK 44711/SMK 47615/
SX4K 64206/SMK 61841

televised on 22 october 1985 at a concert in the musikverein vienna
wiener philharmoniker
lp: deutsche grammophon 419 7711
cd: 419 7712/477 5193
dvd video: 073 4170
video edition includes bernstein's spoken introduction

shostakovich/**symphony no 14**
recorded on 8 december 1976 in the manhattan centre
new york   lp: columbia M 37270
philharmonic   cd: SMK 47617/SX4K 64206
kubiak, bushkin

piano concerto no 1
recorded on 8 april 1962 in the manhattan centre
new york   lp: columbia ML 5792/MS 6392/
philharmonic   MP 38892/BRG 72349-72350/
previn, piano   SBRG 72349-72350/73400
vacchiano, trumpet   cd: MPK 44850/SMK 47618

piano concerto no 2
recorded 6 january 1958 in the saint george's hotel brooklyn
new york   lp: columbia ML 5337/MS 6043/
philharmonic   BRG 72170/SBRG 72170/60338/
bernstein conducts   philips ABL 3300/SABL 134/
from the piano   A01420L/835 525AY

polka/the age of gold
recorded on 22 october 1970 in philharmonic hall
new york   lp: columbia M 34127
philharmonic   cd: MLK 44724/SMK 47607/
                            SMK 64076

JEAN SIBELIUS (1865-1957)
symphony no 1
recorded on 11 march 1967 at a concert in philharmonic hall
new york   cd: disco archivia 563
philharmonic

recorded on 14 march 1967 in philharmonic hall
new york   lp: columbia M5S 784/M 30232/
philharmonic   61804
                            cd: SM2K 47619/SM4K 87329/
                            502 3162/SX4K 64207

recorded on 24 february 1990 at a concert in the musikverein vienna
wiener   cd: deutsche grammophon
philharmoniker   431 3512/474 9362

sibelius/**symphony no 2**
recorded on 16 may 1966 in philharmonic hall
new york philharmonic
lp: columbia MS 7337/M5S 784/
M 31827/MY 38477/61805
cd: MYK 38477/SM2K 47619/
SMK 61848/SM4K 87329/
502 3162/SX4K 64207

televised on 6 october 1986 at a concert in the musikverein vienna
wiener philharmoniker
lp: deutsche grammophon 419 7721
cd: 419 7722/431 0442/
431 0502/474 9362
also unpublished video recording

symphony no 3
recorded on 18 october 1965 in philharmonic hall
new york philharmonic
lp: columbia M5S 784/61809
cd: SM2K 47619/SM4K 87329/
502 3162/SX4K 64207

symphony no 4
recorded on 1 february 1966 in philharmonic hall
new york philharmonic
lp: columbia M5S 784/M 32843/
MQ 32843/61807
cd: SM2K 47622/SM4K 87329/
502 3162/SX4K 64207

symphony no 5
recorded on 27 march 1961 in the manhattan centre
new york philharmonic
lp: columbia ML 6149/MS 6749/
M5S 784/MY 38474/BRG 72356/
SBRG 72356/61808
cd: MYK 38474/SM2K 47622/
SBK 63060/SM4K 87329/
SX10K 89750/502 3162/
SX4K 64207

recorded on 1-2 september 1987 at concerts in the musikverein vienna
wiener philharmoniker
cd: deutsche grammophon
427 6472/474 9362

sibelius/**symphony no 6**
recorded on 9 may 1967 in philharmonic hall
new york philharmonic
lp: columbia M5S 784/61806
cd: SM2K 47622/SM4K 87329/
502 3162/SX4K 64207

symphony no 7
recorded on 28 march 1960 in the manhattan centre
new york philharmonic
lp: columbia M5S 784/61806
cd: SM2K 47622/SM4K 87329/
502 3162/SX4K 64207

recorded between 29 september-4 october 1988 at concerts in the musikverein
wiener philharmoniker
cd: deutsche grammophon
427 6472/474 9362

violin concerto
recorded on 15 january 1963 in philharmonic hall
new york philharmonic francescatti
lp: columbia ML 6131/MS 6731/
Y 33522/MP 38770/61809
cd: SMK 47540/SB2K 63260

finlandia
recorded on 16 february 1965 in philharmonic hall
new york philharmonic
lp: columbia MY 36718/MYX 39131/
60105
cd: MYK 36718/SFK 46706/
SMK 47549/SMK 63156/SM4K 87329

pohjola's daughter
recorded on 1 may 1964 in the manhattan centre
new york philharmonic
lp: columbia ML 6149/MS 6749/
MY 38474/BRG 72356/
SBRG 72356/61808
cd: MYK 38474/SM2K 47619/
SB4K 48271/SMK 61848/SX10K 89750/
SM4K 87329/502 3162

sibelius/**the swan of tuonela/4 legends**
recorded on 8 march 1973 in the columbia studios new york city
new york philharmonic   lp: columbia M 32843/MQ 32843/ MY 36718/MYX 39141/60105
cd: MYK 36718/SMK 47549/ SMK 63156/SM4K 87329

valse triste
recorded on 8 december 1969 in philharmonic hall
new york philharmonic   lp: columbia MS 7527/MY 36718/ MYX 39141/M 39447/61804
cd: MYK 36718/MLK 39447/ SFK 46707/SMK 47549/SBK 48271/ MLK 62617/SMK 63156/SM4K 87329

luonnotar, for soprano and orchestra
recorded on 19 october 1965 in philharmonic hall
new york philharmonic
curtin   lp: columbia M 30232/61807
cd: SM2K 47619/SMK 61848/ SM4K 87329/502 3162

4 songs for soprano and orchestra: svarta rosor; men min fogel märks kock icke; varen flyktar hastigt; säf säf susa
recorded on 2 october 1965 at a concert in philharmonic hall
new york philharmonic
curtin   cd: new york philharmonic NYP 2003

BEDRICH SMETANA (1824-1884)
the bartered bride, overture
recorded on 28 january 1963 in philharmonic hall
new york philharmonic	lp: columbia ML 6279/MS 6879/ D3S 818/M 31817/MG 35188/ BRG 72461/SBRG 72461 cd: SFK 46713/SMK 47601/ SMK 60561/SK 92729

dance of the comedians, furiant and polka/the bartered bride
recorded on 1 february 1965 in the manhattan centre
new york philharmonic	lp: columbia ML 6279/MS 6879/ ML 6388 (dance only)/MS 6988 (dance only)/M 31817/M 30645 (polka only)/M3X 31068 (dance only)/ BRG 72461/SBRG 72461/60334 cd: SMK 60561/SMK 61836/SK 92729/ SMK 64075 (dance only)/SFK 89109 (dance only)/SFK 46714 (dance only)/ MLK 44723 (dance only)

the moldau/ma vlast
recorded on 23 november 1964 in the manhattan centre
new york philharmonic	lp: columbia ML 6279/MS 6879/ MS 7246/M3X 31068/M 31817/ BRG 72461/SBRG 72461 cd: SFK 46706/SMK 47547/ SMK 60561

JOHN STAFFORD SMITH (1750-1836)
the star-spangled banner
recorded on 14 november 1943 at a concert in carnegie hall
new york philharmonic	lp: new york philharmonic NYP 83 cd: new york philharmonic 19054-1196

recorded at bernstein's public conducting debut

recorded on 23 september 1962 at the opening concert in philharmonic hall
new york philharmonic	lp: columbia L2L 1007/L2S 1008

recorded on 28 april 1975 in the manhattan centre
new york philharmonic	lp: promotional USA 1776

JOHN PHILIP SOUSA (1854-1932)
hands across the sea, march
recorded on 24 october 1968 in philharmonic hall
new york philharmonic   lp: columbia M 30943/MG 35919
cd: MDK 45734/SMK 63154/ SBK 89305

semper fidelis, march
recorded on 26 october 1967 in philharmonic hall
new york philharmonic   lp: columbia M 30943/MG 35919
cd: MDK 45734/SMK 63154/ SBK 89305/S3K 90578

stars and stripes forever, march
recorded on 26 october 1967 in philharmonic hall
new york philharmonic   lp: columbia M 30943/MG 35919
cd: MLK 44725/SFK 46709/ MDK 45734/SMK 63154/SMK 64077/ SFK 89109/SBK 89305

the thunderer, march
recorded on 12 october 1970 in philharmonic hall
new york philharmonic   lp: columbia M 30943/MG 35919
cd: MDK 45734/SMK 63154/ SBK 89305

washington post, march
recorded on 26 october 1967 in philharmonic hall
new york philharmonic   lp: columbia M 30943/MG 35919
cd: MDK 45734/SMK 63154/ SBK 89305

JOHANN STRAUSS I (1804-1849)
radetzky march
recorded on 20 october 1970 in philharmonic hall

new york philharmonic	lp: columbia M 30943/MG 35919 cd: MLK 44725/MDK 45734/ SMK 47627/SMK 63154/SMK 64077/ MLK 66709/SBK 89305

JOHANN STRAUSS II (1825-1899)
an der schönen blauen donau, waltz
recorded on 6 february 1969 in philharmonic hall

new york philharmonic	lp: columbia MS 7288/MG 35918/ MY 37771/DMS 658/S2S 5462 cd: MYK 37771/SFK 46710/ SMK 47627/SM2K 48226

auf der jagd, galop
recorded on 12 january 1971 in philharmonic hall

new york philharmonic	cd: columbia SMK 47627/MLK 64063 *unpublished columbia lp recording*

die fledermaus, overture
recorded on 22 october 1970 in philharmonic hall

new york philharmonic	lp: columbia M 34125 cd: SMK 47601

frühlingsstimmen, waltz
recorded on 24 october 1968 in philharmonic hall

new york philharmonic	lp: columbia MS 7288/MG 35918/ MY 37771 cd: MYK 37771/SFK 46710/ SMK 47627

g'schichten aus dem wienerwald, waltz
recorded on 14 april 1975 in the columbia studios new york city

new york philharmonic	lp: columbia M 34125 cd: SFK 46710/SMK 47627

johann strauss/**kaiserwalzer**
recorded on 6 february 1969 in philharmonic hall
new york philharmonic
lp: columbia MS 7288/MG 35918/ MY 37771/S2S 5462/book of the month club 70-3731
cd: MYK 37771/SFK 46710/ SMK 47627

künstlerleben, waltz
recorded on 12 october 1965 in the manhattan centre
new york philharmonic
lp: columbia MS 7288/MG 35918/ MY 37771/book of the month club 70-3731
cd: MYK 37771/SFK 46710/ SMK 47627

perpetuum mobile
recorded on 22 october 1970 in philharmonic hall
new york philharmonic
cd: columbia SMK 47627/MLK 64063
unpublished columbia lp recording

rosen aus dem süden, waltz
recorded on 12 january 1971 in philharmonic hall
new york philharmonic
lp: columbia M 34125
cd: SMK 47627

tritsch tratsch polka
recorded on 20 october 1970 in philharmonic hall
new york philharmonic
cd: columbia MLK 44725/SFK 46707/ SMK 47627/MLK 64063/SMK 64077
unpublished columbia lp recording

wiener blut, waltz
recorded on 24 october 1967 in philharmonic hall
new york philharmonic
lp: columbia MS 7288/MG 35918/ M3X 31068/MY 37771
cd: MYK 37771/SMK 47627

der zigeunerbaron, overture
recorded on 14 april 1975 in the columbia studios new york city
new york philharmonic
lp: columbia M 34125

RICHARD STRAUSS (1864-1949)
der rosenkavalier
recorded on 13 april 1968 at a performance in the staatsoper vienna

wiener philharmoniker
chor der wiener staatsoper
ludwig, grist, jones, kmennt, berry, kunz

unpublished radio broadcast
excerpts
cd: rca 74321 694272/74321 694282

recorded between 29 march-10 april 1971 in the sofiensaal vienna

wiener philharmoniker
chor der wiener staatsoper
ludwig, popp, jones, domingo, berry, gutstein

lp: columbia M4X 30652/77416
cd: M3K 42564
excerpts
lp: 73179

du wolltest mich nicht deinen mund küssen lassen/salome
recorded between 5-7 may 1977 in the maison de la radio paris

orchestre national
caballe

lp: deutsche grammophon 2530 963
cd: 431 1712/477 5910

dance of the seven veils/salome
recorded on 12 october 1965 in the manhattan centre

new york philharmonic

lp: columbia ML 6222/MS 6822
cd: SMK 47625

recorded between 5-7 may 1977 in the maison de la radio paris

orchestre national

lp: deutsche grammophon 2530 963
cd: 431 1712/477 5910

5 orchesterlieder: cäcilie; wiegenlied; ich liebe dich; morgen; zueignung
recorded between 5-7 may 1977 in the maison de la radio paris

orchestre national
caballe

lp: deutsche grammophon 2530 963
cd: 431 1712/477 5910

strauss/**also sprach zarathustra**
recorded on 5 october 1970 in philharmonic hall
new york philharmonic
lp: columbia M 30443/MQ 30443/ MG 33707
cd: SMK 47626

don juan
recorded on 3 february 1963 in philharmonic hall
new york philharmonic
lp: columbia ML 6222/MS 6822/ MG 33707
cd: SMK 47626

don quixote
recorded on 13 november 1943 at a concert in carnegie hall
new york philharmonic
schuster, lincer
lp: new york philharmonic NYP 83
cd: new york philharmonic 19054-1196
recorded at bernstein's public conducting debut

recorded on 24 october 1968 in philharmonic hall
new york philharmonic
munroe, lincer
lp: columbia M 30067/MG 33707
cd: SMK 47625

festliches präludium
recorded on 2 october 1962 in philharmonic hall
new york philharmonic
power biggs
lp: columbia ML 5798/MS 6398/ BRG 72364/SBRG 72364
cd: SMK 47625

till eulenspiegels lustige streiche
recorded on 20 april 1959 in the saint george's hotel brooklyn
new york philharmonic
lp: columbia ML 5625/ML 5841/ ML 6222/MS 6225/MS 6441/ MS 7165/D3S 785/MG 33707/ 61976
cd: SMK 47626
includes bernstein's spoken introduction

IGOR STRAVINSKY (1882-1971)
capriccio for piano and orchestra
recorded on 19 may 1962 at a concert in carnegie hall
new york philharmonic
lipkin
cd: new york philharmonic NYP 2003

le chant du rossignol
recorded on 16 december 1956 at a concert in carnegie hall
new york philharmonic
cd: new york philharmonic NYP 2003

concerto for piano and wind
recorded on 26 october 1959 in the columbia studios new york city
new york philharmonic
lipkin
lp: columbia ML 5729/MS 6329
cd: SMK 47628

l'histoire du soldat
recorded on 11 august 1947 in the concert theatre tanglewood
members of boston symphony
78: victor M 1197
lp: victor LM 1078/SMA 7014/ TVM1 7083
cd: symposium 1372/ pearl GEMM 0066

mass
recorded on 22 march 1977 in the henry wood hall london
english bach festival orchestra and chorus
trinity boys choir
lp: deutsche grammophon 2530 880
cd: 423 2512/477 5193

les noces
televised on 22 march 1977 in the henry wood hall london
percussion ensemble
english bach festival chorus
mory, parker, mitchinson, hudson, argerich, zimerman, francesch, katsaris
lp: deutsche grammophon 2530 880
cd: 423 2512/477 5193
also unpublished video recording

stravinsky/**octet for wind**
recorded on 11 august 1947 in the concert theatre tanglewood
members of   78: victor M 1197
boston symphony   lp: victor LM 1978/TVM1 7083
                             cd: rca 09026 681052/pearl
                             GEMM 0066

oedipus rex
televised on 15-16 december 1972 at concerts in symphony hall boston
boston symphony   lp: columbia M4X 33032/M 33999
harvard glee club   cd: 88697 008192/private edition usa
troyanos, kollo,   *also unpublished video recording*
flagello, krause

l'oiseau de feu, 1919 concert suite from the ballet
recorded on 28 january 1957 in the columbia studios new york city
new york   lp: columbia ML 5182/MS 6014/
philharmonic   MG 30269/MY 37221/61122/
                             philips ABL 3268/SABL 111/
                             A01405L
                             cd: MYK 37221/SMK 47605/
                             SMK 60694/SBK 64113/SK 93080

recorded on 18 may 1984 at a concert in the frederick mann auditorium
israel   lp: deutsche grammophon 415 1271
philharmonic   cd: 415 1272/435 5952/
                             445 5382/477 5193

petrushka, ballet
recorded on 5 may 1969 in philharmonic hall
new york   lp: columbia MG 30269/MY 37221/
philharmonic   61122
                             cd: MYK 37221/SMK 47629/
                             82876 787492

recorded on 29 april 1982 at a concert in the frederick mann auditorium
israel   cd: deutsche grammophon 410 9962/
philharmonic   445 5382/477 5193

stravinsky/**pulcinella, ballet suite**
recorded on 28 march 1960 in the manhattan centre new york city
new york philharmonic
lp: columbia ML 5729/MS 6329
cd: MK 44709/SMK 47628/
82876 787492

recorded on 18 may 1984 at a concert in the frederick mann auditorium
israel philharmonic
lp: deutsche grammophon 415 1271
cd: 415 1272/435 5952

le sacre du printemps
recorded on 20 january 1958 in the saint george's hotel brooklyn
new york philharmonic
lp: columbia ML 5277/MS 6010/
D2L 349/D2S 749/MG 30269/
61104/philips ABL 3268/SABL 111/
A01450L
cd: MK 30269/SMK 47629/
SX10K 89750

recorded on 7 april 1972 in the abbey road studios london
london symphony
lp: columbia M 31520/MZ 31520/
73104
cd: MK 44709/SMK 60694/516 2402

televised in april 1972 at a concert in the royal festival hall london
london symphony
unpublished video recording

recorded on 29 april 1982 at a concert in the frederick mann auditorium
israel philharmonic
lp: deutsche grammophon 2532 075
cd: 410 5082/445 5382/477 5193

televised in 1982 at a concert in the teatro juarez guanajuato mexico
israel philharmonic
unpublished video recording

scenes de ballet
recorded on 29 april 1982 at a concert in the frederick mann auditorium
israel philharmonic
cd: deutsche gramophon 435 5952/
445 5382/477 5193

stravinsky/**symphonie de psaumes**
recorded on 8 april 1972 in the abbey road studios london
london symphony　　　lp: columbia M 34551/76670
english bach　　　　　cd: MK 44710/SMK 47628/
festival chorus　　　　SBK 61703/88697 008192
televised on 17 june 1982 in washington dc
national symphony　　unpublished video recording
scribner choir

symphony in c
recorded on 23 may 1984 at a concert in the frederick mann auditorium
israel　　　　　　　　cd: deutsche grammophon 477 5193
philharmonic

symphony in three movements
recorded on 25 april 1982 at a concert in the frederick mann auditorium
israel　　　　　　　　cd: deutsche grammophon
philharmonic　　　　　445 5382/477 5193
televised in 1982 at a concert in the teatro juarez guanajuato mexico
israel　　　　　　　　unpublished video recording
philharmonic

FRANZ VON SUPPE (1819-1895)
dichter und bauer, overture
recorded on 21 january 1963 in philharmonic hall
new york　　　　　　lp: columbia ML 6143/MS 6743/
philharmonic　　　　　D3S 818/M 31815/MY 37240/
　　　　　　　　　　　MG 35188/CSS 527/BRG 72389/
　　　　　　　　　　　SBRG 72389
　　　　　　　　　　　cd: MYK 37240/SFK 46713/
　　　　　　　　　　　SMK 47606

leichte kavallerie, overture
recorded on 26 october 1967 in philharmonic hall
new york　　　　　　lp: columbia MS 7085/D3S 818/
philharmonic　　　　　MG 35188/61349
　　　　　　　　　　　cd: SFK 46713/SMK 47606

die schöne galathea, overture
recorded on 10 january 1967 in philharmonic hall
new york　　　　　　lp: columbia MS 7085/D3S 818/61349
philharmonic　　　　　cd: SMK 47532/SMK 61830

PIOTR TCHAIKOVSKY (1840-1893)
symphony no 1 "winter dreams"
recorded on 20 october 1970 in philharmonic hall
new york philharmonic
lp: columbia M 30482/D3M 32996/
BRG 72949/SBRG 72949
cd: SMK 47631/SX5K 64208

symphony no 2 "little russian"
recorded on 24 october 1967 in philharmonic hall
new york philharmonic
lp: columbia M 31195/D3M 32996
cd: SMK 47631/SX5K 64208

symphony no 3 "polish"
recorded on 10 february 1970 in philharmonic hall
new york philharmonic
lp: columbia M 31727/D3M 32996
cd: SMK 47632/SX5K 64208

symphony no 4
recorded on 15 january 1958 at a concert in carnegie hall
new york philharmonic
cd: living stage LS 1081

recorded on 30 september 1958 in the saint george's hotel brooklyn
new york philharmonic
lp: columbia ML 5332/MS 6035/
D3S 781/philips ABL 3267/SABL 122/
A01404L/835 515AY
cd: SMK 61556

televised on 28 april 1975 in the manhattan centre
new york philharmonic
lp: columbia M 33886/MQ 33886/
MY 37766/AL 33886/XM 33886/
XMQ 33886
cd: MYK 33886/SMK 47633/
SX5K 64208
sacd: SS 87982
dvd video: deutsche grammophon
073 4511

recorded on 31 october 1989 at a concert in avery fisher hall
new york philharmonic
cd: deutsche grammophon 429 7782/
431 0462/477 6704

tchaikovsky/**symphony no 5**
recorded on 16 may 1960 in the manhattan centre
new york philharmonic   lp: columbia ML 5712/MS 6312/D3S 781/ BRG 72037/SBRG 72037
cd: SMK 47634/SX5K 64208

televised in 1974 at a concert in the music centre tanglewood
boston symphony   cd: private edition usa
dvd video: deutsche grammophon 073 4511

televised in 1988 at a concert in the music centre tanglewood
boston symphony   unpublished video recording

recorded on 29 november 1988 at a concert in avery fisher hall
new york philharmonic   cd: deutsche grammophon 429 2342/ 469 2142/477 6704

symphony no 6 "pathetique"
recorded on 29-30 june 1953 in carnegie hall
new york philharmonic   lp: american decca DL 9718
cd: deutsche grammophon 477 0002/ andromeda ANDRCD 5115
orchestra described for this recording as stadium concerts orchestra; bernstein's spoken analysis of the symphony issued by musical appreciation society and also included in the deutsche grammophon reissue

recorded on 11 february 1964 in the manhattan centre
new york philharmonic   lp: columbia ML 6089/MS 6689/D3S 781/ BRG 72266/SBRG 72266
cd: SMK 47635/SX5K 64208

televised on 22-23 august 1974 at concerts in the sydney opera house
new york philharmonic   dvd video: kultur 1525

recorded on 16 august 1986 at a concert in avery fisher hall
new york philharmonic   lp: deutsche grammophon 419 6041
cd: 419 6042/431 0462/ 469 2142/477 6704

tchaikovsky/**piano concerto no 1**
recorded on 9 october 1961 in the manhattan centre
new york	lp: columbia ML 5759/MS 6359/
philharmonic	D3L 315/D3S 715/MG 32050/
entremont	BRG 72048/SBRG 72048
	cd: SMK 61828

recorded on 12 march 1973 in the columbia studios new york city
new york	lp: columbia M 33701/MQ 33701/
philharmonic	78315
watts	cd: SMK 47630

violin concerto
recorded on 5 march 1973 in the columbia studios new york city
new york	cd: columbia SMK 47637
philharmonic	*unpublished columbia lp recording*
stern

televised on 25 april 1975 in the columbia studios new york city
new york	dvd video: deutsche grammophon
philharmonic	073 4511
belkin	*also unpublished columbia lp recording*

songs: wait!; night
recorded on 3 march 1969 in the columbia studios new york city
tourel	lp: columbia M 32231
bernstein, piano

andante cantabile, arrangement from the first string quartet
televised on 21 april 1975 in the columbia studios new york city
new york	lp: columbia MY 38484
philharmonic	cd: MYK 38484/SFK 46711/
	MLK 62617/SK 92726
	dvd video: deutsche grammophon
	073 4511

tchaikovsky/**capriccio italien**
recorded on 11 february 1960 in the saint george's hotel brooklyn
new york philharmonic lp: columbia ML 5658/ML 5877/ ML 6227/MS 6258/MS 6477/ MS 6827/MS 7513/MG 31264/ MG 35270/MY 36728/3P 6871/ BRG 72147/SBRG 72147/60115
cd: MYK 36728/MLK 39440/ SFK 46711/SMK 47595/ SMK 61556/SK 93076

recorded on 15 may 1984 at a concert in the frederick mann auditorium
israel philharmonic cd: deutsche grammophon 415 3792/ 439 9832/477 6704

casse noisette, suite from the ballet
recorded on 2 may 1960 in the manhattan centre
new york philharmonic lp: columbia ML 5593/MS 6193/ D3S 785/M 31806/MY 37238
cd: MYK 37238/SMK 47636/ SMK 63162/SFK 63303
sacd: SS 87982

polonaise/evgeny onegin
recorded on 12 january 1971 in philharmonic hall
new york philharmonic lp: columbia M 34127/MY 36728/ 3P 6871/60115
cd: MYK 36728/SMK 47636/ SMK 63162

waltz/evgeny onegin
recorded on 28 april 1975 in the manhattan centre
new york philharmonic lp: columbia M 34127/MY 36728/ 3P 6871/60115
cd: MYK 36728/SFK 46707

tchaikovsky/**francesca da rimini**
recorded on 31 october 1960 in the manhattan centre
new york lp: columbia ML 5658/MS 6258/
philharmonic MG 33270/60115
cd: SMK 47633/SX5K 64208

recorded on 23 october 1978 at a concert in the frederick mann auditorium
israel lp: deutsche grammophon 2531 211
philharmonic cd: 439 9832/477 6704

recorded on 31 october 1989 at a concert in avery fisher hall
new york cd: deutsche grammophon 429 7782
philharmonic

hamlet, fantasy overture
recorded on 19 october 1970 in philharmonic hall
new york lp: columbia M 34128
philharmonic cd: SMK 47635/SX5K 64208/
SK 93076

recorded on 15 may 1984 at a concert in the frederick mann auditorium
israel cd: deutsche grammophon
philharmonic 415 3792/477 6704

1812, ouverture solennelle
recorded on 2 october 1962 in philharmonic hall
new york lp: columbia ML 5877/ML 6227/
philharmonic MS 6477/MS 6827/MS 7503/
MG 31264/MQ 32055/MY 36723/
MYX 39141/M 39433/BRG 72147/
SBRG 72147/60113
cd: MYK 36723/MLK 39433/
SFK 46711/SMK 47634/SX5K 64208/
MLK 64055/SK 93076

recorded on 15 may 1984 at a concert in the frederick mann auditorium
israel cd: deutsche grammophon 415 3792/
philharmonic 439 9832/477 6704

164
tchaikovsky/**marche slave**
recorded on 21 january 1963 in philharmonic hall
new york philharmonic
lp: columbia ML 5877/ML 6227/
MS 6477/MS 6827/MG 33270/
MG 35919/MY 36723/MYX 39141/
3P 6871/BRG 72147/SBRG 72147
cd: MYK 36723/MGT 39803/
SMK 42392/SFK 46711/SMK 47634/
SX5K 64208/SK 93076

recorded on 15 may 1984 at a concert in the frederick mann auditorium
israel philharmonic
cd: deutsche grammophon
415 3792/477 6704

romeo and juliet, fantasy overture
recorded on 28 january 1957 in the columbia studios new york city
new york philharmonic
lp: columbia ML 5182/MS 6014/
MG 33270/MY 36723/MYX 39141/
3P 6871/60113
cd: MYK 36723/MGT 39803/
SFK 46711/SMK 47632/
SX5K 64208/SK 93076

recorded on 23 october 1978 at a concert in the frederick mann auditorium
israel philharmonic
lp: deutsche grammophon 2531 211
cd: 439 9832/477 6704

recorded on 31 october 1989 at a concert in avery fisher hall
new york philharmonic
cd: deutsche grammophon
429 2342/469 2142

serenade for strings
recorded on 22 october 1970 in philharmonic hall
new york philharmonic
lp: columbia M 34128
cd: SMK 47637

tchaikovsky/**waltz/sleeping beauty**
recorded on 12 january 1971 in philharmonic hall
new york philharmonic lp: columbia M 34127
cd: MLK 44725/SFK 46708/
SMK 47636/SMK 63162/SMK 64077

swan lake, selections from acts 2 and 3 of the ballet
recorded on 13 may 1969 in philharmonic hall
new york philharmonic lp: columbia M 30056/MQ 30056/
MY 37238/61205
cd: MYK 37238/SMK 47636/
SMK 63162

AMBROISE THOMAS (1811-1896)
mignon, overture
recorded on 21 january 1963 in philharmonic hall
new york philharmonic lp: columbia ML 6143/MS 6743/
D3S 818/M 31815/MY 37240/
BRG 72389/SBRG 72389
cd: MYK 37240/SMK 47601

raymonda, overture
recorded on 21 january 1963 in philharmonic hall
new york philharmonic lp: columbia ML 6143/MS 6743/
D3S 818/M 31815/MY 37240/
BRG 72389/SBRG 72389
cd: MYK 37240

televised in 1981 at a concert in the theatre des champs-elysees
orchestre national unpublished video recording

RANDALL THOMPSON (1899-1984)
symphony no 2
recorded on 22 october 1968 in philharmonic hall
new york philharmonic lp: columbia MS 7392
cd: SMK 60594

VIRGIL THOMSON (1896-1989)
four saints in three acts, scenes
recorded on 7 may 1960 at a concert in carnegie hall
new york philharmonic
choral arts society
venora, allen,
eckert, voketaitis,
boatwright
cd: new york philharmonic NYP 9904

the river seine at night
recorded on 14 october 1961 at a concert in carnegie hall
new york philharmonic
cd: new york philharmonic NYP 2003

EDGAR VARESE (1885-1965)
arcana
recorded on 29 november 1958 at a concert in carnegie hall
new york philharmonic
cd: new york philharmonic NYP 2003

integrales
recorded 8 october 1966 at a concert in philharmonic hall
new york philharmonic
cd: new york philharmonic NYP 9904

RALPH VAUGHAN WILLIAMS (1872-1958)
symphony no 4
recorded on 21 october 1965 in philharmonic hall
new york philharmonic
lp: columbia MS 7177/BRG 72727/ SBRG 72727
cd: SMK 47638/SBK 89779
sacd: SS 87892

fantasia on greensleeves
recorded on 8 december 1969 in philharmonic hall
new york philharmonic
lp: columbia M 30573/MY 38484
cd: MYK 38484/MLK 44724/SFK 46715/ SMK 47638/MLK 62617/SMK 64076/ SK 92726/SBK 89770

fantasia on a theme of thomas tallis
recorded on 21 december 1976 in the manhattan centre
new york philharmonic
lp: columbia MY 38484
cd: MYK 38484/SMK 47638/ SK 92726/SBK 89779

serenade to music
recorded on 23 september 1962 at the opening concert in philharmonic hall
new york philharmonic
addison, amara, farrell, chookasian, tourel, verrett, bressler, tucker, vickers, bell, flagello, london
lp: columbia L2L 1007/L2S 1008/ MS 7177/BRG 72727/SBRG 72727
cd: SMK 47638/SMK 61874/ SBK 89779

GIUSEPPE VERDI (1813-1901)
ballet music/aida
recorded on 24 january 1968 in philharmonic hall
new york philharmonic
lp: columbia MS 7415/61165
cd: SFK 46714/SMK 47600

grand march/aida
recorded on 24 january 1968 in philharmonic hall
new york philharmonic
lp: columbia MS 7271/MG 35919
cd: MLK 44724/MDK 45734/
SMK 47600/SMK 63154/
SMK 64076/SBK 89305

falstaff
recorded on 21 march 1964 at a performance in the metropolitan opera house
metropolitan opera orchestra and chorus
tucci, raskin, elias, resnik, alva, colzani, sereni
unpublished met broadcast

recorded on 14 march 1966 at a performance in the staatsoper vienna
wiener philharmoniker
chor der wiener staatsoper
ligabue, sciutti, rössel-majdan, resnik, oncina, panerai, fischer-dieskau
unpublished radio broadcast
according to monika wolf in her discography of fischer-dieskau excerpts from this performance were issued on cd by arkadia; also unpublished video recording of rehearsal extracts

recorded between 18-30 march 1966 in the sofiensaal vienna
wiener philharmoniker
chor der wiener staatsoper
ligabue, sciutti, rössel-majdan, resnik, oncina, panerai, fischer-dieskau
lp: columbia M3L 350/M3S 750/
BRG 72493-72495/SBRG 72493-72495/77392
cd: M2K 42535

verdi/**requiem mass**
recorded between 23-25 february 1970 in the royal albert hall london
london symphony　　　lp: columbia M2 30060/M2Q 30060/
orchestra and chorus　　77231
arroyo, veasey,　　　　cd: M2K 30060/M2K 77231/
domingo, raimondi　　　SM2K 47639/SM2K 89379/
　　　　　　　　　　　516 0282

televised in february 1970 at a concert in saint paul's cathedral london
london symphony　　　dvd video: kultur 1525
orchestra and chorus
arroyo, veasey,
domingo, raimondi

HEITOR VILLA LOBOS (1887-1959)
bachianas brasileiras no 5
recorded on 6 february 1963 in philharmonic hall
new york　　　　　　lp: columbia ML 5914/MS 6514/
philharmonic　　　　　BRG 72186/SBRG 72186/61059
devrath　　　　　　　cd: SMK 47544/SMK 60571

ANTONIO VIVALDI (1675-1741)
le 4 stagioni
recorded on 13 may 1963 (spring), 27 january 1964 (summer and winter) and 11 february 1964 (autumn) in the manhattan centre
new york　　　　　　lp: columbia ML 6144/MS 6744/
philharmonic　　　　　BRG 72363/SBRG 72363
corigliano　　　　　　cd: SMK 47642/SMK 63161
bernstein conducts
from the harpsichord

concerto for diverse instruments rv 558
recorded on 15 december 1958 in the saint george's hotel brooklyn
new york　　　　　　lp: columbia ML 5459/MS 6131/
philharmonic　　　　　BRG 72243/SBRG 72243/60335
　　　　　　　　　　　cd: SMK 47642/SMK 63161

flute concerto rv 441
recorded on 15 december 1958 in the saint george's hotel brooklyn
new york　　　　　　lp: columbia ML 5459/MS 6131/
philharmonic　　　　　BRG 72243/SBRG 72243/60335
wummer　　　　　　　cd: SMK 47642/SMK 63161

vivaldi/**oboe concerto rv 454**
recorded on 15 december 1958 in the saint george's hotel brooklyn
new york   lp: columbia ML 5459/MS 6131/
philharmonic   BRG 72243/SBRG 72243/60335
gomberg   cd: SMK 47642/SMK 63161

piccolo concerto rv 444
recorded on 15 december 1958 in the saint george's hotel brooklyn
new york   lp: columbia ML 5459/MS 6131/
philharmonic   BRG 72243/SBRG 72243/60335
heims   cd: SMK 47642/SMK 63161

JOSEF FRANZ WAGNER (1856-1908)
unter dem doppeladler, march
recorded on 12 october 1970 in philharmonic hall
new york   lp: columbia M 30943/MG 35919
philharmonic   cd: MDK 45734/SMK 63154/
                           SBK 89305
MG 35919 incorrectly named composer as sousa

RICHARD WAGNER (1813-1883)
der fliegende holländer, overture
recorded on 26 january 1968 in philharmonic hall
new york   lp: columbia M 31011/D3M 32992/
philharmonic   BRG 72870/SBRG 72870
                           cd: SMK 47643

götterdämmerung, scenes: zu neuen taten; ein freier kam; mime hiess ein mürrischer zwerg; brünnhild' heilige braut!
recorded between 24-26 january 1970 at concerts in philharmonic hall
new york   cd: new york philharmonic NYP 2003/
philharmonic   gala GL 100 613
farrell, thomas

starke scheite schichtet mir dort/götterdämmerung
recorded on 30 september 1961 in the manhattan centre new york city
new york lp: columbia ML 5753/MS 6353/
philharmonic D3M 32992
farrell cd: SMK 47644/MDK 46288

recorded between 24-26 january 1970 at concerts in philharmonic hall
new york cd: new york philharmonic NYP 2003/
philharmonic gala GL 100 613
farrell

siegfried's rhine journey/götterdämmerung
recorded between 24-26 january 1970 at concerts in philharmonic hall
new york cd: new york philharmonic NYP 2003/
philharmonic gala GL 100 613

siegfried's funeral march/götterdämmerung
recorded between 24-26 january 1970 at concerts in philharmonic hall
new york cd: new york philharmonic NYP 2003/
philharmonic gala GL 100 613

lohengrin, act one prelude
recorded on 25 january 1968 in philharmonic hall
new york cd: columbia SMK 47643
philharmonic *unpublished columbia lp recording*

lohengrin, act three prelude
recorded on 26 october 1967 in philharmonic hall
new york lp: columbia MS 7141/M2X 795/
philharmonic D3M 32992/61196
  cd: MLK 44725/SMK 47643/
  MLK 64061/SMK 64077

wagner/**die meistersinger von nürnberg, overture**
recorded on 27 april 1964 in the manhattan centre
new york philharmonic   lp: columbia M 31011/D3M 32992/ BRG 72870/SBRG 72870
cd: SMK 47643
recording completed on 1 may 1964

recorded 8 june 1964 at a concert in symphony hall boston
boston pops orchestra   cd: boston symphony orchestra CD 3
recorded at bernstein's twenty-fifth reunion concert

die meistersinger von nürnberg, act three prelude
recorded on 27 april 1964 in the manhattan centre
new york philharmonic   columbia unpublished

dance of the apprentices and entry of the masters/die meistersinger von nürnberg
recorded on 27 april 1964 in the manhattan centre
new york philharmonic   lp: columbia MS 7141/D3M 32992/ 61196

rienzi, overture
recorded on 2 february 1968 in philharmonic hall
new york philharmonic   lp: columbia M 31011/D3M 32992/ BRG 72870/SBRG 72870
cd: SMK 47643

siegfried, act three
recorded on 21 may 1985 at a concert in the staatsoper vienna
wiener philharmoniker
vinzing, ludwig, king, stewart   cd: private edition vienna

tannhäuser, overture
recorded on 26 october 1967 in philharmonic hall
new york philharmonic   lp: columbia MS 7141/D3M 32992/ 61196
cd: SMK 47644

wagner/entry of the guests/tannhäuser
recorded on 26 october 1967 in philharmonic hall
new york philharmonic
lp: columbia MS 7141/MS 7271/ MS 7511/D3M 32992/MG 35919/ 61196
cd: MDK 45734/SMK 47643/ SMK 63154/SBK 89305

tristan und isolde
televised between 11-13 january 1981 (act one), on 27 april 1981 (act two) and on 8 november 1981 (act three) at concerts in the herkulessaal munich
sinfonieorchester und chor des bayerischen rundfunks
behrens, minton, hofmann, weikl, sotin, steinbach, moser, zednik, grumbach

lp: philips 6769 091
cd: 410 4472/438 2412/475 7020
excerpts
cd: 411 0362/438 5012
also unpublished video recording of these concert performances

tristan und isolde, scenes
recorded on 26 february 1969 at a concert in philharmonic hall
new york philharmonic
farrell, simon, thomas

lp: roger frank FWR 69
cd: gala GL 100 613

recorded in 1972 at a concert in the music centre tanglewood
boston symphony   cd: disco archivia 557

tristan und isolde, prelude and liebestod
recorded on 9 may 1967 in philharmonic hall
new york philharmonic
lp: columbia MS 7141 (liebestod)/ M 31011 (prelude)/D3M 32992/ M3X 33024/BRG 72870 (prelude)/ SBRG 72870 (prelude)/ 61196 (liebestod)
cd: SMK 47644
recording completed on 20 may 1967

televised in 1973 in the wgbh studios boston
boston symphony   unpublished video recording

wagner/**die walküre, act one**
recorded on 23 may 1968 at a concert in carnegie hall
new york   lp: penzance records PR 31
philharmonic   cd: gala GL 100 613
farrell, king,
langdon

ride of the valkyries/die walküre
recorded on 26 october 1967 in philharmonic hall
new york   lp: columbia MS 7141/MS 7246/
philharmonic   MS 7511/MS 7519/MG 30074/
                         M3X 31068/D3M 32992/61196
                         cd: MLK 44725/SMK 47643/
                         MLK 62368/SMK 64077

die walküre, act three scenes two and three (beginning at war es so schmählich?)
recorded on 21 may 1985 at a concert in the staatsoper vienna
wiener   cd: private edition vienna
philharmoniker
vinzing, stewart

magic fire music/die walküre
recorded on 25 january 1968 in philharmonic hall
new york   lp: columbia MS 7141/D3M 32992/
philharmonic   61196
                         cd: SMK 47643

wesendonk-lieder
recorded on 30 september 1961 in the manhattan centre
new york   lp: columbia ML 5733/MS 6353/
philharmonic   D3M 32992
farrell   cd: SMK 47644

CARL MARIA VON WEBER (1786-1826)
aufforderung zum tanz, arranged by berlioz
recorded on 12 october 1965 in the manhattan centre
new york philharmonic   lp: columbia M 33585/M 35861

euryanthe, overture
recorded on 16 january 1968 in philharmonic hall
new york philharmonic   lp: columbia M 33585
cd: SMK 47601

televised in 1983 at a concert in the musikverein vienna
wiener philharmoniker   unpublished video recording

der freischütz, overture
recorded on 27 march 1963 in philharmonic hall
new york philharmonic   lp: columbia M 33585
cd: SMK 47601

oberon, overture
recorded on 10 october 1960 in the manhattan centre
new york philharmonic   lp: columbia ML 5623/MS 6223/ M 33585
cd: SMK 47601

ANTON VON WEBERN (1883-1945)
symphony op 21
recorded on 4 december 1965 at a concert in philharmonic hall
new york philharmonic   cd: new york philharmonic NYP 9701

six orchestral pieces op 6
recorded on 19 january 1958 at a concert in carnegie hall
new york philharmonic   cd: new york philharmonic NYP 2003

ERMANNO WOLF-FERRARI (1876-1948)
i gioielli della madonna, intermezzo
recorded on 2 february 1968 in philharmonic hall
new york philharmonic   cd: columbia MLK 44724/SMK 64076
unpublished columbia lp recording

il segreto di susanna, overture
recorded on 24 january 1968 in philharmonic hall
new york philharmonic   lp: columbia M2X 795/D3S 818

IANNIS XENAKIS (born 1922)
pithoprakta
recorded on 5 january 1964 at a concert in philharmonic hall
new york philharmonic   cd: new york philharmonic NYP 2003

CHARLES ZIMMERMAN (1861-1916)
ancors aweigh, march
recorded on 12 october 1970 in philharmonic hall
new york philharmonic   lp: columbia M 30943/MG 35919
cd: MDK 45734/SMK 63154/ SBK 89305

TRADITIONAL
the british grenadiers
recorded on 12 october 1970 in philharmonic hall
new york philharmonic   lp: columbia M 30943/MG 35919
cd: MDK 45734/SMK 63154/ SBK 89305

THE JOY OF CHRISTMAS: CAROLS WITH THE MORMON TABERNACLE CHOIR
recorded on 3-4 september 1963 in the salt lake tabernacle
new york philharmonic   lp: columbia ML 5899/MS 6499
cd: SFK 63303

THE YOUNG PEOPLE'S CONCERTS 1958-1972
a television series introduced by leonard bernstein

what does music mean?
with music by ravel, rossini, strauss, beethoven, mussorgsky and tchaikovsky
recorded on 18 january 1958

new york philharmonic	vhs video: sony SHV 48319
	dvd video: kultur 1503

what is american music?
with music by gershwin, chadwick, dvorak, macdowell, gilbert, copland, schuman, thomson and thompson
recorded on 1 february 1958

new york philharmonic	vhs video: sony SHV 48320
	dvd video: kultur 1503

what is orchestration?
with music by rimsky-korsakov and ravel
recorded on 8 march 1958

new york philharmonic	vhs video: sony SHV 48321
	dvd video: kultur 1503

what makes music symphonic?
with music by mozart, tchaikovsky, beethoven and brahms
recorded on 13 december 1958

new york philharmonic	vhs video: sony SHV 48322
	dvd video: kultur 1503

what is classical music?
with music by mozart, beethoven, handel, bach and haydn
recorded on 24 january 1959

new york philharmonic	vhs video: sony SHV 48323
	dvd video: kultur 1503

humour in music
with music by haydn, prokofiev, mahler, shostakovich, copland and brahms
recorded on 28 february 1959

new york philharmonic	vhs video: sony SHV 48324
	dvd video: kultur 1503

young people's concerts/continued
what is a concerto?
with music by vivaldi, bach, mozart, mendelssohn and bartok
recorded on 28 march 1959
new york   vhs video: sony SHV 48325
philharmonic   dvd video: kultur 1503

folk music in the concert hall
with music by mozart, chavez, canteloube and ives
recorded on 9 april 1961
new york   vhs video: sony SHV 48326
philharmonic   dvd video: kultur 1503

what is impressionism?
with music by debussy and ravel
recorded on 1 december 1961
new york   vhs video: sony SHV 48327
philharmonic   dvd video: kultur 1503

what is a melody?
with music by by tchaikovsky, wagner, mozart, hindemith and brahms
recorded on 21 december 1962
new york   vhs video: sony SHV 48328
philharmonic   dvd video: kultur 1503

what is sonata form?
with music by mozart, bizet and prokofiev
recorded on 6 november 1964
new york   vhs video: sony SHV 48329
philharmonic   dvd video: kultur 1503

a tribute to sibelius
with music by sibelius
recorded on 19 february 1965
new york   vhs video: sony SHV 48330
philharmonic   dvd video: kultur 1503

musical atoms: a study of intervals
with music by wagner, brahms and vaughan williams
recorded on 29 november 1965
new york   vhs video: sony SHV 48331
philharmonic   dvd video: kultur 1503

young people's concerts/continued
what is a mode?
with music by debussy, mussorgsky and bernstein
recorded on 23 november 1966

new york	vhs video: sony SHV 48332
philharmonic	dvd video: kultur 1503

berlioz takes a trip
with music by berlioz
recorded on 25 may 1969

new york	vhs video: sony SHV 48333
philharmonic	dvd video: kultur 1503

who is gustav mahler?
with music by mahler
recorded on 7 february 1960

new york	vhs video: sony SHV 48334/
philharmonic	S10HV 53490
	dvd video: kultur 1503

happy birthday, igor stravinsky!
with music by stravinsky
recorded on 26 march 1962

new york	vhs video: sony SHV 48335/
philharmonic	S10HV 53490
	dvd video: kultur 1503

the latin american spirit
with music by fernandez, villa-lobos, revueltas, copland and bernstein
recorded on 8 march 1963

new york	vhs video: sony SHV 48336/
philharmonic	S10HV 53490
	dvd video: kultur 1503

jazz in the concert hall
with music by schuller, copland and austin
recorded on 11 march 1964

new york	vhs video: sony SHV 48337/
philharmonic	S10HV 53490
	dvd video: kultur 1503

young people's concerts/concluded
the sound of an orchestra
with music by haydn, brahms, debussy, stravinsky and copland
recorded on 14 december 1965
new york philharmonic
vhs video: sony SHV 48338/
S10HV 53490
dvd video: kultur 1503

a birthday tribute to shostakovich
with music by shostakovich
recorded on 5 january 1966
new york philharmonic
vhs video: sony SHV 48339/
S10HV 53490
dvd video: kultur 1503

a toast to vienna in 3/4 time
with music by strauss, mozart, beethoven and mahler
recorded on 25 december 1967
new york philharmonic
vhs video: sony SHV 48340/
S10HV 53490
dvd video: kultur 1503

quiz concert: how musical are you?
with music by brahms, mozart, prokofiev and rimsky-korsakov
recorded on 26 may 1968
new york philharmonic
vhs video: sony SHV 48341/
S10HV 53490
dvd video: kultur 1503

two ballet birds
with music by tchaikovsky and stravinsky
recorded on 14 september 1969
new york philharmonic
vhs video: sony SHV 48342/
S10HV 53490
dvd video: kultur 1503

fidelio: a celebration of life
with music by beethoven
recorded on 29 march 1970
new york philharmonic
vhs video: sony SHV 48343/
S10HV 53490
dvd video: kultur 1503

JOSEPH ACHRON (1886-1943)
hebrew melody for violin and orchestra
recorded in 1947 at a concert in the hollywood bowl
los angeles   cd: doremi DHR 7736
philharmonic
elman

ADOLPHE ADAM (1803-1856)
giselle, suite from the ballet
recorded on 5 march 1968 in the town hall
philadelphia   lp: columbia M 30463/61242
orchestra   cd: SBK 46341

ISAAC ALBENIZ (1860-1909)
iberia, suite arranged by arbos
recorded on 10 january 1956 in the broadwood hotel
philadelphia   lp: columbia M2L 237
orchestra

HUGO ALFVEN (1872-1960)
swedish rhapsody no 1
recorded on 16 february 1953 in the town hall
philadelphia   lp: columbia A 1645/AL 35/
orchestra   ML 5181
recorded on 21 december 1959 in the town hall
philadelphia   lp: columbia ML 5596/MS 6196/
orchestra   61266
                          cd: SBK 38917/SBK 60265
recorded on 11 march 1968 in the town hall
philadelphia   lp: columbia MS 7674
orchestra

ALFREDO D'AMBROSIO (1871-1914)
canzonetta
recorded in 1926
ormandy, violin   78: cameo 1159

DAVID AMRAM (born 1930)
the trail of beauty, for mezzo-soprano, oboe and orchestra
recorded on 3 march 1977 at a concert in the academy of music
philadelphia   cd: disco archivia 725
orchestra
taylor, lancie

CARL PHILIPP EMMANUEL BACH (1714-1788)
concerto for orchestra, arranged by steinberg
recorded on 17 march 1957 in the broadwood hotel
philadelphia orchestra
lp: columbia ML 5742/MS 6342
cd: MH2K 62345/88697 279872

JOHANN CHRISTIAN BACH (1735-1782)
sinfonia op 18 no 1
recorded on 10 april 1960 in the broadwood hotel
philadelphia orchestra
lp: columbia ML 5580/MS 6180
cd: MH2K 62345/88697 279872

sinfonia op 18 no 3
recorded on 25 december 1944 at a concert in the nbc studios new york city
nbc symphony
unpublished radio broadcast

recorded on 17 march 1957 in the town hall
philadelphia orchestra
lp: columbia ML 5742/MS 6342
cd: MH2K 62345/88697 279872

JOHANN SEBASTIAN BACH (1685-1750)
mass in b minor
recorded on 25-26 april 1962 in the town hall
philadelphia orchestra
temple university choir
steber, elias,
verreau, cross
lp: columbia M3L 780/M3S 680/
BRG 72114-72115/SBRG
73114-72114

osteroratorium
recorded on 17 april 1963 in the town hall
philadelphia orchestra
temple university choir
raskin, forrester,
lewis, beattie
lp: columbia ML 5939/MS 6539/
BRG 72163/SBRG 72163
cd: SBK 60261

johannes-passion
recorded on 17-18 april 1968 in the town hall
philadelphia orchestra
singing city choir
raskin, forrester, lewis,
shirley, treigle, paul
lp: columbia M3 30517

bach/**herzliebster jesu mein/matthäus-passion, arrangement**
recorded on 27 march 1940 in the academy of music
philadelphia 78: victor 18166/hmv (australia) ED 296
orchestra cd: biddulph BID 83069-83070

wir setzen uns mit tränen nieder/matthäus-passion
recorded on 3 november 1958 in the broadwood hotel
philadelphia lp: columbia MS 6058/philips ABL 3304/
orchestra A01441L
mormon tabernacle
choir

gloria sei dir gesungen/cantata no 140
recorded on 20 october 1940 in the academy of music
philadelphia 78: victor 18166/hmv (australia) ED 296
orchestra
maynor

concerto for 3 pianos bwv 1063
recorded on 9 december 1962 in the town hall
philadelphia lp: columbia ML 5895/MS 6495/
orchestra BRG 72150/SBRG 72150
robert, gaby and cd: SBK 67179
jean casadesus

violin concerto bwv 1041
recorded on 24 december 1955 in the academy of music
philadelphia lp: columbia ML 5087/philips ABL 3138/
orchestra A01239L/philips fontana 697 203EL/
stern melodiya M10 46429-46430
  cd: SX11K 67193

violin concerto bwv 1042
recorded on 24 december 1955 in the academy of music
philadelphia lp: columbia ML 5087/MG 33328/
orchestra philips ABL 3138/A01239L/G05650R/
oistrakh melodiya M10 46429-46430/eterna 825 612
  cd: naxos 811 1246

bach/**air**/**orchestral suite no 3**
recorded on 7 november 1954 in the town hall
philadelphia   45: philips ABE 10250/409 175AE
orchestra   lp: columbia ML 5065/philips
                            SBL 5207/S04614L
recorded on 30 may 1958 at a concert in the moscow conservatory
philadelphia   cd: scora classics SCORACD 001
orchestra
recorded on 30 march 1959 in the broadwood hotel
philadelphia   lp: columbia MS 6081/MS 7072/
orchestra   MG 30072
                            cd: 88697 279872
recorded on 10 march 1971 in the academy of music
philadelphia   lp: victor ARL1 1959
orchestra

ein feste burg, orchestral arrangement
recorded on 6 may 1968 in the town hall
philadelphia   lp: columbia MG 30072
orchestra   cd: 88697 279872

ein feste burg, choral arrangement
recorded on 3 november 1958 in the broadwood hotel
philadelphia   lp: columbia MS 6058/philips
orchestra   ABL 3304/A01441L
mormon tabernacle choir

herzlich tut mein verlangen, orchestral arrangement
recorded on 8 january 1935
minneapolis symphony

jesu meine freude, orchestral arrangement
recorded on 22 january 1947 in the academy of music
philadelphia   78: columbia M 846
orchestra   lp: columbia ML 2058/ML 4797/
                            philips SBR 6223/S06653R
recorded on 11 march 1968 in the town hall
philadelphia   lp: columbia MS 7405/MG 30072
orchestra   cd: 88697 279872
recorded on 12 june 1972 in the academy of music
philadelphia   lp: victor ARL1 1959
orchestra

bach/**jesu meine freude, choral arrangement**
recorded on 3 november 1958 in the broadwood hotel
philadelphia   lp: columbia MS 6058/philips
orchestra   ABL 3304/A01441L
mormon tabernacle
choir

komm süsser tod, orchestral arrangement
recorded on 15 april 1954 in the town hall
philadelphia   lp: columbia ML 5065/philips
orchestra   SBL 5207/S04614L

recorded on 6 may 1968 in the town hall
philadelphia   lp: columbia MG 30072
orchestra   cd: 88697 279872

komm süsser tod, choral arrangement
recorded on 21 may 1962 in the salt lake tabernacle
philadelphia   lp: columbia MS 6679
orchestra
mormon tabernacle
choir

ach gott vom himmel sieh darein, orchestral arrangement
recorded on 7 november 1954 in the town hall
philadelphia   lp: columbia ML 5065
orchestra

schafe können sicher weiden, orchestral arrangement
recorded on 6 may 1968 in the town hall
philadelphia   lp: columbia MG 30072
orchestra   cd: 88697 279872

bach/schafe können sicher weiden, choral arrangement
recorded on 3 november 1958 in the broadwood hotel
philadelphia orchestra
mormon tabernacle choir
lp: columbia MS 6058/philips ABL 3304/A01441L

wachet auf, orchestral arrangement
recorded on 4 december 1947 in the town hall
philadelphia orchestra
78: columbia M 846
lp: columba ML 2058

recorded on 11 march 1968 in the town hall
philadelphia orchestra
lp: columbia MG 30072
cd: 88697 279872

little suite/comprising 4 pieces from the anna magdalene notebook
recorded on 8 may 1968 in the town hall
philadelphia orchestra
lp: columbia MG 30072
cd: SBK 62640/88697 279872

recorded on 25-26 april 1973 in the academy of music
philadelphia orchestra
lp: victor ARL1 1959

arioso/cantata no 156
recorded on 7 november 1954 in the town hall
philadelphia orchestra
lp: columbia ML 5065/philips SBL 5207/S04614L

recorded on 30 may 1958 at a concert in the moscow conservatory
philadelphia orchestra
cd: scora classics SCORACD 001

recorded on 27 february 1968 in the town hall
philadelphia orchestra
lp: columbia MG 30072
cd: 88697 279872

ave maria, arrangement by gounod
recorded between 14-16 may 1924 in new york
concert theatre orchestra
78: cameo 611

bach/**fantasia and fugue in c minor, arrangement**
recorded on 15 april 1954 in the town hall
philadelphia lp: columbia ML 5065/philips
orchestra SBL 5207/S04614L

fantasia and fugue in g, arrangement
recorded on 23 october 1955 in the town hall
philadelphia lp: columbia ML 5065/philips
orchestra SBL 5207/S04614L

recorded on 6 may 1968 in the town hall
philadelphia lp: columbia MG 30072
orchestra

fugue in g minor, arrangement
recorded on 19 december 1954 in the town hall
philadelphia lp: columbia ML 5065/philips
orchestra SBL 5207/S04614L

recorded on 11 march 1968 in the town hall
philadelphia lp: columbia MG 30072
orchestra cd: 88697 279872

seven organ fugues arranged for quadrophony by arthur harris
recorded between 18-20 october 1971 in the academy of music
philadelphia lp: victor ARD1 0026
orchestra

prelude and fugue in c, arrangement
recorded on 19 december 1954 in the town hall
philadelphia lp: columbia ML 5065/philips
orchestra SBL 5207/S04614L

recorded on 19 may 1968 in the town hall
philadelphia lp: columbia MS 7146/MG 30072
orchestra cd: 88697 279872

sinfonia from the weihnachtsoratorium
recorded on 12 june 1972 in the academy of music
philadelphia lp: victor ARL1 1959
orchestra

bach/**passacaglia and fugue in c, arrangement**
recorded on 13 october 1946 in the town hall
philadelphia					78: columbia 12993-12996D
orchestra					lp: columbia ML 2058/ML 4797
recorded on 27 august 1947 at a concert in the hollywood bowl
los angeles				cd: melodram MEL 16512/
philharmonic				andromeda ANDRCD 5133
recorded on 10 april 1960 in the broadwood hotel
philadelphia				lp: columbia ML 5580/MS 6180/
orchestra					MG 30072
							cd: 88697 279872
recorded on 28 september 1981 in the academy of music
philadelphia				cd: disco archivia 741
orchestra

toccata and fugue in d, arrangement
recorded on 31 october 1947 in the town hall philadelphia
philadelphia				78: columbia M 846/english
orchestra					columbia LX 1181
							lp: columbia ML 2058/ML 4797/
							philips SBR 6223/S06653R
recorded on 31 january 1960 in the broadwood hotel
philadelphia				lp: columbia ML 5580/MS 6180/
orchestra					MS 7501/MS 7437/MGP 7/
							MG 30072
							cd: 88697 279872
recorded on 8 february 1973 in the academy of music
philadelphia				lp: victor ARL1 1959/VCS 7079
orchestra
recorded in 1974 at a concert in the academy of music
philadelphia				cd: disco archivia 750
orchestra

toccata, adagio and fugue in c, arrangement
recorded on 31 january 1960 in the broadwood hotel
philadelphia				lp: columbia ML 5580/MS 6180/
orchestra					MG 30072
							cd: 88697 279872
recorded on 20 october 1971 in the academy of music
philadelphia				lp: victor ARL1 1959
orchestra					*recording completed in january 1974*

WILHELM FRIEDEMANN BACH (1710-1784)
sinfonia in d
recorded on 17 march 1957 in the broadwood hotel
philadelphia lp: columbia ML 5742/MS 6342
orchestra cd: MH2K 62345/88697 279872

HENK BADINGS (1907-1987)
concerto for 2 violins and orchestra
recorded on 22 june 1963 at a concert in the kurzaal scheveningen
residentie unpublished radio broadcast
orkest
krebbers, olof

MILY BALAKIREV (1837-1910)
islamey, oriental fantasy
recorded on 26 february 1961 in the town hall
philadelphia lp: columbia ML 6275/MS 6875/
orchestra BRG 72455/SBRG 72455

GEORGE BARATI (1913-1996)
chamber concerto
recorded in december 1962 in the town hall
philadelphia lp: columbia ML 5779/MS 6379
orchestra

SAMUEL BARBER (1910-1981)
adagio for strings
recorded on 14 april 1957 in the broadwood hotel
philadelphia lp: columbia ML 5187/MS 6224/
orchestra M 30066/philips ABL 3200/
  A01332L
  cd: 88697 279872

recorded in 1973 at a concert in the academy of music
phiadelphia cd: disco archivia 722
orchestra

recorded on 1 february 1978 in the academy of music
philadelphia lp: angel 38270/emi EG 29 0615
orchestra cd: 762 5052

barber/**essay no 1**
recorded on 20 october 1940 in the academy of music
philadelphia   78: victor 18062
orchestra   cd: biddulph WHL 064-065/membran
                                    205 235/222 343/231 058

essay no 2
recorded on 31 december 1944 at a concert in the nbc studios new york city
nbc symphony   unpublished radio broadcast
recorded on 5 september 1955 at a concert in the funkhaus cologne
sinfonieorchester   unpublished radio broadcast
des westdeutschen
rundfunks
recorded in 1976 at a concert in the academy of music
philadelphia   cd: disco archivia 741
orchestra

toccata festiva for organ and orchestra
recorded on 7 october 1962 in the town hall
philadelphia   lp: columbia ML 5798/MS 6398
orchestra   cd: russ oppenheim ROCD 0057
power biggs

the lovers, for baritone, chorus and orchestra
recorded in 1973 at a concert in the academy of music
philadelphia   cd: disco archivia 722
orchestra and chorus

JAMES CARROLL BARTLETT (1850-1929)
a dream
recorded on 8 december 1940 at a concert in the detroit masonic temple
detroit   lp: legendary recordings LR 138
symphony   cd: video artists international
björling   VAI 1189

BELA BARTOK (1881-1945)
music for strings, percussion and celesta
recorded on 20 november 1978 in the academy of music
philadelphia   lp: angel 37608/emi ASD 3655/
orchestra   1C065 03506/2C069 03506/
                                   3C065 03506
                                   cd: 747 1172

bartok/**concerto for orchestra**
recorded on 14 february 1954 in the town hall
philadelphia　　　　　　lp: columbia ML 4973/philips ABL 3090/
orchestra　　　　　　　A01231L/A01370L
recorded on 13 october 1963 in the town hall
philadelphia　　　　　　lp: columbia ML 6026/MS 6626/
orchestra　　　　　　　BRG 72282/SBRG 72282
　　　　　　　　　　　cd: SBK 48263/88697 279872
recorded on 16 april 1979 in the academy of music
philadelphia　　　　　　lp: victor ARC1 3421/ARC1 4308/
orchestra　　　　　　　RL 13421

divertimento for strings
philadelphia　　　　　　lp: columbia M 32874
orchestra　　　　　　　cd: russ oppenheim ROCD 0058

piano concerto no 2
recorded between 10-12 november 1969 in the academy of music
philadelphia　　　　　　lp: victor LSC 3159/LSB 4010/
orchestra　　　　　　　AGL1 4090
weissenberg　　　　　　cd: 09026 613962/74321 886902

piano concerto no 3
recorded on 19 april 1946 in the town hall
philadelphia　　　　　　78: columbia M 674/english columbia
orchestra　　　　　　　LX 1271-1273
sandor　　　　　　　　lp: columbia ML 4239/philips A01370L
　　　　　　　　　　　cd: pearl GEM 0173

violin concerto no 1
recorded on 26 march 1961 in the town hall
philadelphia　　　　　　lp: columbia ML 5677/MS 6277/
orchestra　　　　　　　BRG 72009/SBRG 72009
stern　　　　　　　　　cd: SMK 64502/SX9K 67194

two orchestral images op 10
recorded on 31 march 1963 in the philadelphia athletic club
philadelphia　　　　　　lp: columbia ML 6189/MS 6789/
orchestra　　　　　　　BRG 72445/SBRG 72455
　　　　　　　　　　　cd: SBK 48263/88697 279872

four orchestral pieces op 12
recorded on 10 november 1969 in the academy of music
philadelphia　　　　　　lp: victor LSC 3159/LSB 4010/
orchestra　　　　　　　AGL1 4090

bartok/**bluebeard's castle**
recorded on 20 november 1960 in the town hall
philadelphia   lp: columbia ML 5825/MS 6425/
orchestra   BRG 72121/SBRG 72121
elias, hines   cd: private edition usa

the miraculous mandarin, suite from the ballet
recorded on 15 november 1962 in the town hall
philadelphia   lp: columbia ML 6189/MS 6789/
orchestra   BRG 72445/SBRG 72445
                       cd: SBK 46446/SBK 48263/
                       88697 279872
recorded on 18 november 1978 in the academy of music
philadelphia   lp: angel 37608/emi ASD 3655/
orchestra   1C065 03506/2C069 03506/
                       3C065 03506
                       cd: 747 1172/565 1752

LESLIE RAYMOND BASSETT (born 1923)
echoes from an invisible world
recorded in 1976 at a concert in the academy of music
philadelphia   cd: disco archivia 748
orchestra

LUDWIG VAN BEETHOVEN (1770-1827)
symphony no 1
recorded on 10 january 1946 in the academy of music
philadelphia   78: victor M 409/hmv DB 3178-3182
orchestra
recorded on 24 march 1965 in the town hall
philadelphia   lp: columbia D7S 745
orchestra

symphony no 2
recorded on 17 january 1962 in the town hall
philadelphia   lp: columbia D7S 745
orchestra

symphony no 3 "eroica"
recorded on 9 april 1961 in the town hall
philadelphia   lp: columbia ML 5666/MS 6266/
orchestra   D7S 745
recorded on 29 september 1980 in the academy of music
philadelphia   lp: victor ARC1 4582/
orchestra   ATC1 4032

beethoven/**symphony no 4**
recorded on 9 january 1935 in minneapolis
minneapolis				78: victor M 274/hmv DB 2767-2771
symphony
recorded on 20 september 1965 in the town hall
philadelphia			lp: columbia D7S 745
orchestra
symphony no 5
recorded on 23 october 1955 in the town hall
philadelphia			lp: columbia ML 5098/philips
orchestra			ABL 3230/A01379L/G03500L/
				GBR 6509/G05609R
recorded on 13 june 1965 at a concert in the musikverein vienna
wiener				unpublished radio broadcast
philharmoniker
recorded on 14 february 1966 in the town hall
philadelphia			lp: columbia M 31634/D7S 745
orchestra			cd: SB2K 63266
recorded in 1974 at a concert in the academy of music
philadelphia			cd: disco archivia 750
orchestra
recorded in 1977 at a concert in the hill auditorium ann arbor
university of michigan		lp: university of michigan SM 0007
symphony orchestra
symphony no 6 "pastoral"
recorded on 26 january 1966 in the town hall
philadelphia			lp: columbia MS 7444/D7S 745
orchestra			cd: SB2K 63266
symphony no 7
recorded on 19 november 1944 in the town hall
philadelphia			78: columbia M 551
orchestra			lp: columbia ML 4011
recorded on 11 july 1954 at a concert in recklinghausen
sinfonieorchester		unpublished radio broadcast
des westdeutschen
rundfunks
recorded on 29 may 1958 at a concert in the moscow conservatory
philadelphia			cd: scora classics SCORACD 001
orchestra
recorded on 27 april 1964 in the town hall
philadelphia			lp: columbia D7S 745
orchestra			cd: SB2K 63266
recorded in 1970 at a concert in the academy of music
philadelphia			cd: disco archivia 750
orchestra

194
beethoven/**symphony no 8**
recorded on 10 december 1961 in the town hall
philadelphia orchestra
lp: columbia M2S 738/D7S 745/ M 31634
cd: SB2K 63266

televised on 9 june 1963 at a concert in the musikverein vienna
wiener philharmoniker
laserdisc: toshiba TOLW 3741

symphony no 9 "choral"
recorded on 20-21 march 1945 in the town hall
philadelphia orchestra
westminster choir
roman, szantho, jagel, moscona
78: columbia M 591
lp: columbia SL 150
recording completed on 12 january 1946; this was the first recording of the work to be published in lp format

recorded between 5-29 september 1964 in the town hall
philadelphia orchestra
mormon tabernacle choir
amara, chookasian, alexander, macurdy
lp: columbia D7S 745/D2S 720/ MS 7016/
cd: SB2K 63240

recorded in 1974 at a concert in the academy of music
philadelphia orchestra and chorus
valente, carlson, mccoy, devlin
cd: disco archivia 745

symphony no 9, second movement
recorded on 26 june 1944 at a concert in the town hall sydney
sydney symphony orchestra
cd: 434 8952
this was a cd-set celebrating the first sixty years of the sydney symphony orchestra

beethoven/**piano concerto no 1**
recorded on 1 february 1954 in the town hall
philadelphia lp: columbia ML 4914/philips ABL 3164/
orchestra ABR 4040/A01221L/A01627R/philips
serkin fontana EFR 2034/664 007ER
 recording completed on 14 february 1954
recorded on 14 january 1965 in the town hall
philadelphia lp: columbia ML 6238/MS 6838/D4L 340/
orchestra D4S 740/MY 37807/BRG 72430/
serkin SBRG 72430/61916
 cd: MK 43359/MYK 37807

piano concerto no 2
recorded on 14 february 1954 in the town hall
philadelphia lp: columbia ML 5037/philips GL 5744/
orchestra G03640L/philips fontana EFR 2035/
serkin 664 008ER/697 202EL/699 028CL
 recording completed on 24 april 1955
recorded on 13 january 1965 in the town hall
philadelphia lp: columbia ML 6239/MS 6839/D4L 340/
orchestra D4S 740/BRG 72431/SBRG 72431/
serkin 61916
recorded in 1976 at a concert in the academy of music
philadelphia cd: disco archivia 742
orchestra
serkin

piano concerto no 3
recorded on 27 june 1943 at a concert in the academy of music
philadelphia cd: music and arts CD 1114
orchestra
rubinstein
recorded on 24 december 1947 in the town hall
philadelphia 78: columbia M 917
orchestra lp: columbia ML 4302/Y 34601/english
arrau columbia 33CX 1080/french columbia
 FCX 142/italian columbia QCX 10075/
 philips SBR 6252/S06681R
 cd: dante HPC 124/membran 205 235/
 205 236
recorded on 22 march 1953 in the town hall
philadelphia lp: columbia ML 4738/philips fontana
orchestra EFR 2036/664 009ER
serkin
recorded on 10 march 1971 in the academy of music
philadelphia lp: victor LSC 3238/LSB 4052
orchestra cd: GD 60419/disco archivia 749
cliburn

beethoven/**piano concerto no 4**
recorded on 4 april 1938 at a concert in the academy of music
philadelphia orchestra hofmann
cd: philadelphia orchestra centennial collection/ marston 52044

recorded on 28 december 1947 in the academy of music
philadelphia orchestra casadesus
78: columbia M 744/english columbia LX 1198-1201
lp: columbia ML 4074
cd: membran 205 235/231 058/ dante HPC 160

recorded 10 march 1955 in the town hall
philadelphia orchestra serkin
lp: columbia ML 5037/philips ABL 3164/ GL 5744/A01221L/G03640L/philips fontana EFR 2037/664 010ER/ 697 202EL/699 028CL

recorded on 28 january 1962 in the town hall
philadelphia orchestra serkin
lp: columbia ML 6145/MS 6745/ D4L 340/D4S 740/BRG 72360/ SBRG 72360

recorded on 15 december 1966 in the town hall
philadelphia orchestra istomin
lp: columbia MS 7199

recorded in 1974 at a concert in the academy of music
philadelphia orchestra serkin
cd: disco archivia 752

piano concerto no 5 "emperor"
recorded on 19 november 1950 in the academy of music
philadelphia orchestra serkin
78: columbia M 989
lp: columbia ML 4373/english columbia 33CX 1070/italian columbia QCX 10041/ philips GL 5748/G03644L/philips fontana EFR 2014/664 011ER/697 207EL
cd: SM3K 47269

recorded on 26 january 1958 in the town hall
philadelphia orchestra istomin
lp: columbia ML 5318/philips GBL 5516/ G03521L

recorded on 14 june 1963 at a concert in the royal festival hall london
philharmonia orchestra rubinstein
cd: bbc legends BBCL 41302

violin concerto
recorded on 5 november 1950 in the academy of music
philadelphia			78: polish columbia LNX 8058-8062
orchestra			lp: columbia ML 4371/A 1086/english
francescatti			columbia 33CX 1011/french columbia
				FCX 126/italian columbia QCX 126/
				philips A01314L/GBL 5506/G03517L
				cd: biddulph 802 052

recorded on 5 october 1959 at a concert in montreux
concertgebouw			cd: music and arts CD 1168
orkest
milstein

recorded in 1976 at a concert in the academy of music
philadelphia			cd: disco archivia 748
orchestra
kogan

violin romance no 2
recorded on 5-6 april 1952 in the town hall
philadelphia			lp: columbia ML 4629
orchestra
krachmalnick

triple concerto
recorded on 16 april 1964 in the town hall
philadelphia			lp: columbia D2L 320/D2S 720/
orchestra			BRG 72346/SBRG 72346
istomin, stern,			cd: SB3K 48397/SM2K 66941/
rose				SBK 46549

coriolan overture
recorded on 23 december 1951 in the academy of music
philadelphia			45: columbia A 1595
orchestra			lp: columbia AL 15

recorded in 1974 at a concert in the academy of music
philadelphia			cd: disco archivia 752
orchestra

egmont overture
recorded on 23 december 1951 in the academy of music
philadelphia			lp: columbia AL 15
orchestra

beethoven/**leonore no 3 overture**
recorded on 29 may 1958 at a concert in the moscow conservatory
philadelphia   cd: scora classics SCORACD 001
orchestra
recorded on 21 june 1958 at a concert in cologne
philadelphia   unpublished radio broadcast
orchestra
recorded on 6 june 1963 at a concert in the musikhalle hamburg
sinfonieorchester   cd: originals
des norddeutschen
rundfunks
recorded in 1977 at a concert in the hill auditorium ann arbor
university of michigan   lp: university of michigan
symphony orchestra   SM 0007

leonore no 3 overture, bars 499-638
recorded on 14 september 1949 at a rehearsal in the konserthuset stockholm
stockholm   cd: bis BISCD 424
philharmonic

abscheulicher wo eilst du hin?/fidelio
recorded on 17 october 1937 in the academy of music
philadelphia   78: victor 14972/hmv DB 3439
orchestra   lp: victor LM 6705/LM 20144/
flagstad   CAL 462/SP 33-555/
                     top classic TC 9046
                     cd: preiser 89141/simax PSC 1821

wellington's victory
recorded on 16 november 1970 in the academy of music
philadelphia   lp: victor LSC 3204/LSB 4031
orchestra   cd: VD 87731

turkish march/die ruinen von athen
recorded on 3 february 1963 in the town hall
philadelphia
orchestra
recorded on 23-24 march 1968 in the academy of music
philadelphia
orchestra

minuetto in g, arrangement
recorded on 15 may 1968 in the town hall
philadelphia
orchestra

beethoven/**missa solemnis**
recorded on 29-30 march 1967 in the philadelphia hotel
philadelphia   lp: columbia Y2 30083
orchestra   cd: SBK 53517
singing city choirs
arroyo, forrester,
lewis, siepi

christus am ölberge, oratorio
recorded on 17 april 1963 in the town hall
philadelphia   lp: columbia ML 6241/MS 6841
orchestra   cd: MPK 45878
temple university choir
raskin, lewis, beattie

allelujah/christus am ölberge
recorded on 22 may 1962 in the salt lake tabernacle
philadelphia   lp: columbia MS 6679
orchestra
mormon tabernacle
choir

ah perfido, concert scena
recorded on 17 october 1937 in the academy of music
philadelphia   78: victor M 439/hmv DB 3441
orchestra   and DA 1625
flagstad   lp: victor LM 6705/LM 20144/
                            CAL 462/VIC 1208/VIC 1517/
                            PVM1 9068/AG 26 41399/
                            preiser LV 1372
                            cd: nimbus NI 7847/pickwick
                            GLRS 105/simax PSC 1821/
                            preiser 89141

recorded on 15 november 1953 in the town hall
philadelphia   columbia unpublished
orchestra
steber

ARTHUR BENJAMIN (1893-1960)
jamaican rumba
recorded on 3 may 1965 in the town hall
philadelphia   lp: columbia 62907
orchestra

ALBAN BERG (1885-1935)
violin concerto
recorded on 30 january 1969 at a concert in the academy of music
philadelphia orchestra
kogan
cd: philadelphia orchestral centennial collection

lulu suite
recorded on 27 march 1967 in the town hall
philadelphia orchestra
lp: columbia MS 7041
cd: russ oppenheim ROCD 0059
recording completed on 4 april 1967

three fragments from wozzeck
recorded on 1 november 1947 in the town hall
philadelphia orchestra
78: english columbia LX 1158-1159
lp: columbia ML 2140

THEODOR BERGER (1905-1992)
violin concerto
recorded on 13 june 1965 at a concert in the musikverein vienna
wiener philharmoniker
odnoposoff
unpublished radio broadcast

IRVING BERLIN (1888-1989)
god bless america
recorded on 5 september 1964 in the salt lake tabernacle
philadelphia orchestra
mormon tabernacle choir
lp: columbia MS 6721

HECTOR BERLIOZ (1803-1869)
symphonie fantastique
recorded on 30 october 1950 in the town hall
philadelphia   lp: columbia ML 4467/A 1069/
orchestra   philips A01159L

recorded on 14 december 1960 in the town hall
philadelphia   lp: columbia ML 5648/MS 6248/
orchestra   BRG 72032/SBRG 72032
                            cd: SBK 46329

recorded on 16 december 1976 in the academy of music
philadelphia   lp: victor ARL1 2674
orchestra   cd: 09026 380492

harold en italie
recorded on 21 january 1965 in the town hall
philadelphia   lp: columbia M 30116
orchestra   cd: SBK 53255
de pasquale

grande messe des morts
recorded on 1-2 april 1964 in the philadelphia athletic club
philadelphia   lp: columbia M2S 730/BRG 72400-
orchestra   72401/SBRG 72400-72401
temple university   cd: SBK 62659
choir
valletti

ballet des sylphes et menuet des follets/la damnation de faust
recorded on 15 november 1953 in the town hall
philadelphia   lp: columbia ML 5261
orchestra

marche hongroise/la damnation de faust
recorded on 15 november 1953 in the town hall
philadelphia   lp: columbia ML 5261
orchestra

recorded on 16 june 1972 in the academy of music
philadelphia   lp: victor AGL1 4298
orchestra   cd: disco archivia 745

berlioz/**repose of the holy family/l'enfance du christ**
recorded on 25 december 1944 at a concert in the nbc studios new york city
nbc symphony　　　　　　unpublished radio broadcast

marche troyenne/les troyens
recorded on 15 may 1968 in the town hall
philadelphia　　　　　　lp: columbia 61301
orchestra

LEONARD BERNSTEIN (1918-1990)
chichester psalms
recorded in 1973 at a concert in the academy of music
philadelphia　　　　　　cd: disco archivia 722
orchestra
and chorus

WILLIAM BILLINGS (1746-1800)
david's lament/the singing master's assistant
recorded on 3 november 1958 in the broadwood hotel
philadelphia　　　　　　lp: columbia MS 6068/MS 6679/
orchestra　　　　　　　　philips A01439L
mormon tabernacle
choir

GEORGES BIZET (1838-1875)
symphony in c
recorded on 4 december 1955 in the town hall
philadelphia　　　　　　lp: columbia ML 5289
orchestra

recorded on 27-28 march 1974 in the academy of music
philadelphia　　　　　　lp: victor ARL1 3640
orchestra

bizet/l'arlesienne, suite no 1 from the incidental music
recorded on 14 may 1955 in the town hall
philadelphia lp: columbia ML 5035/philips ABL 3171/
orchestra A01247L

recorded on 26 january 1958 in the town hall
philadelphia lp: columbia ML 5946/MS 6546/
orchestra M 31848
  cd: SMK 47531/SBK 48159

recorded on 18 november 1975 in the academy of music
philadelphia lp: victor ARL1 3343/ARL1 3640
orchestra cd: GD 60787
  recording completed in december 1976 and january 1976

l'arlesienne, suite no 2 from the incidental music
recorded on 14 may 1955 in the town hall
philadelphia lp: columbia ML 5035/philips ABL 3171/
orchestra A01247L

recorded on 22 january 1963 in the town hall
philadelphia lp: columbia ML 5946/MS 6546/
orchestrta M 31848
  cd: SMK 47531/SBK 48159

recorded on 7 january 1976 in the academy of music
philadelphia lp: victor ARL1 3343/AGL1 5252
orchestra cd: GD 60787

carmen, suite no 1 from the opera
recorded on 26 january 1958 in the town hall
philadelphia lp: columbia ML 5356/MS 6051/
orchestra Y 33293
  cd: SMK 47531/SBK 48159

recorded in october 1975 in the academy of music
philadelphia lp: victor ARL1 3343/AGL1 5252
orchestra cd: GD 60787
  recording completed in january and october 1976

bizet/**carmen, suite no 2 from the opera**
recorded on 26 january 1958 in the town hall
philadelphia orchestra
lp: columbia ML 5356/MS 6051/ Y 33293
cd: SMK 47531/SBK 48159

recorded between 6-12 may 1976 in the academy of music
philadelphia orchestra
lp: victor ARL1 3343/AGL1 5252
cd: GD 60787
recording completed on 18 november 1976

marche des contrebandiers/carmen
recorded on 25 april 1972 in the academy of music
philadelphia orchestra
lp: victor AGL1 4298

les voici!/carmen
recorded on 9 june 1967 in the salt lake tabernacle
philadelphia orchestra
mormon tabernacle choir
lp: columbia MS 7061

ERNEST BLOCH (1880-1959)
suite modale for flute and orchestra
recorded on 5 april 1962 in the town hall
philadelphia orchestra
panitz
lp: columbia MS 6977

schelomo for cello and orchestra
recorded on 29 january 1961 in the town hall
philadelphia orchestra
rose
lp: columbia ML 5653/MS 6253/ BRG 72580/SBRG 72580
cd: SBK 48278

LUIGI BOCCHERINI (1743-1805)
minuetto
recorded on 10 april 1968 in the town hall
philadelphia orchestra   lp: columbia

ALEXANDER BORODIN (1833-1887)
in the steppes of central asia
recorded on 15 march 1959 in the town hall
philadelphia orchestra   lp: columbia ML 5392/ML 6275/ MS 6073/MS 6875/BRG 72455/ SBRG 72455

nocturne from the string quartet, arranged by sargent
recorded on 14 april 1957 in the broadwood hotel
philadelphia orchestra
45: philips ABE 10039/409 074AE
lp: columbia ML 5187/ML 5624/ MS 6224/MS 6575/MS 7072/ M 30066/philips ABL 3200/A01332L
cd: 88697 279872

recorded between 6-16 february 1972 in the academy of music
philadelphia orchestra   lp: victor

polovtsian dances/prince igor
recorded on 18 december 1944 in the academy of music
philadelphia orchestra
78: columbia 12269D/english columbia LX 1027/canadian columbia 12019

recorded on 14 march 1959 in the town hall
philadelphia orchestra
45: philips ABE 10240/SABE 200
lp: columbia ML 5392/ML 5857/ MS 6073/MS 6457/MS 6958/ MG 30947/BPG 62153/SBPG 62153
cd: classic fm CFMCD 40

recorded on 13 january 1971 in the academy of music
philadelphia orchestra
lp: victor CRL3 0985
cd: disco archivia 745

JOHANNES BRAHMS (1833-1897)
symphony no 1
recorded on 5 november 1950 in the town hall
philadelphia orchestra   lp: columbia ML 4477

recorded on 8 february 1959 in the town hall
philadelphia orchestra   lp: columbia ML 5385/MS 6067

recorded on 29 may 1959 at a concert in the moscow conservatoire
philadelphia orchestra   lp: melodiya M10 47161

recorded on 19 may 1968 in the town hall
philadelphia orchestra   lp: columbia D3M 31636/M 31821
     cd: SB2K 63287

symphony no 2
recorded on 26 february 1940 in the academy of music
philadelphia orchestra   78: victor M 694

recorded on 14 january 1945 at a concert in the nbc studios new york city
nbc symphony   unpublished radio broadcast

recorded on 15 february 1953 in the town hall
philadelphia orchestra   lp: columbia ML 4827
     cd: biddulph 802 252

recorded on 21 june 1958 at a concert in cologne
philadelphia orchestra   unpublished radio broadcast

recorded on 6 april 1966 in the town hall
philadelphia orchestra   lp: columbia D3M 31636

recorded in 1976 at a concert in the academy of music
philadelphia orchestra   cd: disco archivia 742

brahms/**symphony no 3**
recorded on 19 april 1946 in the town hall
philadelphia   78: columbia M 642
orchestra   lp: columbia ML 4088

recorded on 5 september 1955 at a concert in the sendesaal cologne
sinfonieorchester   unpublished radio broadcast
des westdeutschen
rundfunks

recorded on 31 january 1967 in the town hall
philadelphia   lp: columbia D3M 31616
orchestra   *recording completed on 13 march 1967*

symphony no 4
recorded on 19 november 1944 in the town hall
philadelphia   78: columbia M 567
orchestra   lp: columbia ML 4017

recorded on 25 october 1967 in the town hall
philadelphia   lp: columbia D3M 31616
orchestra   cd: emi 575 1272

recorded in 1971 at a concert in the academy of music
philadelphia   cd: disco archivia 746
orchestra

piano concerto no 1
recorded on 11 december 1945 at a concert in carnegie hall new york
philadelphia   cd: philadelphia orchestra
orchestra   centennial collection
kapell

recorded on 9 april 1961 in the town hall
philadelphia   lp: columbia ML 5704/MS 6304/
orchestra   D3L 341/D3S 741/BRG 72017/
serkin   SBRG 72017
                                  cd: MK 42261/MBK 46272

brahms/**piano concerto no 2**
recorded on 15 march 1945 in the academy of music

philadelphia	78: columbia M 584/canadian columbia
orchestra	D 142/english columbia LX 1276-1281/
serkin	swiss columbia LZX 250-255
	lp: columbia ML 4014/english columbia
	33CX 1027/italian columbia QCX 10010/
	german columbia/C 90303/WCX 1027

recorded on 11 march 1956 in the broadwood hotel

philadelphia	lp: columbia ML 5117/philips ABL 3161/
orchestra	A01270L/philips fontana 697 204EL/
serkin	699 022CL
	cd: SM3K 47269

recorded on 4 april 1960 in the town hall

philadelphia	lp: columbia ML 5491/MS 6715/D3L 341/
orchestra	D3S 741/BRG 72002/SBRG 72002
serkin	cd: MBK 46273

recorded on 12 june 1971 at a concert in the academy of music

philadelphia	cd: arkadia CDHP 600
orchestra	
pollini	

recorded on 23 november 1971 in the academy of music

philadelphia	lp: victor LSC 3253/SB 6869
orchestra	cd: 09026 630712
rubinstein	

brahms/**violin concerto**
recorded on 23 february 1945 in the academy of music
philadelphia 78: columbia M 603/canadian columbia
orchestra D 205/english columbia LX 983-987
szigeti lp: columbia ML 4015
cd: MPK 52535

recorded on 11 march 1956 in the town hall
philadelphia lp: columbia ML 5114/philips ABL 3229/
orchestra A01376L/L09410L/S06678R
francescatti cd: biddulph 802 252

recorded on 2 november 1959 in the town hall
philadelphia lp: columbia ML 5486/MS 6153/D3S 721/
orchestra BRG 72094/SBRG 72094/philips fontana
stern SCFL 129/699 055CL/876 006CY
cd: SBK 46335/SX11K 67193

recorded in 1973 at a concert in the academy of music
philadelphia cd: disco archivia 740
orchestra
fujikawa

double concerto
recorded on 21 december 1939 in the academy of music
philadelphia 78: victor M 815/hmv DB 6120-6123/
orchestra DB 11131-11134/australian hmv ED 376-379
heifetz lp: victor LCT 1016
feuermann cd: naxos 811 0940/810 7001/pearl
GEMMCD 9293/membran 205 235/
231 058
*pearl edition claims to be taken from previously
unpublished test pressings*

recorded on 14 april 1964 in the town hall
philadelphia lp: columbia MS 7251/D2S 720/BRG
orchestra 72295/SBRG 72295
stern cd: MPK 44842/SM2K 66941/
rose SBK 46335/SBK 44842

serenade no 2
recorded on 28 march 1955 in the town hall
philadelphia lp: columbia ML 5129
orchestra cd: SB2K 63287

brahms/**haydn variations**
recorded on 19 april 1946 in the academy of music
philadelphia   78: columbia M 322
orchestra   lp: columbia ML 2066

recorded on 28 april 1963 in the town hall
philadelphia   lp: columbia MS 7298
orchestra   cd: SB2K 63287

recorded on 22 may 1969 in the academy of music
philadelphia   lp: victor ARL1 3001
orchestra   cd: GD 60536

handel variations, arranged by rubbra
recorded on 20 may 1962 in the town hall
philadelphia   lp: columbia M2L 286/M2S 686/
orchestra   MS 7298
                            cd: SB2K 63287

academic festival overture
recorded on 14 january 1945 at a concert in the nbc studios new york city
nbc symphony   unpublished radio broadcast

recorded on 18 june 1966 in the town hall
philadelphia   lp: columbia MG 31190
orchestra   cd: SB2K 63287

tragic overture
recorded on 1 june 1959 at a concert in the sendesaal cologne
sinfonieorchester   unpublished radio broadcast
des westdeutschen
rundfunks

recorded in 1971 at a concert in the academy of music
philadelphia   cd: disco archivia 746
orchestra

recorded on 28 february 1977 in the academy of music
philadelphia   lp: victor ARL1 3001
orchestra

brahms/**hungarian dance no 2, arrangement**
recorded in 1927 in new york
ormandy and his   78: judson 854
salon orchestra   cd: biddulph WHL 064-065

hungarian dance no 5, arrangement
recorded on 2 june 1945 in the academy of music
philadelphia   78: columbia M 588
orchestra   lp: columbia ML 2017

recorded on 15 november 1953 in the town hall
philadelphia   lp: columbia ML 5223
orchestra

recorded on 12 december 1967 in the town hall
philadelphia   lp: columbia MS 6993/MS 7146
orchestra   cd: russ oppenheim ROCD 0069

recorded on 12 june 1972 in the academy of music
philadelphia   lp: victor
orchestra

hungarian dance no 6, arrangement
recorded on 15 november 1953 in the town hall
philadelphia   lp: columbia ML 5223
orchestra

hungarian dance nos 11, 12, 13, 14, 15 and 16, arrangements
recorded on 21 april 1979 in the academy of music
philadelphia   lp: victor
orchestra

brahms/**hungarian dance no 17, arrangement**
recorded on 13 april 1957 in the town hall
philadelphia   lp: columbia ML 5223/MS 6241
orchestra   cd: SBK 46534/SB3K 48398

hungarian dance no 18, arrangement
recorded on 8-9 january 1935 in minneapolis
minneapolis   78: victor 1796/hmv DA 1543
symphony

recorded on 13 april 1957 in the town hall
philadelphia   lp: columbia ML 5223/MS 6241
orchestra   cd: SBK 46534/SB3K 48398

hungarian dance no 19, arrangement
recorded on 8-9 january 1935 in minneapolis
mineapolis   78: victor 1796/hmv DA 1543
symphony

recorded on 13 april 1957 in the town hall
philadelphia   lp: columbia ML 5223/MS 6241
orchestra   cd: SBK 46534/SB3K 48398

brahms/**hungarian dance no 20, arrangement**
recorded on 8-9 january 1935 in minneapolis
minneapolis   78: victor 1796/hmv DA 1543
symphony

recorded on 13 april 1957 in the town hall
philadelphia   lp: columbia ML 5223/MS 6241
orchestra   cd: SBK 46534/SB3K 48398

hungarian dance no 21, arrangement
recorded on 8-9 january 1935 in minneapolis
minneapolis   78: victor 1796/hmv DA 1543
symphony

recorded on 13 april 1957 in the town hall
philadelphia   lp: columbia ML 5223/MS 6241
orchestra   cd: SBK 46534/SB3K 48398

ein deutsches requiem
recorded on 20 may 1962 in the broadwood hotel
philadelphia   lp: columbia M2L 286/M2S 686
orchestra   *excerpts*
mormon tabernacle   lp: columbia MS 6679/
choir   philips A01439L
curtin, hines

selig sind die da leid tragen/ein deutsches requiem
recorded on 5 november 1958 in the broadwood hotel
philadelphia   lp: columbia MS 6058/philips
orchestra   ABL 3304/A01441L
mormon tabernacle
choir

brahms/**alto rhapsody**
recorded on 8 january 1939 in the academy of music
philadelphia   78: victor M 555/hmv DB 3837 and
orchestra   DA 1700
pennsylvania   cd: GD 87911/pearl GEMMCD 9405/
university choir   biddulph LAB 150/urania
anderson   URN 22320

recorded on 1 september 1969 in the academy of music
philadelphia   lp: victor ARL1 3001
orchestra
temple university
choir
verrett

lieder with orchestra: dein blaues auge; der schmied; immer leiser wird mein schlummer
recorded on 8 january 1939 in the academy of music
philadelphia   78: victor M 555/hmv DB 3838
orchestra   lp: victor LM 2712
anderson   cd: pearl GEMMCD 9405/memoir
                      CDMOIR 432/biddulph LAB 150/
                      GD 40007

von ewiger lieber, version with orchestra
recorded on 8 january 1939 in the academy of music
philadelphia   cd: philadelphia orchestra
orchestra   centennial collection
anderson   *unpublished victor 78rpm recording*

BENJAMIN BRITTEN (1913-1976)
four sea interludes and passacaglia/peter grimes
recorded on 26 september 1977 in the academy of music
philadelphia   lp: victor ARL1 2744
orchestra

britten/**variations and fugue on a theme of purcell**/young
person's guide to the orchestra
recorded on 3 february 1957 in the town hall
philadelphia   lp: columbia ML 5183/MS 6027/
orchestra   Y 34616/61427/philips ABL 3193/
ritchard, narrator   A01325L/835 509AY
                        cd: SBK 62638

recorded on 27-28 march 1974 in the academy of music
philadelphia   lp: victor ARL1 2743
orchestra   cd: RD 82743/GD 60878
bowie, narrator

MAX BRUCH (1838-1920)
violin concerto no 1
recorded on 10 january 1956 in the town hall
philadelphia   lp: columbia ML 5097/BRG 72612/
orchestra   SBRG 72612/philips ABL 3168/
stern   A01253L/GL 5749/G03646L/
                        philips fontana EFL 2526/
                        697 211EL/699 040CL
                        cd: SX11K 67193

recorded on 22 february 1966 in the town hall
philadelphia   lp: columbia MS 7003
orchestra   cd: SMK 66830/88697 008172
stern

kol nidrei for cello and orchestra
recorded on 28 december 1947 in the town hall
philadelphia   78: columbia 12882D/english
orchestra   columbia LX 1095
piatigorsky   cd: MHK 62876

ANTON BRUCKNER (1824-1896)
symphony no 4 "romantic"
recorded on 9 october 1967 in the town hall
philadelphia orchestra   lp: columbia M 31920
    cd: SBK 47653

recorded on 3 march 1977 at a concert in the academy of music
philadelphia orchestra   cd: disco archivia 725

symphony no 5
recorded on 13 april 1965 in the town hall
philadelphia orchestra   lp: columbia M2S 768/77222
    cd: SBK 48160

symphony no 7
recorded between 5-7 january 1935 in minneapolis
minneapolis symphony   78: victor M 276/hmv DB 2626-2633
    cd: dante LYS 288/membran 205 235/222 343/231 058
    205 235 and 231 058 incorrectly described orchestra as philadelphia

recorded on 3 october 1968 in the academy of music
philadelphia orchestra   lp: victor LSC 3059/SB 6803

te deum
recorded on 13 april 1963 in the town hall
philadelphia orchestra
temple university choir
stader, vanni, kolk, gramm   lp: columbia M2S 768/77222

JOHN ALDEN CARPENTER (1876-1951)
adventures in a perambulator, suite for orchestra
recorded between 17-23 january 1934 in minneapolis
minneapolis symphony   78: victor M 238
    excerpts
    78: victor M 1063

ALFREDO CASELLA (1883-1947)
paganiniana
recorded on 4 april 1960 in the town hall
philadelphia   lp: columbia ML 5605/MS 6205
orchestra   cd: russ oppenheim ROCD 0057

MARIO CASTELNUOVO-TEDESCO (1895-1968)
guitar concerto no 1
recorded on 14 december 1965 in the town hall
philadelphia   lp: columbia MS 6834/M3X 31508/
orchestra   BRG 72439/SBRG 72439/77334
williams

EMANUEL CHABRIER (1841-1894)
espana
recorded on 28 november 1954 in the town hall
philadelphia   45: philips ABE 10159
orchestra   lp: columbia ML 4983/philips SBL 5234/
                       S04643L

recorded on 24 february 1963 in the town hall
philadelphia   lp: columbia ML 5878/MS 6478/
orchestra   M2X 786/SPR 43
                       cd: SBK 38917/SBK 60265

recorded on 11 january 1972 in the academy of music
philadelphia   lp: victor ARD1 0002/CRL3 0985/
orchestra   CRL3 2182
                       cd: 74321 242132

marche joyeuse
recorded on 28 december 1966 in the town hall
philadelphia   lp: columbia MS 6979/MG 32314/
orchestra   61292

larghetto for horn and orchestra
recorded on 5-6 april 1952 in the town hall
philadelphia   lp: columbia ML 4629
orchestra
jones

GUSTAVE CHARPENTIER (1860-1956)
depuis le jour/louise
recorded on 20 october 1940 in the academy of music
philadelphia   78: victor 17698
orchestra   lp: hmv CSLP 504
maynor   cd: philadelphia orchestra
                        centennial collection

ERNEST CHAUSSON (1855-1899)
poeme pour violon et orchestre
recorded on 5 november 1950 in the academy of music
philadelphia   lp: columbia ML 2194/ML 5253/
orchestra   english columbia 33C 1029/french
francescatti   columbia FC 1017/philips A01275L
                        cd: MH2K 62339/membran 222 343

FREDERIC CHOPIN (1810-1849)
piano concerto no 1
recorded on 23 november 1952 in the town hall
philadelphia   lp: columbia ML 4651/philips S06632R
orchestra
sandor

recorded on 12 february 1961 in the town hall
philadelphia   lp; columbia ML 5652/MS 6252/
orchestra   78207
brailowsky

recorded on 31 december 1964 in the town hall
philadelphia   lp: columbia ML 6112/MS 6712/
orchestra   Y 32369/BRG 72338/SBRG 72338/
gilels   61799/melodiya D019897-019898/
                         S10 05395 96
                         cd: SBK 46336

recorded on 18 august 1969 in the academy of music
philadelphia   lp: victor LSC 3147/SB 6837/
orchestra   CRL3 2282
cliburn   cd: GD 87945

recorded on 22 october 1980 in the academy of music
philadelphia   lp: victor ARC1 4580/ATC1 4097
orchestra   cd: RD 85317/74321 178922
ax

piano concerto no 2
recorded on 1 november 1959 in the town hall
philadelphia   lp: columbia ML 5494/MS 6159/
orchestra   Y 34618/philips A01467L/835 560AY
istomin

recorded on 1 october 1968 in the academy of music
philadelphia   lp: victor LSC 3055/SB 6797/
orchestra   RL 43195
rubinstein   cd: GD 60404/09026 630692

recorded on 13 february 1978 in the academy of music
philadelphia   lp: victor ARL1 2868
orchestra   cd: RD 85317/74321 178922
ax

chopin/ **grand fantasy on polish airs for piano and orchestra**
recorded on 1 october 1968 in the academy of music
philadelphia   lp: victor LSC 3055/SB 6797
orchestra   cd: GD 60404/09026 630692
rubinstein

nocturne in e flat, arrangement
recorded on 16 february 1966 in the town hall
philadelphia   lp: columbia MS 6883
orchestra

les sylphides, suite from the ballet arranged by douglas
recorded on 9 may 1954 in the town hall
philadelphia   lp: columbia CL 741/philips NBL
orchestra   5019/GBL 5533/GBR 6527/
                       N02114L/S06607R/G03514L/
                       G03547R
                       excerpts
                       45: philips NBE 11055/409 524NE/
                       SBF 170

recorded on 31 march 1963 in the town hall
philadelphia   lp: columbia ML 5908/MS 6508/
orchestra   BRG 72188/SBRG 72188/61016
                       cd: SBK 46550
                       excerpts
                       lp: columbia D3S 789

JEREMIAH CLARKE (1674-1707)
trumpet voluntary, arrangement
recorded on 5-6 april 1952 in the town hall
philadelphia   lp: columbia ML 4629
orchestra
krauss

recorded on 28 december 1966 in the town hall
philadelphia   lp: columbia MS 6979/MS 7267/
orchestra   61292
johnson   cd: SBK 62640

MICHAEL COLGRASS (born 1932)
as quiet as
recorded in 1971 at a concert in the academy of music
philadelphia   cd: disco archivia 750
orchestra

CARLTON COOLEY (born 1898)
air and dance for viola and orchestra
recorded on 4 december 1961 in the town hall
philadelphia   lp: columbia ML 6191/MS 6791
orchestra
cooley

AARON COPLAND (1900-1990)
appalachian spring, suite from the ballet
recorded on 28 march 1955 in the town hall
philadelphia   lp: columbia ML 5157
orchestra   cd: SBK 63467

recorded on 1 may 1969 in the academy of music
philadelphia   lp: victor LSC 3184/LSB 4018/
orchestra   ARL1 0109

billy the kid, suite from the ballet
recorded on 18 december 1955 in the town hall
philadelphia   lp: columbia ML 5157
orchestra   cd: SBK 63467

recorded on 28 may 1969 in the academy of music
philadelphia   lp: victor LSC 3184/LSB 4018
orchestra   cd: GD 86802

fanfare for the common man
recorded on 13 november 1963 in the town hall
philadelphia   lp: columbia MS 6684/MS 7289/
orchestra   MS 7521/MG 31190/BRG 72384/
                             SBRG 72384
                             cd: SBK 62401

recorded on 11 january 1972 in the academy of music
philadelphia   lp: victor
orchestra

copland/**a lincoln portrait**
recorded on 15 november 1962 in the town hall
philadelphia   lp: columbia MS 6684/BRG 72384/
orchestra   SBRG 72384
stevenson, speaker   cd: SBK 62401

hoe down/rodeo
recorded on 6 may 1968 in the town hall
philadelphia   lp: columbia
orchestra

ARCANGELO CORELLI (1653-1713)
christmas concerto
recorded on 25 december 1944 at a concert in the nbc studios new york city
nbc symphony   unpublished radio broadcast

recorded on 30 march 1959 in the broadwood hotel
philadelphia   lp: columbia ML 5402/MS 6081
orchestra

suite for strings, arranged by pinelli
recorded on 28 december 1947 in the academy of music
philadelphia   78: columbia 12836D/english
orchestra   columbia LX 1214
                              lp: philips S06655R

recorded on 8 february 1959 in the broadwood hotel
philadelphia   lp: columbia ML 5417/MS 6095/
orchestra   61639
                              cd: SBK 62640

PAUL CRESTON (1906-1985)
concertino for marimba and orchestra
recorded on 5 april 1962 in the town hall
philadelphia   lp: columbia MS 6977
orchestra
owen

chant of 1942
recorded on 12 june 1959 at a concert in the deutsches museum munich
sinfonieorchester   unpublished radio broadcast
des bayerischen
rundfunks

CLAUDE DEBUSSY (1862-1918)
la mer
recorded on 25 january 1959 in the town hall
philadelphia orchestra	lp: columbia ML 5397/MS 6077/ MG 30950
	cd: SBK 53256

recorded in 1971 at a concert in the academy of music
philadelphia orchestra   cd: disco archivia 748

recorded on 23 march 1972 in the academy of music
philadelphia orchestra   lp: victor ARL1 0029/ARD1 0029/ CRL3 2182

televised between 24-26 june 1977 at concerts in the academy of music
philadelphia orchestra   laserdisc: polygram (japan) 070 2261
    dvd video: philips (japan) CDV 102/ euroarts 207 2268

prelude a l'apres-midi d'un faune
recorded on 3 december 1947 in the town hall
philadelphia orchestra   78: columbia 12917D

recorded on 18 december 1955 in the town hall
philadelphia orchestra   lp: columbia AL 26/ML 5112

recorded on 24 june 1957 at a concert in the funkhaus cologne
sinfonieorchester des westdeutschen rundfunks   unpublished radio broadcast

recorded on 14 march 1959 in the broadwood hotel
philadelphia orchestra   lp: columbia ML 5397/MS 6077/ M2S 738/MG 30950
    cd: SBK 53256

recorded on 19 january 1971 in the academy of music
philadelphia orchestra   lp: victor LSC 3284/ARL1 0029/ ARD1 0029/CRL3 2182/ARL2 3384
    cd: 09026 612112/disco archivia 741

debussy/**first rhapsody for clarinet and orchestra**
recorded on 4 december 1961 in the town hall
philadelphia   lp: columbia MS 6977
orchestra
gigliotti

nuages/trois nocturnes
recorded on 20 december 1944 in the academy of music
philadelphia   78: columbia M 247
orchestra   lp: columbia ML 4020

recorded on 18 december 1955 in the town hall
philadelphia   lp: columbia ML 5112
orchestra

recorded on 14 march 1964 in the town hall
philadelphia   lp: columbia MS 6697/MG 30950
orchestra   cd: SBK 53256

fetes/trois nocturnes
recorded on 20 december 1944 in the academy of music
philadelphia   78: columbia M 247
orchestra   lp: columbia ML 4020

recorded on 18 december 1955 in the town hall
philadelphia   lp: columbia ML 5112
orchestra

recorded on 14 march 1964 in the town hall
philadelphia   lp: columbia MS 6697/MG 30950
orchestra   cd: SBK 53256

sirenes/trois nocturnes
recorded on 18 december 1955 in the town hall
philadelphia   lp: columbia ML 5112
orchestra
temple university
choir

recorded on 14 march 1964 in the town hall
philadelphia   lp: columbia MS 6697/MG 30950
orchestra   cd: SBK 53256
temple university
choir

debussy/**iberia/images pour orchestre**
recorded on 11 march 1951 in the town hall
philadelphia   lp: columbia ML 4344/philips A01100L
orchestra

danse sacree et danse profane
recorded in october 1962 in the town hall
philadelphia   lp: columbia MS 6977
orchestra
costello, harp

le martyre de saint sebastien, mystery play
recorded on 2 february 1958 in the town hall
philadelphia   lp: columbia M2L 266/M2S 609/
orchestra   BRG 72078-72079/SBRG
chorus   72078-72079
güden, whitemore,
zorina

la demoiselle elue, cantata
recorded on 14 march 1947 in the academy of music
philadelphia   78: columbia M 761
orchestra   lp: columbia ML 4075
pennsylvania
university choir
sayao, nadell

air de lia/l'enfant prodigue
recorded on 20 october 1940 in the academy of music
philadelphia   78: victor 17698
orchestra
maynor

tarantelle styrienne, arrangement by ravel
recorded on 14 march 1959 in the town hall
philadelphia   lp: columbia
orchestra

debussy/**clair de lune, arrangement from the suite bergamasque**
recorded on 19 december 1954 in the town hall
philadelphia orchestra   lp: columbia ML 4983

recorded on 17 february 1963 in the town hall
philadelphia orchestra   lp: columbia ML 5878/ML 5975/ MS 6478/MS 6575/MS 6883/ MS 7523/MG 30950/62907

recorded on 6 january 1971 in the academy of music
philadelphia orchestra   lp: victor LSC 3284/CRL3 2182
cd: 09026 612112

general lavine eccentric, arrangement of the piano prelude
recorded on 3 may 1965 in the town hall
philadelphia orchestra   lp: columbia MS 6993

reverie, arrangement of the piano piece
recorded on 12 february 1964 in the town hall
philadelphia orchestra   lp: columbia MS 6993

recorded on 30 september 1971 in the academy of music
philadelphia orchestra   lp: victor

LEO DELIBES (1836-1891)
coppelia, suite from the ballet
recorded on 31 march 1963 in the town hall
philadelphia orchestra   lp: columbia ML 5908/MS 6508/ BRG 72188/SBRG 72188/61016/ MG 35186
cd: SBK 46550
excerpts
lp: columbia D3S 789

valse et entr'acte/coppelia
recorded on 14 january 1935 in minneapolis
minneapolis symphony   78: victor 1743/hmv DA 1493

4 pieces from la source: scene d'amour; variations; scherzo polka; pas des voiles
recorded on 19 january 1934 in minneapolis
minneapolis symphony   78: victor M 220/hmv DA 1402-1403

sylvia, suite from the ballet
recorded on 31 march 1963 in the town hall
philadelphia orchestra   lp: columbia ML 5908/MS 6508/ M 31845/BRG 72188/SBRG 72188/61016/MG 35186
cd: SBK 46550

cortege de bacchus et pizzicato polka/sylvia
recorded on 20 january 1934 in minneapolis
minneapolis symphony   78: victor M 220/hmv DA 1401-1402

FREDERICK DELIUS (1863-1934)
brigg fair
recorded on 8 april 1962 in the town hall
philadelphia orchestra
lp: columbia ML 5776/MS 6376/ BRG 72086/SBRG 72086/61426/ 30056
cd: SBK 62645

dance rhapsody no 2
recorded on 2 november 1961 in the town hall
philadelphia orchestra
lp: columbia ML 5776/MS 6376/ BRG 72086/SBRG 72086/61426
cd: SBK 62645

in a summer garden
recorded on 20 november 1960 in the town hall
philadelphia orchestra
lp: columbia ML 5776/MS 6376/ BRG 72086/SBRG 72086/61426
cd: SBK 62645

on hearing the first cuckoo in spring
recorded on 2 march 1962 in the town hall
philadelphia orchestra
lp: columbia ML 5776/MS 6376/ BRG 72086/SBRG 72086/61426/ 30056
cd: SBK 62645

LUIGI DENZA (1846-1922)
funiculi funicula
recorded on 8 december 1940 at a ford sunday evening concert in the masonic temple detroit
detroit symphony björling
lp: ed smith records UORC 254/ legendary recordings LR 138
cd: video artists international VAI 1189

GRIGORAS DINICU (1889-1949)
hora staccato, arrangement
recorded on 12 december 1967 in the town hall
philadelphia orchestra
lp: columbia MS 7146
cd: russ oppenheim ROCD 0069

GAETONO DONIZETTI (1797-1848)
una furtiva lagrima/l'elisir d'amore
recorded on 2 october 1938 at a ford sunday evening concert in the masonic temple detroit
detroit   lp: ed smith records EJS 414
symphony
gigli

recorded on 28 august 1947 at a concert in the hollywood bowl
los angeles   lp: ed smith records EJS 457
philharmonic   cd: melodram MEL 16215/
lanza   andromeda ANDRCD 5133
                                 also issued in cd by gala

recorded in 1975 at a concert in the academy of music
philadelphia   cd: bella voce BLV 107 009
orchestra
pavarotti

vien leonora!/la favorita
recorded on 10 march 1940 at a ford sunday evening concert in the masonic temple detroit
detroit   lp: ed smith records EJS 214/EJS 531
symphony
thomas

o mio fernando!; o suora mia!/la favorita
recorded in 1975 at a concert in the academy of music
philadelphia   cd: bella voce BLV 107 009
orchestra
verrett, pavarotti

chacun le sait; il faut partir/la fille du regiment
recorded on 23 november 1941 at a ford sunday evening concert in the masonic temple detroit
detroit   lp: ed smith records EJS 235
symphony
pons

de surprise...au partir mon coeur renomme/rosamonda d'inghilterra
recorded on 23 november 1941 at a ford sunday evening concert in the masonic temple detroit
detroit   lp: ed smith records EJS 235
symphony
pons

FRANTISEK DRDLA (1869-1944)
souvenir for violin and harp
recorded on 30 august 1928 in new york
ormandy, violin   78: okeh 41147
goldner, harp   cd: biddulph WHL 064-065

RICCARDO DRIGO (1846-1930)
valse bluette for solo violin
recorded in 1926 in new york
ormandy, violin   78: cameo 1159

valse bluette, orchestral arrangement
recorded on 30 january 1934 in minneapolis
minneapolis   78: victor 1757
symphony

PAUL DUKAS (1865-1935)
l'apprenti sorcier
recorded on 22 april 1947 in the academy of music
philadelphia   78: columbia 12584D/english
orchestra   columbia LX 1068
                      lp: columbia AL 26

recorded on 2 october 1963 in the town hall
philadelphia   lp: columbia ML 6024/MS 6624/
orchestra   MS 7437
                      cd: SBK 46329

recorded on 28 september 1971 in the academy of music
philadelphia   lp: victor ARD1 0002/CRL3 0985/
orchestra   CRL3 2182
                      cd: 09026 612112/74321 242132

ANTONIN DVORAK (1841-1904)
symphony no 7
recorded on 19 october 1976 in the academy of music
philadelphia   lp: victor ARL1 3555
orchestra   cd: 09026 381182

symphony no 8
recorded on 28 february 1977 in the academy of music
philadelphia   lp: victor ARL1 4264
orchestra   cd: 09026 381182

symphony no 9 "from the new world"
recorded on 18 december 1944 in the academy of music
philadelphia   78: columbia M 570
orchestra   lp: columbia ML 4023

recorded on 8 april 1956 in the town hall
philadelphia   lp: columbia ML 5115/philips
orchestra   SBL 5216/GBL 5558/S04625L/
                        G03546L

recorded on 7 november 1966 in the town hall watford
london   lp: columbia MS 7089/61053/
symphony   30110
                        cd: SBK 46331/SX2K 64339

recorded in 1974 at a concert in the academy of music
philadelphia   cd: disco archivia 744
orchestra

recorded on 12 may 1976 in the academy of music
philadelphia   lp: victor ARL1 2949
orchestra   cd: VD 60537/74321 178982

violin concerto
recorded on 22 march 1965 in the town hall
philadelphia   lp: columbia MS 6876/BRG 72457/
orchestra   SBRG 72457
stern   cd: SMK 66827/SX11K 67193/
                        SBK 46337

dvorak/**romance for violin and orchestra**
recorded on 22 february 1966 in the town hall
philadelphia orchestra stern
lp: columbia MS 6876/BRG 72457/ SBRG 72457
cd: SMK 66827/SX11K 67193

cello concerto
recorded on 17 january 1946 in the academy of music
philadelphia orchestra piatigorsky
78: columbia M 658
lp: columbia ML 4022/Y 34602
cd: MHK 62876/membran 205 235/ 222 343/231 058

recorded on 24 november 1963 in the town hall
philadelphia orchestra rose
lp: columbia MS 6714/BRG 72296/ SBRG 72206/61036
cd: SBK 46337

scherzo capriccioso
recorded on 22 january 1934 in minneapolis
minneapolis symphony
78: victor 8413/hmv DB 2520

recorded on 11 june 1968 in the academy of music
philadelphia orchestra
lp: victor LSC 3085
cd: VD 60537/74321 178982

carnival overture
recorded on 19 december 1957 in the town hall
philadelphia orchestra
lp: columbia ML 5242/philips GBL 5558/G03546L

slavonic dance no 8
recorded in september 1971 in the academy of music
philadelphia orchestra
lp: victor
cd: disco archivia 741

slavonic dance no 10
recorded on 2 june 1945 in the academy of music
philadelphia orchestra
78: columbia M 588
lp: columbia ML 2017

dvorak/**humoresque for solo violin**
recorded between 18-20 june 1926 in new york
ormandy, violin   78: cameo 983/romeo 243

humoresque, orchestral arrangement
recorded on 7 december 1966 in the town hall
philadelphia   lp: columbia MS 7146
orchestra   cd: russ oppenheim ROCD 0069

GOTTFRIED VON EINEM (1918-1996)
capriccio for orchestra
recorded on 5 june 1959 at a concert in the herkulessaal munich
sinfonieorchester   cd: orfeo C199 891B
des bayerischen
rundfunks

EDWARD ELGAR (1857-1934)
enigma variations
recorded on 8 april 1962 in the town hall
philadelphia   lp: columbia M 31074/BRG 72982/
orchestra   SBRG 72982
recorded in 1971 at a concert in the academy of music
philadelphia   cd: disco archivia 749
orchestra

cockaigne overture
recorded on 20 january 1963 in the town hall
philadelphia   lp: columbia M 31074/BRG 72982/
orchestra   SBRG 72982

pomp and circumstance, march no 1
recorded on 28 march 1955 in the town hall
philadelphia
orchestra
recorded on 21 may 1962 in the salt lake tabernacle
philadelphia   lp: columbia MS 6419
orchestra
mormon tabernacle
choir
recorded on 3 february 1963 in the town hall
philadelphia   lp: columbia ML 5874/MS 6474/
orchestra   MS 7267
                        cd: disco archivia 745

GEORGE ENESCU (1881-1955)
rumanian rhapsody no 1
recorded on 16 january 1934 in minneapolis
minneapolis   78: victor 1701-1702/
symphony   hmv DA 1433-1434

recorded on 1 august 1941 in the academy of music
philadelphia   78: victor M 830/hmv DB 6130/
orchestra   australian hmv ED 230

recorded on 10 november 1957 in the town hall
philadelphia   lp: columbia ML 5242/ML 5299/
orchestra   MS 6018/M 31846
                      cd: SBK 38917/SBK 60265

recorded on 11 january 1972 in the academy of music
philadelphia   lp: victor CRL3 0985
orchestra

rumanian rhapsody no 2
recorded on 10 november 1957 in the town hall
philadelphia   lp: columbia ML 5242/ML 5299/
orchestra   MS 6018/M 31846
                      cd: SBK 38917/SBK 60265

MANUEL DE FALLA (1876-1946)
noches en los jardines de espana
recorded on 2 november 1961 in the town hall
philadelphia   lp: columbia ML 6029/MS 6629/
orchestra   BRG 72239/SBRG 72239
entremont   cd: SBK 62643

recorded on 2 january 1969 in the academy of music
philadelphia   lp: victor LSC 3165/SB 6841/
orchestra   AGL1 5205
rubinstein   cd: RD 85666/09026 614962/
                      09026 618632

falla/el sombrero de 3 picos, dances from the ballet
recorded on 11 march 1968 in the town hall
philadelphia　　　　　　lp:　columbia MS 7673
orchestra

danza ritual del fuego/el amor brujo
recorded on 8 february 1965 in the town hall
philadelphia　　　　　　lp:　columbia 62907
orchestra

recorded on 14 january 1971 in the academy of music
philadelphia　　　　　　lp:　victor
orchestra　　　　　　　　cd:　disco archivia 741

GABRIEL FAURE (1845-1924)
elegie for cello and orchestra
recorded on 4 december 1961 in the town hall
philadelphia　　　　　　lp:　columbia ML 6191/MS 6791
orchestra
munroe

recorded on 27 march 1967 in the town hall
philadelphia　　　　　　lp:　columbia M 30113
orchestra　　　　　　　　cd:　SBK 48278
rose

sicilienne/pelleas et melisande
recorded on 14 january 1971 in the academy of music
philadelphia　　　　　　lp:　victor
orchestra　　　　　　　　cd:　09026 612112

FRIEDRICH VON FLOTOW (1812-1883)
m'appari/martha
recorded on 2 october 1938 at a ford sunday evening concert in the masonic temple detroit
detroit symphony　　　　lp:　ed smith records EJS 414
gigli

STEPHEN FOSTER (1826-1864)
beautiful dreamer
recorded on 5 september 1964 in the salt lake tabernacle
philadelphia orchestra lp: columbia MS 6721
mormon tabernacle choir

camptown races, arrangement
recorded on 3 may 1965 in the town hall
philadelphia orchestra lp: columbia MS 7072

CESAR FRANCK (1822-1890)
symphony in d minor
recorded on 23 february 1945 in the academy of music
philadelphia orchestra
78: columbia M 608
lp: columbia ML 4024

recorded on 23 december 1953 in the town hall
philadelphia orchestra lp: columbia ML 4939/philipa ABR 4048/ GBL 5628/A01641R/G03607L

recorded on 5 february 1961 in the town hall
philadelphia orchestra
lp: columbia ML 5697/MS 6297/ Y 33922/BRG 72031/SBRG 72031/ 61356
cd: SBK 60287

recorded on 6 june 1963 at a concert in the musikhalle hamburg
sinfonieorchester des norddeutschen rundfunks cd: originals

variations symphoniques pour piano et orchestre
recorded on 16 november 1958 in the broadwood hotel
philadelphia orchestra
casadesus
lp: columbia ML 5388/MS 6070/ Y 31274/61356
cd: MPK 46730/SMK 61725/ SBK 60287/503 3852

franck/**praise ye the lord**/psalm 150
recorded on 22 may 1962 in the salt lake tabernacle
philadelphia   lp: columbia MS 6679
orchestra
mormon tabernacle
choir

GIOVANNI GABRIELI (1553-1612)
sonata pian e forte/symphoniae sacrae
recorded on 28 march 1955 in the town hall
philadelphia   lp: columbia
orchestra

GEORGE GATES (born 1920)
o my father
recorded on 3 november 1958 in the broadwood hotel
philadelphia   lp: columbia MS 6068
orchestra
mormon tabernacle
choir

GEORGE GERSHWIN (1898-1937)
an american in paris
recorded on 5 january 1967 in the town hall
philadelphia   lp: columbia MS 7258/MS 7518/
orchestra   MG 30073
                        cd: SBK 62402
recorded in 1976 at a concert in the academy of music
philadelphia   cd: disco archivia 746
orchestra

piano concerto
recorded on 1 january 1967 in the town hall
philadelphia   lp: columbia MS 7013/MG 30073/
orchestra   61240
entremont   cd: SBK 46338
recorded in 1976 at a concert in the academy of music
philadelphia   cd: disco archivia 746
orchestra
wild

porgy and bess, symphonic suite arranged by bennett
recorded on 5 january 1967 in the town hall
philadelphia   lp: columbia MS 7258/MG 30073
orchestra   cd: SBK 62402

gershwin/**rhapsody in blue**
recorded on 20 may 1945 in the academy of music
philadelphia 78: columbia M 251/english
orchestra columbia DX 1212-1213
levant 45: philips NBE 11126/409 571NE
lp: columbia ML 4026/CL 700/
CS 8461/english columbia 33S 1003/
philips A01293L/S04633L
cd: MPK 47681
recorded on 4 january 1967 in the town hall
philadelphia lp: columbia MS 7013/MG 30073/
orchestra 61240
entremont cd: SBK 62643
recorded in 1976 at a concert in the academy of music
philadelphia cd: disco archivia 746
orchestra
wild

LOUIS GESENSWAY (born 1906)
commemoration symphony
recorded in 1971 at a concert in the academy of music
philadelphia cd: disco archivia 747
orchestra
four squares of philadelphia
recorded on 11 march 1955 in the town hall
philadelphia lp: columbia ML 5108
orchestra

ALBERTO GINASTERA (1916-1983)
concerto for strings
philadelphia lp: columbia M 32874
orchestra cd: russ oppenheim ROCD 0057

UMBERTO GIORDANO (1867-1948)
un di all azzurro spazio/andrea chenier
recorded on 28 august 1947 at a concert in the hollywood bowl
los angeles lp: ed smith records EJS 457
philharmonic cd: melodram MEL 16215/
lanza andromeda ANDRCD 5133
also issued on cd by gala

REINHOLD GLIERE (1875-1956)
symphony no 3 "ilya mourometz"
recorded on 25 november 1956 in the town hall
philadelphia			lp: columbia ML 5189
orchestra
recorded on 6 october 1971 in the academy of music
philadelphia			lp: victor LSC 3246/SB 6859
orchestra			cd: 09026 382942
recorded in 1971 at a concert in the academy of music
philadelphia			cd: disco archivia 723
orchestra

russian sailors' dance/the red poppy
recorded on 6 october 1957 in the town hall
philadelphia			lp: columbia MS 6958/M2X 786/
orchestra			BRG 72153/SBRG 72153
recorded on 16 february 1972 in the academy of music
philadelphia			lp: victor
orchestra

MIKHAIL GLINKA (1804-1857)
russlan and lyudmila, overture
recorded on 12 january 1946 in the academy of music
philadelphia			78: columbia 19010D
orchestra			lp: columbia ML 2043
recorded on 15 march 1959 in the broadwood hotel
philadelphia			lp: columbia ML 5414/ML 6275/
orchestra			MS 6092/MS 6875/BRG 72455/
				SBRG 72455/MG 35188/philips
				ABL 3306/SABL 110/
				A01440L/835 539AY
televised on 30 june-1 july 1978 at concerts in the academy of music
philadelphia			dvd video: euroarts 207 2278
orchestra

CHRISTOPH WILLIBALD GLUCK (1714-1787)
dance of the blessed spirits/orfeo ed euridice
recorded on 10 may 1949 in the town hall
philadelphia			78: columbia M 894
orchestra

ballet suite of movements from orfeo ed euridice, armide and iphigenie in aulis
recorded between 8-15 may 1968 in the town hall
philadelphia			lp: columbia
orchestra

LOUIS GOTTSCHALK (1829-1869)
cakewalk, ballet suite
recorded on 17 february 1952 in the town hall
philadelphia   lp: columbia ML 4616
orchestra

grand walkaround/cakewalk
recorded on 6 may 1968 in the town hall
philadelphia   lp: columbia
orchestra   cd: SBK 63034

MORTON GOULD (1913-1996)
american salute/when johnny comes marching home
recorded on 3 february 1963 in the town hall
philadelphia   lp: columbia MS 6474/MS 6721/
orchestra   MS 7267/MG 32314
         cd: SBK 63034/EC3K 60153

gospel train/spirituals
recorded on 3 may 1965 in the town hall
philadelphia   lp: columbia
orchestra

CHARLES GOUNOD (1818-1893)
waltz/faust
recorded on 20 april 1967 in the town hall
philadelphia   lp: columbia D3S 789/BPG 63254/
orchestra   SBPG 63254/61301

soldiers' chorus/faust
recorded on 9 june 1967 in the salt lake tabernacle
philadelphia   lp: columbia MS 7061
orchestra
mormon tabernacle
choir

marche funebre d'une marionette
recorded on 3 february 1963 in the town hall
philadelphia   lp: columbia
orchestra

gounod/**sanctus/messe solennelle de sainte cecilie**
recorded on 3 november 1958 in the broadwood hotel
philadelphia lp: columbia MS 6068
orchestra
mormon tabernacle
choir

fac ut portem/requiem
recorded on 22 may 1962 in the salt lake tabernacle
philadelphia lp: columbia MS 6367
orchestra
mormon tabernacle
choir

PERCY GRAINGER (1882-1961)
country gardens; shepherds hey
recorded between 16-23 january 1934 in minneapolis
minneapolis 78: victor 1665/hmv DA 1400
symphony

londonderry air; molly on the shore
recorded between 16-23 january 1934 in minneapolis
minneapolis 78: victor 8734/hmv DB 2685
symphony

ENRIQUE GRANADOS (1867-1916)
danza espanola/andaluza, arrangement
recorded on 7 december 1966 in the town hall
philadelphia lp: columbia MS 7146
orchestra cd: russ oppenheim ROCD 0069

EDVARD GRIEG (1843-1907)
piano concerto
recorded on 6 march 1942 in the academy of music
philadelphia 78: victor M 900/hmv DB 6234-6236/
orchestra DB 9004-9006
rubinstein cd: 09026 608972/09026 618832/
  membran 205 235/222 343/231 058

recorded on 1 february 1958 in the town hall
philadelphia lp: columbia ML 5282/MS 6016/
orchestra D3S 715/MG 32050/61040/philips
entremont ABL 3250/SABL 123/A01375L/
  835 503AY/610 304VR/836 404VZ
  cd: SBK 46543

recorded on 12 august 1968 in the academy of music
philadelphia lp: victor LSC 3065/LSC 3198/
orchestra LSC 3306/SB 6810/CRL3 2282
cliburn cd: GD 87834

peer gynt, first suite from the incidental music
recorded on 22 november 1947 in the academy of music
philadelphia 78: columbia M 291
orchestra lp: columbia ML 4132
  excerpts
  45: columbia A 1645
  lp: columbia AL 35

recorded on 14 may 1955 in the town hall
philadelphia lp: columbia ML 5035/philips ABL 3171/
orchestra A01247L/GBL 5525/G03513L
  excerpts
  45: philips ABE 10019/409 017AE

recorded on 21 december 1959 in the broadwood hotel
philadelphia lp: columbia ML 5181/ML 5257/
orchestra ML 5596/MS 6196/61286

recorded in april 1972 in the academy of music
philadelphia lp: victor ARL1 2613/RL 12613
orchestra cd: 74321 212952

grieg/peer gynt, second suite from the incidental music
recorded on 14 may 1955 in the town hall
philadelphia orchestra
lp: columbia ML 5035/philips ABL 3171/ A01247L/GBL 5525/G03513L
excerpts
45: philips ABE 10019/409 017AE

recorded in december 1974 and february 1975 in the academy of music
philadelphia orchestra
blegen
lp: victor ARL1 2613/RL 12613
cd: 74321 212952

two elegaic melodies
recorded on 18 october 1967 in the town hall
philadelphia orchestra
lp: columbia MS 7103/61286
cd: SBK 53257
last spring only
cd: 88697 279872

march of the dwarfs/lyric suite
recorded on 1 may 1965 in the town hall
philadelphia orchestra
lp: columbia M2X 786

nocturne/lyric suite
recorded on 15 may 1968 in the town hall
philadelphia orchestra
lp: columbia M 30066
cd: SBK 53257/88697 279872

homage march/sigurd jorsalfar
recorded on 5 march 1968 in the town hall
philadelphia orchestra
lp: columbia M 30066/61286
cd: SBK 53257

norwegian dance no 2
recored on 27 february 1968 in the town hall
philadelphia orchestra
lp: columbia M 30066
cd: SBK 53257

landkjenning, arrangement of the song
recorded on 22 may 1962 in the salt lake tabernacle
philadelphia orchestra
mormon tabernacle choir
lp: columbia MS 6679

CHARLES TOMLINSON GRIFFES (1884-1920)
the pleasure dome of kubla khan
recorded on 17 january 1934 in minneapolis
minneapolis symphony
78: victor 7957
cd: biddulph WHL 064-065/ membran 205 235/231 058
membran editions incorrectly describe orchestra as philadelphia

poem for flute and orchestra
recorded on 5-6 june 1952 in the town hall
philadelphia orchestra
lp: columbia ML 4629

FERD GROFE (1892-1972)
grand canyon suite
recorded on 23 december 1957 in the town hall
philadelphia orchestra
lp: columbia ML 5286/MS 6003/ M 30046/61266/philips ABL 3294/ SABL 106/A01414L/835 508AY
cd: SBK 62402
excerpts
45: philips ABE 10253/SABE 2006/ 740 101AV
lp: columbia MS 7289

ALEXANDRE GUILMANT (1837-1911)
morceau symphonique for trombone and orchestra
recorded on 4 december 1961 in the town hall
philadelphia orchestra
smith
lp: columbia ML 6191/MS 6791

DAVID GUION (1892-1961)
de lawd's baptizin', spiritual
recorded on 24 september 1939 at a ford sunday evening concert in the masonic temple detroit
detroit symphony   lp: ed smith records UORC 370
tibbett

JACQUES HALEVY (1799-1862)
quand du seigneur/la juive
recorded on 24 january 1970 at a concert in the academy of music
philadelphia   lp: private issue MMR 566
orchestra
domingo

JOHAN HALVORSEN (1864-1935)
entry march of the boyars
recorded on 7 december 1966 in the town hall
philadelphia   lp: columbia MS 6979/MS 7267/
orchestra   61292

GEORGE FRIDERIC HANDEL (1685-1759)
concerto grosso op 3 no 6, arrangement
recorded on 31 december 1944 at a concert in the nbc studios new york city
nbc symphony   unpublished radio broadcast

recorded on 21 may 1945 in the academy of music
philadelphia   78: columbia 12280D
orchestra   lp: columbia ML 2054/philips S06655R

concerto in g minor for oboe and strings
recorded on 5-6 april 1952 in the town hall
philadelphia   lp: columbia ML 4629
orchestra
tabuteau

concerto from the fireworks music
televised between 24-26 june 1977 at concerts in the academy of music
philadelphia   dvd video: euroarts 207 2278
orchestra

handel/**music for the royal fireworks, suite**
recorded on 12 april 1959 in the broadwood hotel
philadelphia orchestra
lp: columbia ML 5417/MS 6095/
MG 31190/BPG 62503/
SBPG 62503/61639

water music, suite
recorded on 12 january 1946 in the academy of music
philadelphia orchestra
78: columbia M 279
45: philips ABE 10057/409 053AE
lp; columbia ML 2054/ML 4797/
philips SBR 6223/S06653R/
S06655R

recorded on 1 april 1959 in the broadwood hotel
philadelphia orchestra
lp: columbia ML 5417/MS 6095/
MS 7515/61639

recorded on 5 february 1970 in the academy of music
philadelphia orchestra
lp: victor LSC 3226
cd: russ oppenheim ROCD 0069
recording completed in april and may 1971

messiah, abridged version
recorded on 2-3 november 1958 in the town hall
philadelphia orchestra
mormon tabernacle choir
farrell, lipton, cunningham, warfield
lp: columbia M2L 263/M2S 607/
philips fontana 699 050-051CL/
876 002-003CY
excerpts
lp: MS 6679/philips A01439L
cd: SBK 48172

handel/**hallelujah chorus/messiah**
recorded on 21 may 1962 in the salt lake tabernacle
philadelphia			lp: columbia MS 6367
orchestra			cd: MDK 48296
mormon tabernacle
choir

choruses from judas maccabaeus and xerxes
recorded on 21 may 1962 in the salt lake tabernacle
philadelphia			lp: columbia MS 5679
orchestra			cd: MDK 48296
mormon tabernacle
choir

largo/xerxes, arrangement
recorded on 15 may 1968 in the town hall
philadelphia			lp: columbia
orchestra

orchestral arrangements from alexander's feast, judas maccabaeus, messiah, samson and the cuckoo and the nightingale
recorded in april-may 1971 in the academy of music
philadelphia			lp: victor
orchestra			cd: russ oppenheim ROCD 0069
				excerpts
				cd: GD 64302

HOWARD HANSON (1896-1981)
serenade for flute and strings
recorded on 4 december 1947 in the academy of music
philadelphia			78: columbia M 851
orchestra			lp: columbia ML 4177
kincaid

ROY HARRIS (1898-1979)
symphony no 3
recorded on 21 june 1958 at a concert in cologne
philadelphia orchestra   unpublished radio broadcast

recorded on 20 march 1974 in the academy of music
philadelphia orchestra   lp: victor ARL1 1682

symphony no 7
recorded on 22 october 1955 in the town hall philadelphia
philadelphia orchestra
lp: columbia ML 5095
cd: american archives ALB 256

chinese dance
recorded on 3 may 1965 in the town hall philadelphia
philadelphia orchestra   lp: columbia

american overture/when johnny comes marching home
recorded on 12 january 1935 in minneapolis
minneapolis symphony
78: victor 8629
cd: biddulph WHL 064-065

KARL AMADEUS HARTMANN (1905-1963)
symphony no 6
recorded on 12 june 1959 at a concert in the deutsches museum munich
sinfonieorchester des bayerischen rundfunks   unpublished radio broadcast

FRANZ JOSEF HAYDN (1732-1809)
symphony no 7 "le midi"
recorded on 2 april 1950 in the town hall
philadelphia orchestra   lp: columbia ML 4673/philips A01171L

symphony no 45 "farewell"
recorded on 16 december 1951 in the town hall
philadelphia   lp: columbia ML 4673/philips A01171L
orchestra   *recording completed on 17 february 1952*

symphony no 88
recorded on 28 december 1947 in the academy of music
philadelphia   78: columbia M 803
orchestra   lp: columbia ML 4109

recorded on 5 september 1955 in the sendesaal cologne
sinfonieorchester   unpublished radio broadcast
des westdeutschen
rundfunks

symphony no 96 "miracle"
recorded on 11 december 1961 in the town hall
philadelphia orchestra   lp: columbia ML 6212/MS 6812

symphony no 99
recorded on 15 april 1954 in the town hall
philadelphia orchestra   lp: columbia ML 5316/philips A01422L

symphony no 100 "military"
recorded on 23 december 1953 in the town hall
philadelphia orchestra   lp: columbia ML 5316/philips A01422L

recorded on 13 june 1965 at a concert in the musikverein vienna
wiener   unpublished radio broadcast
philharmoniker

250
haydn/**symphony no 101 "the clock"**
recorded on 10 may 1949 in the town hall
philadelphia 78: columbia M 894
orchestra lp: columbia ML 4268/english
columbia 33CX 1028/italian
columbia 33QCX 10006/austrian
columbia 33VCX 518/philips
GBL 5521/G03526L

recorded on 28 january 1962 in the town hall
philadelphia lp: columbia ML 6212/MS 6812
orchestra

sinfonia concertante for wind and orchestra
recorded on 23 february 1958 in the town hall
philadelphia lp: columbia ML 5374/MS 6061
orchestra cd: SBK 62649
lancie, garfield,
krachmalnick, munroe

trumpet concerto in e flat
recorded on 9 october 1967 in the town hall
philadelphia lp: columbia
orchestra cd: SBK 62649
johnson

serenade from the string quartet in f, arrangement
recorded on 10 april 1968 in the town hall
philadelphia lp: columbia
orchestra

die himmel erzählen die ehre gottes/die schöpfung
recorded on 3 november 1958 in the broadwood hotel
philadelphia lp: columbia MS 6058/philips
orchestra ABL 3304/A01441L
mormon tabernacle
choir

MICHAEL HEAD (1900-1976)
when I think upon the maidens
recorded on 12 november 1939 at a ford sunday evening concert in the masonic temple detroit

detroit   lp: ed smith records EJS 564
symphony
thomas

VICTOR HERBERT (1859-1924)
march of the toys/babes in toyland
recorded on 3 february 1953 in the town hall

philadelphia   lp: columbia ML 5376
orchestra

selections from naughty marietta and the fortune teller
recorded on 13 may 1952 in th town hall

philadelphia   lp: columbia ML 5376
orchestra

american fantasy
recorded on 13 may 1952 in the town hall

philadelphia   45: columbia A 1030
orchestra   lp: columbia AL 21/ML 5376

an irish rhapsody
recorded on 13 may 1952 in the town hall

philadelphia   45: columbia A 1030
orchestra   lp: columbia AL 21/ML 5376

pan americana
recorded on 13 may 1952 in the town hall

philadelphia   45: columbia A 1030
orchestra   lp: columbia AL 21/ML 5376

FERDINAND HEROLD (1791-1833)
zampa overture
recorded on 20 march 1973 in the academy of music

philadelphia   lp: victor AGL1 3657
orchestra

PAUL HINDEMITH (1895-1963)
mathis der maler, symphony
recorded on 20 october 1940 in the academy of music
philadelphia   78: victor M 854/hmv DB 5997-5999/
orchestra   australian hmv ED 165-167

recorded on 23 november 1952 in the town hall
philadelphia   lp: columbia ML 4816/philips
orchestra   ABL 3051/A01138L

recorded on 5 june 1959 at a concert in the herkulessaal munich
sinfonieorchester   cd: orfeo C199 891B
des bayerischen
rundfunks

recorded on 17 january 1962 in the town hall
philadelphia   lp: columbia ML 5962/MS 6562/
orchestra   61347
     cd: SBK 53258

recorded on 12 november 1967 at a concert in the concertgebouw amsterdam
concertgebouw   cd: q-disc 97019/RCO 05001
orkest

concert music for brass and strings
recorded on 1 november 1953 in the town hall
philadelphia   lp: columbia ML 4816/philips
orchestra   ABL 3051/A01138L

recorded on 11 july 1954 at a concert in recklinghausen
sinfonieorchester   unpublished radio broadcast
des westdeutschen
rundfunks

recorded on 20 november 1978 in the academy of music
philadelphia   lp: angel 37536/emi ASD 3743/
orchestra   1C065 03505/2C069 03505/
     3C065 03505
     cd: emi 565 1752

hindemith/**nobilissima visione**
recorded on 2 march 1947 in the academy of music
philadelphia 78: columbia M 841
orchestra lp: columbia ML 4177/philips
ABL 3390/A01492L

symphonic metamorphoses on themes of carl maria von weber
recorded on 28 december 1961 in the town hall
philadelphia lp: columbia ML 5962/MS 6562
orchestra cd: SBK 53258

recorded on 25 february 1978 in the academy of music
philadelphia lp: angel 37536/emi ASD 3743/
orchestra 1C065 03505/2C069 03505/
3C065 03505
cd: emi 565 1752

GUSTAV HOLST (1874-1934)
the planets
recorded on 18 december 1975 in the academy of music
philadelphia lp: victor ARL1 1797/AGL1 3885/
orchestra RCL1 1921
mendelssohn club cd: GD 61270/09026 612702/
choir 74321 179052

televised between 24-26 june 1977 at concerts in the academy of music
philadelphia dvd video: philips (japan) CDV 102/
orchestra euroarts 207 2268
mendelssohn club
choir

psalm 148
recorded on 5 november 1958 in the broadwood hotel
philadelphia lp: columbia MS 6068
orchestra
mormon tabernacle
choir

ARTHUR HONEGGER (1892-1955)
jeanne d'arc au bucher
recorded on 16 november 1952 in the town hall
philadelphia lp: columbia SL 178/philips ABL
orchestra 3033-3034/A01128-01129L
temple university
and saint peters choirs
yeend, long, lipton,
lloyd, smith, zorina,
gerome

concertino for flute and orchestra
recorded on 15 january 1935 in minneapolis
minneapolis 78: victor 8765
symphony
norton

JULIA HOWE (1819-1910)
battle hymn of the republic
recorded on 5 november 1958 in the broadwood hotel
philadelphia lp: columbia MS 6068/MS 6721/
orchestra MS 7072
mormon tabernacle cd: MDK 48294
choir

recorded in 1973 at a concert in the academy of music
philadelphia cd: disco archivia 745
orchestra
and chorus

ENGELBERT HUMPERDINCK (1854-1921)
evening prayer/hänsel und gretel, arrangement
recorded on 24 march 1965 in the town hall
philadelphia lp: columbia MS 6883/MS 7267
orchestra

JACQUES IBERT (1890-1962)
escales
recorded on 28 february 1954 in the town hall
philadelphia orchestra   lp: columbia ML 4983
recorded on 24 june 1957 at a concert in the sendesaal cologne
sinfonieorchester des westdeutschen rundfunks   unpublished radio broadcast
recorded on 20 november 1960 in the town hall
philadelphia orchestra
lp: columbia ML 5878/MS 6478
cd: SBK 62644
recorded between 4-6 february 1970 in the academy of music
philadelphia orchestra
lp: victor CRL3 2182
cd: 74321 242132

divertissement
recorded between 20-22 january 1963 in the town hall
philadelphia orchestra
lp: columbia ML 5849/MS 6449/ BRG 72123/SBRG 72123
cd: SBK 62644

VINCENT D'INDY (1851-1931)
symphonie montagnard pour piano et orchestre
recorded on 16 november 1958 in the broadwood hotel
philadelphia orchestra
casadesus
lp: columbia ML 5388/MS 6070/ Y 31274
cd: MPK 46730/SM2K 61725/ 503 4002

MIKHAIL IPPOLITOV-IVANOV (1859-1935)
procession of the sardar/caucasian sketches
recorded on 7 december 1966 in the town hall
philadelphia orchestra
lp: columbia MS 6979/M2X 786/ 61292
cd: SBK 62647
recorded on 8 february 1973 in the academy of music
philadelphia orchestra
lp: victor
cd: 09026 612092

JOSIF IVANOVICI (1845-1902)
donauwellen, waltz
recorded on 20 april 1967 in the town hall
philadelphia orchestra
lp: columbia MS 7032/D3S 789/ BPG 63254/SBPG 63254

CHARLES IVES (1874-1954)
symphony no 1
recorded on 13 march 1967 in the town hall
philadelphia orchestra   lp: columbia MS 7111/D3S 783/77424
                             cd: SBK 89290

symphony no 2
recorded on 7 february 1973 in the academy of music
philadelphia orchestra   lp: victor ARL1 0663
                             cd: RD 63316

symphony no 3
recorded on 3 october 1968 in the academy of music
philadelphia orchestra   lp: victor LSC 3060

holidays symphony
recorded on 7 october 1974 in the academy of music
philadelphia orchetra   lp: victor ARL1 1249

variations on america, arranged by william schuman
recorded on 8 may 1968 in the town hall
philadelphia orchestra   lp: columbia MS 7289/77424

three places in new england
recorded on 17 february 1964 in the town hall
philadelphia orchestra   lp: columbia MS 6684/MS 7015/MS 7111/BRG 72384/SBRG 72384/72646/77424
                             cd: SBK 89290

recorded on 11 december 1974 in the academy of music
philadelphia orchestra   lp: victor APL1 1682

ARNAS JAERNEFELT (1869-1958)
praeludium for small orchestra
recorded on 24 february 1968 in the town hall
philadelphia   lp: columbia
orchestra

NORMAN DELLO JOIO (born 1913)
air power, orchestral suite
recorded on 14 march 1957 in the town hall
philadelphia   lp: columbia ML 5214/MS 6029
orchestra   cd: american archives ALB 250

variations, chaconne and finale
philadelphia
orchestra

DMITRY KABALEVSKY (1904-1987)
cello concerto
recorded on 3 may 1982 in the academy of music
philadelphia   lp: columbia M 37840/MK 37840
orchestra   cd: SMK 37840
ma

colas breugnon, overture
recorded on 15 november 1965 at a concert in the herkulessaal munich
sinfonieorchester   cd: emi 575 1272
des bayerischen
rundfunks

recorded on 24 january 1970 at a concert in the academy of music
philadelphia   lp: private edition MMR 566
orchestra

recorded in 1974 at a concert in the academy of music
philadelphia   cd: disco archivia 741
orchestra

the comedians, suite for small orchestra
recorded on 8 april 1956 in the town hall
philadelphia   lp: columbia CL 719
orchestra

kabalevsky/**galop/the comedians**
recorded on 23 march 1964 in the town hall philadelphia
philadelphia   lp: columbia MS 7072
orchestra

recorded on 16 june 1972 in the academy of music
philadelphia   lp: victor
orchestra

KENT KENNAN (1913-2004)
night soliloquy for flute and orchestra
recorded on 2 april 1950 in the town hall
philadelphia   78: columbia M 940
orchestra
kincaid

ARAM KHACHATURIAN (1903-1978)
gayaneh, suite from the ballet
recorded on 8 april 1956 in the town hall
philadelphia   lp: columbia CL 719
orchestra

sabre dance/gayaneh
recorded on 23 march 1963 in the town hall
philadelphia   lp: columbia MS 6624/MS 6934/
orchestra   MS 6958

recorded on 15 june 1972 in the academy of music
philadelphia   lp: victor
orchestra

dance of the young maidens/gayaneh
recorded on 13 april 1966 in the town hall
philadelphia   lp: columbia
orchestra

galop/masquerade
recorded on 13 april 1966 in the town hall
philadelphia   lp: columbia
orchestra

TIKHON KHRENNIKOV (1913-2007)
symphony in b flat
recorded on 7 january 1945 at a concert in the nbc studios new york city
nbc symphony   unpublished radio broadcast

ZOLTAN KODALY (1882-1967)
concerto for orchestra
recorded on 8 february 1967 in the town hall
philadelphia   lp: columbia MS 7034/BRG 72627/
orchestra   SBRG 72627
                         cd: russ oppenheim ROCD 0058

hary janos, suite from the incidental music
recorded on 17 january 1934 in minneapolis
minneapolis   78: victor M 197/hmv DB 2456-2458
symphony

recorded on 24 january 1946 in the academy of music
philadelphia   78: columbia M 912/english columbia
orchestra   LX 1130-1132/LCX 131-133
                         lp: columbia ML 4036

recorded on 28 december 1961 in the town hall
philadelphia   lp: columbia MS 6746
orchestra

recorded on 29 october 1975 in the academy of music
philadelphia   lp: victor ARL1 1325
orchestra   cd: russ oppenheim ROCD 0058

dances from galanta
recorded on 9 december 1962 in the town hall
philadelphia   lp: columbia MS 7034/BRG 72627/
orchestra   SBRG 72627
                         cd: SBK 62404

dances of marosszek
recorded on 15 november 1962 in the town hall
philadelphia   lp: columbia MS 7034/BRG 72627/
orchestra   SBRG 72627
                         cd: SBK 62404

FRITZ KREISLER (1875-1962)
caprice viennois, arrangement
recorded on 19 january 1934 in minneapolis
minneapolis   78: victor M 211/hmv DB 2352
symphony

liebesfreud, arrangement
recorded on 19 january 1934 in minneapolis
minneapolis   78: victor M 211/hmv DB 2352
symphony

recorded on 20 december 1967 in the town hall
philadelphia   lp: columbia MS 7146
orchestra

liebesleid, arrangement
recorded on 19 january 1934 in minneapolis
minneapolis   78: victor M 211/hmv DA 1399
symphony

schön rosmarin, arrangement
recorded on 19 january 1934 in minneapolis
minneapolis   78: victor M 211/hmv DA 1399
symphony

tambourin, arrangement
recorded on 19 january 1934 in minneapolis
minneapolis   78: victor M 211/hmv DB 2352
symphony

EDOUARD LALO (1823-1892)
symphonie espagnole pour violon et orchestre
recorded on 19 november 1944 in the academy of music
philadelphia   78: columbia M 564
orchestra   cd: pearl GEMMCD 9259
milstein   *recording completed on 15 march 1945*

recorded in july 1955 at a concert in paris
orchestre   cd: music and arts CD 1168
national
milstein

recorded on 10 january 1956 in the town hall
philadelphia   lp: columbia ML 5097/BRG 72616/
orchestra   SBRG 72616/philips ABL 3168/
stern   A01253L/S06664R
                        cd: SX9K 67194

recorded on 13 february 1967 in the town hall
philadelphia   lp: columbia MS 7003/77418
orchestra   cd: 88697 008172
stern

cello concerto
recorded on 27 march 1967 in the town hall
philadelphia   lp: columbia M 30113
orchestra   cd: SBK 48278
rose

BENJAMIN LEES (born 1924)
concerto for string quartet and orchestra
recorded in 1970 at a concert in the academy of music
philadelphia   cd: disco archivia 747
orchestra

FRANZ LEHAR (1870-1948)
eva, waltz
recorded on 26 june 1953 in the town hall
philadelphia   45: columbia A 1832/A 1867/
orchestra   philips 409 511NE
                     lp: columbia AL 48/ML 4893

gold und silber, waltz
recorded on 26 june 1953 in the town hall
philadelphia   45: columbia A 1832/A 1867/
orchestra   philips 409 511NE
                     lp: columbia AL 48/ML 4893/MS 6352

dein ist mein ganzes herz/das land des lächelns, arrangement
recorded on 26 june 1953 in the town hall
philadelphia   45: columbia A 1832
orchestra   lp: columbia AL 48/ML 4893

die lustige witwe, waltz
recorded on 26 june 1953 in the town hall
philadelphia   45: columbia A 1832/A 1867/
orchestra   philips 409 511NE
                     lp: columbia AL 48/ML 4893

viljalied/die lustige witwe, arrangement
recorded on 26 june 1953 in the town hall
philadelphia   45: columbia A 1832/philips 409 511NE
orchestra   lp: columbia AL 48/ML 4893

RUGGERO LEONCAVALLO (1858-1919)
vesti la giubba/i pagliacci
recorded on 2 october 1938 at a ford sunday evening concert in the masonic temple detroit

detroit symphony   lp: ed smith records EJS 414
gigli

bell chorus/i pagliacci
recorded on 10 june 1967 in the salt lake tabernacle
philadelphia   lp: columbia MS 7061
orchestra
mormon tabernacle
choir

FRANZ LISZT (1811-1886)
piano concerto no 1
recorded on 17 february 1952 in the academy of music
philadelphia   lp: columbia ML 4665/Y 34601/
orchestra   philips GBR 6511/G05614R
arrau   cd: MHK 62338

recorded on 8 february 1959 in the town hall
philadelphia   lp: columbia ML 5389/MS 6071
orchestra   cd: SBK 48167
entremont

piano concerto no 2
recorded on 25 january 1959 in the town hall
philadelphia   lp: columbia ML 5389/MS 6071
orchestra   cd: SBK 48167
entremont

recorded on 7 may 1970 in the academy of music
philadelphia   lp: victor LSC 3179
orchestra   cd: GD 87834
cliburn

liszt/**hungarian fantasia for piano and orchestra**
recorded on 17 february 1952 in the academy of music
philadelphia orchestra
arrau
    lp: columbia ML 4665/philips GBL 5583/ GBR 6511/G05373L/G05614R
    cd: MHK 62338/arlecchino ARLA 12/ archipel ARPCD 0260

recorded on 15 may 1968 in the town hall
philadelphia orchestra
i.davis
    lp: columbia M 30306

recorded on 31 october 1981 in the academy of music
philadelphia orchestra
katsaris
    lp: angel 37888/emi ASD 4258/ 1C065 43199/2C069 43199/ 3C065 43199
    cd: piano P21 022A

totentanz for piano and orchestra
recorded on 23 february 1961 in the town hall
philadelphia orchestra
brailowsky
    lp: columbia ML 5652/MS 6252
    cd: SBK 48167

les preludes
recorded on 13 october 1946 in the academy of music
philadelphia orchestra
    78: victor M 453/hmv DB 3490-3491

mephisto waltz/episodes from faust
recorded on 19 december 1957 in the town hall
philadelphia orchestra
    lp: columbia ML 5641/MS 6241

recorded on 23 march 1968 in the town hall
philadelphia orchestra
    lp: columbia M 30306

liszt/**hungarian rhapsody no 1**
recorded on 20 march 1947 in the academy of music
philadelphia　　　　　　　78: columbia 12928D/english columbia
orchestra　　　　　　　　　LX 1107/swiss columbia DZX 41
　　　　　　　　　　　　　45: philips ABE 10159/409 111AE
　　　　　　　　　　　　　lp: columbia ML 4132/CL 722/philips
　　　　　　　　　　　　　SBL 5234/GBL 5583/S04643L/
　　　　　　　　　　　　　G03573L

recorded on 1-2 february 1958 in the town hall
philadelphia　　　　　　　lp: columbia ML 5299/MS 6018/
orchestra　　　　　　　　　M 31846
　　　　　　　　　　　　　cd: SBK 38917/SBK 60265

recorded on 8 january 1969 in the academy of music
philadelphia　　　　　　　lp: victor LSC 3085/ARL1 0111
orchestra

hungarian rhapsody no 2
recorded on 18 april 1946 in the academy of music
philadelphia　　　　　　　78: columbia 12437D/english
orchestra　　　　　　　　　columbia LX 1045
　　　　　　　　　　　　　lp: columbia ML 4132/CL 722/
　　　　　　　　　　　　　philips GBL 5583/GL 5678/
　　　　　　　　　　　　　G03573L

recorded on 1-2 february 1958 in the town hall
philadelphia　　　　　　　lp: columbia ML 5299/MS 6018/
orchestra　　　　　　　　　M 30306/M 31846
　　　　　　　　　　　　　cd: SBK 38917/SBK 60265

recorded on 8 january 1969 in the academy of music
philadelphia　　　　　　　lp: victor LSC 3085/ARL1 0111
orchestra

liebestraum, orchestral arrangement
recorded on 15 may 1968 in the town hall
philadelphia　　　　　　　lp: columbia
orchestra

liebestraum, violin arrangement
recorded between 18-20 june 1926 in new york
ormandy, violin　　　　　　78: cameo 983/romeo 243

EDWARD MACDOWELL (1860-1908)
to a wild rose, arrangement
recorded on 18 june 1966 in the town hall
philadelphia   lp: columbia MS 7103/M 30066
orchestra   cd: 88697 279872

GUSTAV MAHLER (1860-1911)
symphony no 1
recorded on 21 may 1969 in the academy of music
philadelphia   lp: victor LSC 3107
orchestra   *recording includes the blumine movement*

symphony no 2 "resurrection"
recorded on 6-7 january 1935 at concerts in minneapolis
minneapolis   78: victor M 256/hmv DB 2751-2761
symphony   cd: biddulph LHW 032/membran
twin city symphony   205 235/231 058
chorus
bowen, galloghy

recorded on 18-19 march 1970 in the academy of music
philadelphia   lp: victor LMDS 7066/LSB 4003-4004
orchestra
singing city choirs
mandac, finnilä

symphony no 4
recorded in 1972 at a concert in the academy of music
philadelphia   cd: disco archivia 750
orchestra
mandac

veni creator spiritus/symphony no 8
recorded on 29 july 1948 at a concert in the hollywood bowl
los angeles   cd: biddulph WHL 064-065
philharmonic
greater los angeles
and boys' choirs
yeend, beech, beal,
coray, kullmann,
harrell, london

mahler/**symphony no 10, original performing version by deryck cooke**
recorded on 17 november 1965 in the town hall
philadelphia orchestra
lp: columbia M2S 735/D3S 774/ BRG 72408-72409/SBRG 72408-72409/61447
cd: 82876 787422

das lied von der erde
recorded on 9 february 1966 in the town hall
philadelphia orchestra
chookasian, lewis
lp: columbia MS 6946/D3S 774
cd: SBK 53518

ALBERT HAY MALOTTE (1895-1964)
the lord's prayer
recorded on 22 may 1962 in the salt lake tabernacle
philadelphia orchestra
mormon tabernacle choir
lp: columbia MS 6367/BRG 72210/ SBRG 72210

BENEDETTO MARCELLO (1686-1739)
oboe concerto in c minor
philadelphia orchestra
lancie
lp: columbia MS 6977

FRANK MARTIN (1890-1974)
concerto for wind, timpani and strings
recorded on 1 june 1959 at a concert in the funkhaus cologne
sinfonieorchester des westdeutschen rundfunks
unpublished radio broadcast

PIETRO MASCAGNI (1863-1945)
cavalleria rusticana, intermezzo
recorded on 18 october 1967 in the town hall
philadelphia   lp: columbia MS 7103/61301
orchestra   cd: 88697 279872
regina coeli/cavalleria rusticana
recorded on 9 june 1967 in the salt lake tabernacle
philadelphia   lp: columbia MS 7061
orchestra
mormon tabernacle
choir

JULES MASSENET (1842-1912)
le cid, ballet suite
recorded on 6 may 1968 in the town hall
philadelphia   lp: columbia MS 7673
orchestra
elegie, arrangement of the song
recorded on 28 february 1966 in the town hall
philadelphia   lp: columbia M 30066
orchestra   cd: 88697 279872
ah fuyez douce image/manon
recorded on 13 january 1946 at a ford sunday evening concert in the masonic temple detroit
detroit symphony   lp: ed smith records EJS 252
björling
meditation pour violon et orchestre/thais
recorded on 16 february 1966 in the town hall
philadelphia   lp: columbia MS 7103
orchestra
brusilow

HARL MCDONALD (1899-1955)
symphony no 1 "the santa fe trail"
recorded on 20 october 1940 in the academy of muic
philadelphia   78: victor M 754
orchestra
recorded in 1971 at a concert in the academy of music
philadelphia   cd: disco archivia 723
orchestra

mcdonald/**cakewalk/choral symphony**
recorded on 8 january 1939 in the academy of music
philadelphia   78: victor 15377/hmv DB 5777
orchestra

my country at war, symphonic suite
recorded on 20 december 1944 in the academy of music
philadelphia   78: columbia M 592
orchestra

FELIX MENDELSSOHN-BARTHOLDY (1809-1847)
symphony no 3 "scotch"
recorded on 2 november 1977 in the academy of music
philadelphia   lp: victor ARL1 4359
orchestra

symphony no 4 "italian"
recorded on 27 august 1947 at a concert in the hollywood bowl
los angeles   cd: melodram MEL 16215/
philharmonic   andromeda ANDRCD 5133
                                   first movement only

recorded on 24 june 1957 at a concert in the sendesaal cologne
sinfonieorchester   unpublished radio broadcast
des westdeutschen
rundfunks

recorded on 2 october 1963 in the town hall
philadelphia   lp: columbia ML 6028/MS 6628/
orchestra   31014
                                 cd: SBK 63251

recorded in 1974 at a concert in the academy of music
philadelphia   cd: disco archivia 752
orchestra

piano concerto no 1
recorded on 19 december 1957 in the town hall
philadelphia   lp: columbia ML 5456/MS 6128/
orchestra   MS 7185/D3S 741/BRG 72303/
serkin   SBRG 72303/philips fontana
                                 699 053CL
                                 cd: SBK 46542

mendelssohn/**piano concerto no 2**
recorded on 18 october 1959 in the town hall
philadelphia orchestra serkin
lp: columbia ML 5456/MS 6128/ BRG 72303/SBRG 72303/philips fontana 699 053CL
cd: SBK 46542

concerto in a flat for 2 pianos and orchestra
recorded on 16 december 1963 in the town hall
philadelphia orchestra
gold, fizdale
lp: columbia MS 6681/Y 31532

concerto in e for 2 pianos and orchestra
recorded on 16 december 1963 in the town hall
philadelphia orchestra
gold, fizdale
lp: columbia MS 6681/Y 31532

capriccio brillant for piano and orchestra
recorded on 4 april 1967 in the town hall
philadelphia orchestra serkin
lp: columbia MS 7183/MG 32042/ MP 39544
cd: MPK 45690/M2YK 45675/ SBK 48166/SB3K 52516

mendelssohn/**violin concerto**
recorded on 20 december 1941 in the academy of music
philadelphia   cd: biddulph LAB 054
orchestra   *unpublished victor 78rpm recording*
spalding

recorded on 30 october 1950 in the town hall
philadelphia   78: english columbia LX 1445-1447/
orchestra   swiss columbia LZX 268-270/polish
stern   columbia LNX 8039-8041
                         lp: columbia ML 4363/english columbia
                         33CX 1071/french columbia FCX 210/
                         italian columbia QCX 10042/german
                         columbia WCX 1071/philips GL 5749/
                         G03646L/philips fontana EFL 2526/
                         697 211EL
                         cd: SX11K 67193

recorded on 24 december 1955 in the academy of music
philadelphia   lp: columbia ML 5085/MG 22219/
orchestra   BRG 72306/SBRG 72306/philips
oistrakh   ABL 3145/GBR 6507/A01249L/
                         G05602R
                         cd: naxos 811 1246

recorded on 24 march 1958 in the broadwood hotel
philadelphia   lp: columbia ML 5379/MS 6062/
orchestra   MS 7516/D3S 721/M 31835/
stern   BRG 72083/SBRG 72083/61029/
                         philips fontana 699 017CL/876 004CY
                         cd: SMK 66827/88697 279872

recorded in 1971 at a concert in the academy of music
philadelphia   cd: disco archivia 747
orchestra
carol

the hebrides, overture
recorded on 21 april 1979 in the academy of music
philadelphia   lp: victor ARL1 3460
orchestra

mendelssohn/**war march of the priests/athalie**
recorded on 7 december 1966 in the town hall
philadelphia　　　　　　　lp: columbia MS 6979/61292
orchestra　　　　　　　　cd: SBK 63251

scherzo/octet
recorded on 1 march 1959 in the town hall philadelphia
philadelphia　　　　　　　lp: columbia MS 6081
orchestra　　　　　　　　cd: SBK 63251

a midsummer night's dream, incidental music
recorded on 20 april 1976 in the academy of music
philadelphia　　　　　　　lp: victor ARL1 2084/RL 12084
orchestra　　　　　　　　*recording completed between 6-12 may 1976*
mendelssohn
club choir
blegen, von stade

a midsummer night's dream, suite from the incidental music
recorded on 3 february 1957 in the town hall
philadelphia　　　　　　　lp: columbia ML 5221/philips GBL
orchestra　　　　　　　　5525/G03513L
　　　　　　　　　　　　excerpts
　　　　　　　　　　　　45: philips ABE 10250/409 175AE
　　　　　　　　　　　　recording completed on 13 april 1957

recorded on 24 november 1963 in the town hall
philadelphia　　　　　　　lp: columbia ML 6028/MS 6628/
orchestra　　　　　　　　31014
　　　　　　　　　　　　cd: SBK 63251
　　　　　　　　　　　　excerpts
　　　　　　　　　　　　lp: columbia MS 6979/61292

wedding march/a midsummer night's dream
recorded on 12 june 1972 in the academy of music
philadelphia　　　　　　　lp: victor AGL1 4298
orchestra

elias
recorded on 8-9 april 1969 in the academy of music
philadelphia　　　　　　　lp: victor LSC 6190
orchestra
singing city and
columbus choirs
marsh, verrett,
lewis, krause

mendelssohn/**die erste walpurgisnacht**
recorded on 8 may 1978 in the academy of music
philadelphia   lp: victor ARL1 3460
orchestra
mendelssohn
club choir
taylor, norman, estes

GIAN CARLO MENOTTI (1911-2007)
amelia al ballo, overture
recorded on 8 january 1939 in the academy of music
philadelphia   78: victor 15377/hmv DB 5777
orchestra   cd: biddulph WHL 064-065
triple concerto
recorded in 1971 at a concert in the academy of music
philadelphia   cd: disco archivia 724
orchestra
barcarolle/sebastian suite
recorded on 6 march 1966 in the town hall
philadelphia   lp: columbia
orchestra

SOPHIE MENTER (1846-1918)
hungarian concerto for piano and orchestra, arranged by tchaikovsky
recorded on 31 october 1981 in the academy of music
philadelphia   lp: angel 37888/emi ASD 4258/
orchestra   1C065 43199/2C069 43199/
katsaris   3C065 43199
                             cd: piano P21 022A
                             at the time of this premiere recording it was thought that the concerto might have been composed by liszt

GIACOMO MEYERBEER (1791-1864)
les patineurs, suite from the ballet
recorded on 5 march 1968 in the town hall
philadelphia   lp: columbia M 30463/61242
orchestra   cd: SBK 46341
o beau pays/les huguenots
recorded on 24 january 1970 at a concert in the academy of music
philadelphia   lp: private issue MMR 566
orchestra
sutherland

meyerbeer/**coronation march/le prophete**
recorded on 3 february 1963 in the town hall
philadelphia   lp: columbia
orchestra

recorded on 22-23 january 1973 in the academy of music
philadelphia   lp: victor AGL1 4298
orchestra   cd: 09026 612112

NIKOLAY MIASKOVSKY (1881-1950)
symphony no 21
recorded on 22 november 1947 in the academy of music
philadelphia   lp: columbia ML 4239
orchestra   cd: biddulph WHL 064-065/
                                   membran 205 235/231 058

DARIUS MILHAUD (1892-1974)
concerto for percussion and small orchestra
recorded on 28 march 1955 in the town hall
philadelphia   lp: columbia ML 5129
orchestra

WOLFGANG AMADEUS MOZART (1756-1791)
symphony no 30
recorded on 8 april 1962 in the town hall
philadelphia   lp: columbia MS 6722
orchestra   cd: SBK 62827

symphony no 31 "paris"
recorded on 29 january 1961 in the town hall
philadelphia   lp: columbia MS 6722
orchestra   cd: SBK 62827

symphony no 35 "haffner"
recorded on 31 december 1944 at a concert in the nbc studios new york city
nbc symphony   unpublished radio broadcast

mozart/**symphony no 40**
recorded on 10 january 1956 in the town hall
philadelphia   lp: columbia ML 5098
orchestra

recorded in 1974 at a concert in the academy of music
philadelphia   cd: disco archivia 725
orchestra

symphony no 41 "jupiter"
recorded on 28 may 1968 in the academy of music
philadelphia   lp: victor LSC 3056/LSC 6190
orchestra

piano concerto no 17
recorded on 29 january 1970 at a concert in the academy of music
philadelphia   lp: private edition MJA 1970
orchestra   cd: intaglio INCD 7071/stradivarius
richter   STR 33303/STR 33354/musica viva
                                (greece) 88 053/philadelphia
                                centennial collection

piano concerto no 20
recorded on 11 february 1951 in the town hall
philadelphia   lp: columbia ML 4224/philips ABR 4006/
orchestra   A01600R/philips fontana CFL 1038/
serkin   EFL 2524/699 030CL/699 210EL
                                cd: SM3K 47207

recorded on 29 january 1970 at a concert in the academy of music
philadelphia   lp: private edition MJA 1970
orchestra
richter

piano concerto no 21
televised on 9 june 1963 at a concert in the musikverein vienna
wiener   laserdisc: toshiba TOLW 3741
philharmoniker
serkin

piano concerto no 23
recorded on 10 may 1968 in the town hall
philadelphia   columbia unpublished
orchestra
serkin

mozart/**piano concerto no 27**
recorded on 28 january 1962 in the town hall
philadelphia lp: columbia ML 6239/MS 6839/
orchestra MG 31267/BRG 72431/
serkin SBRG 72431
 cd: SM3K 47207

concerto for 2 pianos and orchestra
recorded on 15 december 1960 in the manhattan centre new york city
philadelphia lp: columbia ML 5674/MS 6274/
orchestra BRG 72008/SBRG 72008
robert and gaby cd: SBK 87838/SM3K 46519/
casadesus 503 3962

concerto for 3 pianos and orchestra
recorded on 9 december 1962 in the town hall
philadelphia lp: columbia ML 5895/MS 6495/
orchestra Y 31531/BRG 72150/SBRG 72150
robert, gaby and cd: 503 3962
jean casadesus

violin concerto no 3
recorded on 12 november 1967 at a concert in the concertgebouw amsterdam
concertgebouw cd: q-disc 97019/RCO 05001
orkest
klimov

violin concerto no 4
recorded on 24 december 1955 in the academy of music
philadelphia lp: columbia ML 5085/MG 33328/
orchestra BRG 72306/SBRG 72306/philips
oistrakh ABL 3145/GBR 6506/A01249L/
 G05601R/melodiya D17385-17386/
 M10 46431
 cd: naxos 811 1246

violin concerto no 5
recorded in 1971 at a concert in the academy of music
philadelphia cd: disco archivia 724
orchestra
zukerman

mozart/**sinfonia concertante for 4 wind**
recorded on 23 december 1957 in the town hall
philadelphia   lp: columbia ML 5374/MS 6061
orchestra   cd: SBK 67177
lancie, gigliotti,
garfield, jones

bassoon concerto
recorded on 29 january 1961 in the town hall
philadelphia   lp: columbia M2L 284/M2S 684/
orchestra   MS 6451/BRG 72127-72128/
garfield   SBRG 72127-72128/61657
                       cd: SBK 62652

clarinet concerto
recorded on 16 april 1961 in the town hall
philadelphia   lp: columbia M2L 284/M2S 684/
orchestra   MS 6452/BRG 72127-72128/
gigliotti   SBRG 72127-72128/61657

flute concerto
recorded on 24 april 1960 in the town hall
philadelphia   lp: columbia M2L 284/M2S 684/
orchestra   MS 6451/BRG 72127-72128/
kincaid   SBRG 72127-72128

horn concerto no 1
recorded on 26 february 1961 in the town hall
philadelphia   lp: columbia MS 6785/61095
orchestra
jones

horn concerto no 2
recorded on 3 december 1961 in the town hall
philadelphia   lp: columbia MS 6785/61095
orchestra
jones

horn concerto no 3
recorded on 5 february 1961 in the town hall
philadelphia   lp: columbia MS 6785/61095
orchestra
jones

mozart/**horn concerto no 4**
recorded on 11 march 1962 in the town hall
philadelphia   lp: columbia MS 6785/61095
orchestra
jones

oboe concerto
recorded on 10 december 1961 in the town hall
philadelphia   lp: columbia MS 6452/M2L 284/
orchestra   M2S 684/BRG 72127-72128/
lancie   SBRG 72127-72128/61657
                      cd: SBK 62652

divertimento no 10
recorded on 17 april 1938 in minneapolis
minneapolis   78: victor M 603/australian
symphony   hmv EC 66-67 and ED 62

serenade no 13 "eine kleine nachtmusik"
recorded on 17 january 1934 in minneapolis
minneapolis   78: victor 8588-8589/hmv
symphony   DB 2570 and DA 1440

recorded on 1 april 1959 in the town hall
philadelphia   lp: columbia ML 5402/MS 6081
orchestra

german dances: k600 nos 1-5; k602 no 3; k605 nos 2-3
recorded on 23 january 1934 in minneapolis
minneapolis   78: victor 1722-1723/hmv DA
symphony   6002-6003/australian hmv
                      EC 32-33

minuet from don giovanni, arrangement
recorded on 15 may 1968 in the town hall
philadelphia   lp: columbia
orchestra

mozart/**le nozze di figaro, overture**
recorded on 23 january 1934 in minneapolis
minneapolis   78: victor 14325
symphony

requiem aeternam/requiem
recorded on 20 may 1962 in the town hall
philadelphia   lp: columbia
orchestra
mormon tabernacle
choir

exsultate jubilate, motet
recorded on 15 november 1953 in the town hall
philadelphia   columbia unpublished
orchestra
steber

recorded on 25 april 1974 at a concert in the academy of music
philadelphia   cd: philadelphia orchestra
orchestra   centennial collection
sills

alleluia/exsultate jubilate
recorded on 27 august 1947 at a concert in the hollywood bowl
los angeles   cd: melodram MEL 16215/
philharmonic   andromeda ANDRCD 5133
yeend

MODEST MUSSORGSKY (1839-1881)
night on bare mountain, arranged by rimsky-korsakov
recorded on 19 april 1959 in the town hall
philadelphia   lp: columbia ML 5392/MS 6073/
orchestra   MS 7148/MS 7437/M 30448/
                                    M 31826/MG 30947/61050
                                    cd: SBK 46329

recorded on 21 april 1971 in the academy of music
philadelphia   lp: victor ARD1 0002/CRL3 0985
orchestra   cd: RD 68336/09026 612092

mussorgsky/**pictures at an exhibition, arranged by cailliet**
recorded on 17 october 1937 in the academy of music
philadelphia   78: victor M 442
orchestra   cd: biddulph WHL 046/membran
                        205 235/231 058

pictures at an exhibition, arranged by ravel
recorded on 15 february 1953 in the town hall
philadelphia   lp: columbia ML 4700/philips
orchestra   A01187L/S06631R

recorded in 1958 at a concert in the moscow conservatory
philadelphia   lp: melodiya M10 47183 007
orchestra

recorded on 12 june 1959 at a concert in the deutsches museum munich
sinfonieorchester   unpublished radio broadcast
des bayerischen
rundfunks

recorded on 21 april 1966 in the town hall
philadelphia   lp: columbia MS 7148/M 30448/
orchestra   M 31826/61050
                        cd: 88697 279872
                        recording completed on 18 june 1966

recorded on 25-26 april 1973 in the academy of music
philadelphia   lp: victor ARL1 0451
orchestra   cd: RD 68336/09026 612092

televised in 1978 at a concert in the academy of music
philadelphia   laserdisc: polygram (japan)
orchestra   070 2263
                        dvd video: philips (japan) CDV 102/
                        euroarts 207 2128

gopak/sorotchinsky fair
recorded on 13 april 1966 in the town hall
philadelphia   lp: columbia
orchestra

NICOLAS NABOKOV (1903-1978)
prelude, variations and finale on a theme of tchaikovsky for cello and orchestra
recorded on 5 january 1972 at a concert in the academy of music
philadelphia   cd: intaglio INCD 7521
orchestra
rostropovich

CARL NIELSEN (1865-1931)
symphony no 1
recorded on 8 february 1967 in the town hall
philadelphia   lp: columbia MS 7004/BRG 72606/
orchestra   SBRG 72606
                        cd: S4K 45989/SBK 63040

symphony no 6
recorded on 10 january 1966 in the town hall
philadelphia   lp: columbia MS 6882
orchestra   cd: S4K 45989/SBK 63040

helios overture
recorded on 31 january 1967 in the town hall
philadelphia   lp: columbia MS 7004/BRG 72606/
orchestra   SBRG 72606
                        cd: SBK 63040

overture and act two prelude/maskerade
recorded on 3 february 1966 in the town hall
philadelphia   lp: columbia MS 6882
orchestra

pan and syrinx
recorded on 31 january 1967 in the town hall
philadelphia   lp: columbia MS 7004/BRG 72606/
orchestra   SBRG 72606

an imaginary trip to the faroe islands, rhapsodic overture
recorded on 8 february 1967 in the town hall
philadelphia   lp: columbia MS 7004/BRG 72606/
orchestra   SBRG 72606

JOHN JACOB NILES (1892-1980)
i wonder as i wander, orchestral arrangement of the song
recorded on 13 august 1964 in the town hall
philadelphia orchestra
    lp: columbia MS 7103

OTTOKAR NOVACEK (1866-1900)
moto perpetuo, arrangement
recorded on 7 december 1966 in the town hall
philadelphia orchestra
    lp: columbia MS 7146
    cd: russ oppenheim ROCD 0069

JACQUES OFFENBACH (1819-1880)
gaite parisienne, ballet
recorded on 9 may 1954 in the town hall
philadelphia orchestra
    lp: columbia CL 741/philips NBL 5019/ GBL 5505/N02114L/G03514L/ S06606R
    excerpts
    45: philips ABE 10106/409 116AE

recorded on 30 january 1963 in the town hall
philadelphia orchestra
    lp: columbia MS 6546/M 31848/ BRG 72300/SBRG 72300
    cd: SBK 48279

orfee aux enfers, overture
recorded on 9 may 1954 in the town hall
philadelphia orchestra
    lp: columbia ML 5206/philips ABL 3215/ GBL 5626/A01356L/G03604L

recorded on 4 november 1973 in the academy of music
philadelphia orchestra
    lp: victor AGL1 3657/CRL3 2182
    cd: 09026 612112

barcarolle/les contes d'hoffmann
recorded on 6 may 1968 in the town hall
philadelphia orchestra
    lp: columbia 61301

CARL ORFF (1895-1982)
carmina burana
recorded on 24 april 1960 in the broadwood hotel
philadelphia orchestra
rutgers university choir
presnell, petrak, harsanyi

lp: columbia ML 5498/MS 6163/
BRG 72169/SBRG 72169/philips
ABL 3385/SABL 217/A01472L
cd: SBK 47668

catulli carmina
recorded on 20 april 1967 in the town hall
philadelphia orchestra
temple university choir
blegen, kness

lp: columbia MS 7017/BRG 72611/
SBRG 72611
cd: SBK 61703

IGNACY JAN PADEREWSKI (1860-1941)
menuetto, arrangement
recorded on 1 may 1965 in the town hall
philadelphia orchestra

lp: columbia

NICOLO PAGANINI (1782-1840)
violin concerto no 1
recorded on 15 january 1950 in the town hall
philadelphia orcherstra
francescatti

78: columbia M 936/austrian columbia
LVX 181-183/swiss columbia LZX
274-276
lp: columbia A 1006/ML 4315/
MS 6268/BRG 72151/SBRG
72151/french columbia FCX 140/
philips SBL 5219/S04620L/
G03501L
cd: MPK 46728/SBK 47661/
membran 223 343

paganini/**violin concerto no 1, first movement arranged by kreisler**
recorded on 13 december 1936 in the academy of music
philadelphia   78: columbia M 36/hmv DB 3234-3235
orchestra   cd: biddulph LAB 101/
kreisler   symposium 1282

moto perpetuo, arrangement for orchestra
recorded on 8 january 1935 in minneapolis
minneapolis   78: victor 8661/14325/hmv DB 2823/
symphony   australian hmv ED 31

recorded on 28 march 1955 in the town hall
philadelphia   lp: columbia
orchestra

recorded on 6 december 1966 in the town hall
philadelphia   lp: columbia MS 7146
orchestra

KRZYSZTOF PENDERECKI (born 1933)
threnody for the victims of hiroshima
recorded on 10 january 1969 at a concert in the academy of music
philadelphia   cd: philadelphia orchestra
orchestra   centennial collection/
                             disco archivia 748

utrenja: the entombment of christ
philadelphia   lp: victor LSC 3180/SB 6857
orchestra   cd: 09026 383032
woytowicz, meyer,
mccoy, ladysz, lagger

GIOVANNI PERGOLESI (1710-1736)
glory to god in the highest
recorded on 22 may 1962 in the salt lake tabernacle
philadelphia   lp: columbia MS 6679
orchestra
mormon tabernacle
choir

VINCENT PERSICHETTI (1915-1987)
symphony no 4
recorded on 19 december 1954 in the town hall
philadelphia   lp: columbia ML 5108
orchestra   cd: american archives ALB 276

symphony no 9 "sinfonia janiculum"
recorded on 16 march 1971 in the academy of music
philadelphia   lp: victor LSC 3212
orchestra   cd: disco archivia 749

BURRILL PHILLIPS (1907-1988)
concerto piece for bassoon and strings
recorded on 5-6 april 1952 in the town hall
philadelphia   lp: columbia ML 4629
orchestra
schoenbach

GABRIEL PIERNE (1863-1937)
marche des petits soldats
recorded on 8 may 1968 in the town hall
philadelphia   lp: columbia
orchestra

WALTER PISTON (1894-1976)
symphony no 4
recorded on 15 april 1954 in the town hall
philadelphia   lp: columbia ML 4992
orchestra   cd: american archives ALB 256

symphony no 7
recorded on 10 february 1961 at a concert in the academy of music
philadelphia   cd: philadelphia orchestra
orchestra   centennial collection/
                         disco archivia 746

lincoln centre overture
recorded in 1970 at a concert in the academy of music
philadelphia   cd: disco archivia 747
orchestra

AMILCARE PONCHIELLI (1834-1886)
danza delle ore/la gioconda
recorded on 16 march 1964 in the town hall
philadelphia orchestra   lp: columbia MS 6823/MS 7072/MS 7437
     cd: SBK 48159

recorded on 2 march 1971 in the academy of music
philadelphia orchestra   lp: victor CRL3 0985/VCS 7079

FRANCIS POULENC (1899-1963)
organ concerto
recorded on 7 october 1962 in the town hall
philadelphia orchestra
power biggs   lp: columbia ML 5798/MS 6398
     cd: russ oppenheim ROCD 0057

SERGE PROKOFIEV (1891-1953)
symphony no 1 "classical"
recorded on 13 october 1946 in the academy of music
philadelphia orchestra   78: columbia M 287
     lp: columbia A 1638/ML 2035/english columbia 33C 1025/italian columbia QC 5015

recorded on 18 december 1955 in the town hall
philadelphia orchestra   lp: columbia ML 5289

recorded on 26 march 1961 in the town hall
philadelphia orchestra   lp: columbia ML 5945/MS 6545/M 31812/MGP 7/BRG 72185/SBRG 72185
     cd: SBK 53260

recorded on 12 january 1972 in the academy of music
philadelphia orchestra   lp: victor ARL1 0113/CRL3 2026
     cd: 74321 212922/disco archivia 745

prokofiev/**symphony no 4**
recorded on 6 october 1957 in the town hall
philadelphia   lp: columbia ML 5488/MS 6154
orchestra

symphony no 5
recorded on 14 march 1957 in the town hall
philadelphia   lp: columbia ML 5260/MS 6004/
orchestra   Y 30490/philips SABL 105/
                        835 502AY
                        cd: SBK 53260

recorded on 30 september 1975 in the academy of music
philadelphia   lp: victor ARL1 1869
orchestra   cd: 74321 212922

symphony no 6
recorded on 15 january 1950 in the town hall
philadelphia   78: columbia M 950
orchestra   lp: columbia ML 4328

recorded on 2 november 1961 in the town hall
philadelphia   lp: columbia ML 5889/MS 6489/
orchestra   Y 32885/BRG 72149/
                        SBRG 72149

symphony no 7
recorded on 26 april 1953 in the town hall
philadelphia   lp: columbia ML 4683/philips
orchestra   ABR 4034/A01614R

piano concerto no 2
recorded on 14-15 may 1974 in the academy of music
philadelphia   lp: victor ARL1 0751
orchestra   cd: disco archivia 743
joselson

piano concerto no 4
recorded on 30 march 1958 in the town hall
philadelphia   lp: columbia ML 5805/MS 6405/
orchestra   BRG 72109/SBRG 72109
serkin   cd: MPK 46452

prokofiev/**violin concerto no 1**
recorded on 20 january 1963 in the town hall
philadelphia   lp: columbia ML 6035/MS 6635/
orchestra   BRG 72269/SBRG 72269
stern   cd: SBK 38525/SX9K 67194

violin concerto no 2
recorded on 30 january 1963 in the town hall
philadelphia   lp: columbia ML 6035/MS 6635/
orchestra   BRG 72269/SBRG 72269
stern   cd: SBK 38525/SX9K 67194

lieutenant kije, suite from the incidental music
recorded on 9 december 1962 in the town hall
philadelphia   lp: columbia MS 6545/MS 7528/
orchestra   M 31812/BRG 72185/
     SBRG 72185

recorded on 28-29 october 1974 in the academy of music
philadelphia   lp: victor ARL1 1325
orchestra

the love of three oranges, suite from the opera
recorded on 24 february 1963 in the town hall
philadelphia   lp: columbia ML 5945/MS 6545/
orchestra   M 31812/BRG 72185/
     SBRG 72185
     cd: SBK 53261

march/the love of three oranges
recorded on 15 june 1972 in the academy of music
philadelphia   lp: victor AGL1 4298
orchestra

scythian suite
recorded on 22 november 1947 in the academy of music
philadelphia   78: columbia M 827
orchestra   lp: columbia ML 4142

recorded in 1973 at a concert in the academy of music
philadelphia   cd: disco archivia 740/749
orchestra

prokofiev/**alexander nevsky**
recorded on 21 may 1945 in the academy of music
philadelphia 78: columbia M 580/canadian
orchestra columbia D 141/english columbia
westminster choir LX 977-981
tourel lp: columbia ML 4247

recorded on 24 october 1975 in the academy of music
philadelphia lp: victor ARL1 1151/RL 11151
orchestra *recording completed on 26 february 1976*
mendelssohn club
choir
allen

peter and the wolf
recorded on 17 march 1957 in the town hall
philadelphia lp: columbia ML 5183/MS 6405/
orchestra Y 34616/philips ABL 3193/
ritchard, narrator A01325L/835 509AY
cd: SBK 62638

recorded on 8 october 1975 in the academy of music
philadelphia lp: victor ARL1 2743
orchestra cd: RD 82743/GD 60878
bowie, narrator

GIACOMO PUCCINI (1858-1924)
che gelida manina/la boheme
recorded on 8 december 1940 at a ford sunday evening concert in the masonic temple detroit
detroit symphony lp: legendary recordings LR 138
björling

o soave fanciulla/la boheme
recorded on 28 august 1947 at a concert in the hollywood bowl
los angeles lp: ed smith records EJS 457
philharmonic cd: melodram MEL 16215/
yeend, lanza andromeda ANDRCD 5133
also issued on cd by gala

puccini/**madama butterfly**
recorded on 3 september 1948 at a concert in the hollywood bowl
los angeles　　　　　　cd: eklipse EKRCD 16/video
philharmonic　　　　　artists international VAI 1220
and chorus
steber, carre,
peerce, bonelli

vieni la sera/madama butterfly
recorded on 28 august 1947 at a concert in the hollywood bowl
los angeles　　　　　　lp: ed smith records EJS 457
philharmonic　　　　　cd: melodram MEL 16215/
yeend, lanza　　　　　andromeda ANDRCD 5133
　　　　　　　　　　　also issued on cd by gala

humming chorus/madama butterfly
recorded on 10 june 1967 in the salt lake tabernacle
philadelphia　　　　　lp: columbia MS 7061
orchestra
mormon tabernacle
choir

recondita armonia/tosca
recorded on 12 december 1937 at a ford sunday evening concert in the masonic temple detroit
detroit symphony　　　lp: ed smith records EJS 425
masini

e lucevan le stelle/tosca
recorded on 12 december 1937 at a ford sunday evening concert in the masonic temple detroit
detroit symphony　　　lp: ed smith records EJS 425
masini

recorded on 28 august 1947 at a concert in the hollywood bowl
los angeles　　　　　　lp: ed smith records EJS 457
philharmonic　　　　　cd: melodram MEL 16215/
lanza　　　　　　　　andromeda ANDRCD 5133
　　　　　　　　　　　also issued on cd by gala

HENRY PURCELL (1659-1695)
dido and aeneas, suite from the opera
recorded on 9 august 1939 in the academy of music
philadelphia   78: victor M 647/hmv DB 3975-3976/
orchestra   australian hmv ED 51-52

funeral march for queen mary, arrangement
recorded on 11 january 1972 in the academy of music
philadelphia   lp: victor LSC 3268
orchestra

SERGEI RACHMANINOV (1873-1943)
symphony no 1
recorded on 28 february 1966 in the town hall
philadelphia   lp: columbia MS 6986/D3S 813/
orchestra   BRG 72571/SBRG 72571/77345
         cd: SB2K 63257

symphony no 2
recorded between 18-22 january 1934 in minneapolis
minneapolis   78: victor M 239/hmv DB 2487-2492
symphony

recorded on 11 february 1951 in the town hall
philadelphia   lp: columbia ML 4433
orchestra

recorded on 19 april 1959 in the town hall
philadelphia   lp: columbia ML 5436/MS 6110/
orchestra   D3S 813/73042/77345
         cd: SBK 46335/SB2K 63257/
         88697 279872

recorded on 18-19 december 1973 in the academy of music
philadelphia   lp: victor ARL1 1150
orchestra   cd: 09026 60132/09026 68022/
         09026 68788/emi 575 1272
         this recording comprises the uncut version
         of the symphony

rachmaninov/**symphony no 3**
recorded on 7 november 1954 in the town hall
philadelphia   lp: columbia ML 4961/philips
orchestra   ABL 3111/A01156L

recorded on 20 december 1967 in the town hall
philadelphia   lp: columbia MS 7081/D3S 813/
orchestra   77345
                      cd: SB2K 63257

piano concerto no 1
recorded on 4 december 1939 in the academy of music
philadelphia   78: victor M 865/hmv DB 5706-5708
orchestra   lp: victor LCT 1118/LM 6123/
rachmaninov   MVC 903/TVM9 7018/hmv
                      CSLP 509
                      cd: RD 86659/09026 616582/naxos
                      811 0602/membran 205 235/221 361/
                      231 058/classica d'oro 3002
                      recording completed on 24 february 1940

recorded on 24 february 1963 in the town hall
philadelphia   lp: columbia ML 5917/MS 6517/
orchestra   BRG 72156/SBRG 72156/61310
entremont   cd: SBK 46541

piano concerto no 2
recorded on 8 april 1956 in the town hall
philadelphia   lp: columbia ML 5103/philips
orchestra   SBR 6233/S06677R
istomin

recorded on 24 november 1971 in the academy of music
philadelphia   lp: victor ARL1 0031/ARD1 0031/
orchestra   CRL7 0725/RL 43195
rubinstein   cd: 09026 630602

rachmaninov/**piano concerto no 3**
recorded on 4 december 1939 in the academy of music
philadelphia 78: victor M 710/hmv DB 5707-5713/
orchestra australian hmv ED 201-205
rachmaninov lp: victor LM 6123/MCV 903/
TVM9 7018
cd: RD 85997/09026 616582/
aura AUR 192/naxos 811 0601/
membran 205 235/221 361/231 058/
classica d'oro 3002
recording completed on 24 february 1940

recorded on 27 december 1966 at a concert in philharmonic hall new york
philadelphia lp: melodiya M10 38727-38728
orchestra
gilels

recorded on 15 february 1975 in the academy of music
philadelphia lp: victor ARL1 1324
orchestra
ashkenazy

recorded on 8 january 1978 in carnegie hall new york
new york lp: victor ARL1 2633/CRL1 2633/
philharmonic cd: GD 87754/RD 82633/516 3335/
horowitz 09026 615642/09026 636812
recording completed on 11 january 1978

piano concerto no 4
recorded on 20 december 1941 in the academy of music
philadelphia 78: victor M 972/hmv DB 6284-6287
orchestra lp: victor LM 6123/MCV 903/
rachmaninov TVM9 7018
cd: RD 86659/09026 616582/
naxos 811 0602/membran 221 361/
222 343/classica d'oro 3002

recorded on 2 november 1961 in the town hall
philadelphia lp: columbia ML 5917/MS 6517/
orchestra BRG 72156/SBRG 72156/61310
entremont cd: SBK 46541

rachmaninov/**rhapsody on a theme of paganini**
recorded on 1 february 1958 in the town hall
philadelphia   lp: columbia ML 5282/MS 6016/
orchestra   D3S 715/M 31801/61040/
entremont   philips ABL 3250/SABL 123/
                      A01375L/835 503AY
                      cd: SBK 46541

recorded on 7 may 1970 in the academy of music
philadelphia   lp: victor LSC 3179/LSC 3306/
orchestra   CRL3 2282
cliburn   cd: RD 87945

symphonic dances
recorded on 19 march 1960 in the town hall
philadelphia   lp: columbia ML 5605/MS 6205/
orchestra   61347
                      cd: SBK 48279

the isle of the dead
recorded on 7 november 1954 in the town hall
philadelphia   lp: columbia ML 5043/philips
orchestra   ABL 3156/A01267L

recorded on 22 april 1977 at a concert in the academy of music
philadelphia   cd: philadelphia orchestra
orchestra   centennial collection/disco
                      archivia 746

vocalise for orchestra
recorded on 28 november 1954 in the town hall
philadelphia   lp: columbia ML 4961/philips
orchestra   ABL 3111/A01156L

recorded on 18 october 1967 in the town hall
philadelphia   lp: columbia MS 7081/MS 7103/
orchestra   D3S 813/77345
                      cd: SB2K 63257/88697 279872

rachmaninov/**piano preludes op 23 no 5 and op 32 no 5, arranged for orchestra by cailliet**
recorded on 2 april 1950 in the town hall
philadelphia	lp: columbia ML 2158
orchestra

the bells
recorded on 24 march 1973 in the academy of music
philadelphia	lp: victor ARL1 0193
orchestra
temple university
choir

the bells/version sung in english
recorded on 28 february 1954 in the town hall
philadelphia	lp: columbia ML 5043/philips
orchestra	ABL 3156/A01267L
temple university
choir
yeend, lloyd

three russian songs
recorded on 12 april 1973 in the academy of music
philadelphia	lp: victor ARL1 0193
orchestra
temple university
choir

JEAN PHILIPPE RAMEAU (1683-1764)
la poule/pieces de clavecin, arrangement
recorded on 1 may 1965 in the town hall
philadelphia	lp: columbia
orchestra

MAURICE RAVEL (1875-1937)
piano concerto in g
recorded on 14 december 1960 in the town hall
philadelphia orchestra entremont
lp: columbia ML 6029/MS 6629/
BRG 72239/SBRG 72239/73070
cd: SBK 46338

piano concerto for the left hand
recorded on 22 january 1947 in the academy of music
philadelphia orchestra casadesus
78: columbia M 288/english columbia LX 1088-1089/italian columbia GQX 11461-11462
lp: columbia ML 4075/english columbia 33C 1023/french columbia FC 1032/ italian columbia QC 5011
cd: MH2K 63316/503 3892/philips 456 7392/membran 205 235/ 222 343/231 058

recorded on 12 may 1964 in the manhattan centre new york city
philadelphia orchestra casadesus
lp: columbia ML 5674/MS 6274/ BRG 72008/SBRG 72008
cd: SBK 64350

tzigane pour violon et orchestre
recorded on 13 april 1957 in the town hall
philadelphia orchestra stern
lp: columbia ML 5208
cd: SX9K 67194

alborada del gracioso
recorded on 23 january 1934 in minneapolis
minneapolis symphony
78: victor 8552/hmv DB 2499

recorded on 5 january 1958 in the town hall
philadelphia orchestra
lp: columbia ML 5569/ML 5857/ MS 6169/MS 6457/MG 31190/ Y 33926
cd: SBK 48163

ravel/**bolero**
recorded on 22 march 1953 in the town hall
philadelphia   45: philips ABE 10036/409 044AE
orchestra   lp: columbia ML 4983/ML 5257
                           philips SBR 6201/S06604R

recorded on 24 june 1957 at a concert in the sendesaal cologne
sinfonieorchester   unpublished radio broadcast
des westdeutschen
rundfunks

recorded on 19 march 1960 in the town hall
philadelphia   lp: columbia MS 6169/MS 6478/
orchestra   MS 7673/MGP 7/Y 33926
                           cd: SBK 48163

recorded on 16-17 may 1973 in the academy of music
philadelphia   lp: victor LSC 3302/ARL1 0451/
orchestra   CRL3 2182

daphnis et chloe, first ballet suite
recorded on 2 april 1950 in the town hall
philadelphia   78: columbia M 940
orchestra   lp: columbia ML 4316/philips
                           GBL 5508/G03509L

daphnis et chloe, second ballet suite
recorded on 8 january 1939 in the academy of music
philadelphia   78: victor M 667/hmv DB 5734-5735/
orchestra   australian hmv ED 109-110

recorded on 10 may 1949 in the town hall
philadelphia   78: columbia M 940
orchestra   lp: columbia ML 4316/philips
                           GBL 5508/G03509L

recorded on 5 september 1955 at a concert in the sendesaal cologne
sinfonieorchester   unpublished radio broadcast
des westdeutschen
rundfunks

ravel/daphnis et chloe/second ballet suite/concluded
recorded on 18 december 1955 in the town hall
philadelphia   lp: columbia ML 5112
orchestra

recorded on 21 june 1958 at a concert in cologne
philadelphia   unpublished radio broadcast
orchestra

recorded on 19 april 1959 in the town hall
philadelphia   lp: columbia ML 5397/MS 6077
orchestra   cd: SBK 47664

recorded on 22 june 1963 at a concert in the kurzaal scheveningen
residentie   unpublished radio broadcast
orkest

recorded on 13 january 1971 in the academy of music
philadelphia   lp: victor ARL1 0029/ARD1 0029/
orchestra   CRL3 2182

pavane pour une infante defunte
recorded on 19 december 1954 in the town hall
philadelphia   lp: columbia ML 4983
orchestra

recorded on 3 february 1963 in the town hall
philadelphia   lp: columbia ML 5878/ML 5975/
orchestra   MS 6478/MS 6575/MS 7512

recorded on 28 september 1971 in the academy of music
philadelphia   lp: victor LSC 3284/CRL3 2182
orchestra   cd: 09026 612112

ravel/**rapsodie espagnole**
recorded on 24 january 1946 in the academy of music
philadelphia 78: columbia M 342
orchestra lp: columbia ML 4306/english
columbia 33C 1023/french columbia
FC 1032/italian columbia QC 5011

recorded on 19 march 1950 in the town hall
philadelphia columbia unpublished
orchestra

recorded on 24 february 1963 in the town hall
philadelphia lp: columbia MS 6697
orchestra cd: SBK 38917/SBK 48163

le tombeau de couperin
recorded on 16 november 1958 in the town hall
philadelphia lp: columbia ML 5569/MS 6169/
orchestra Y 33926
cd: SBK 48163

la valse, poeme choreographique
recorded on 22 march 1953 in the town hall
philadelphia lp: columbia ML 4983/philips
orchestra SBR 6201/S06604R

recorded on 5 june 1959 at a concert in the herkulessaal munich
sinfonieorchester cd: orfeo C199 891B
des bayerischen
rundfunks

recorded on 3 february 1963 in the town hall
philadelphia lp: columbia ML 5878/MS 6478/
orchestra MS 7512/M2S 738
cd: SBK 63056

recorded on 30 september 1971 in the academy of music
philadelphia lp: victor ARL2 3384/CRL3 2182
orchestra cd: disco archivia 741

MAX REGER (1873-1916)
piano concerto
recorded on 30 march 1959 in the town hall
philadelphia lp: columbia ML 5635/MS 6235/
orchestra 61711
serkin cd: MPK 46452

OTTORINO RESPIGHI (1879-1936)
aria di corte/antiche danze ed arie
recorded on 12 january 1946 in the academy of music
philadelphia 78: columbia 12973D
orchestra *recording completed on 18 april 1946*

feste romane
recorded on 18 april 1946 in the academy of music
philadelphia 78: columbia M 707
orchestra lp: columbia ML 4142

recorded on 20 november 1960 in the academy of music
philadelphia lp: columbia ML 5675/MS 6275/
orchestra MS 6587/MG 32308/BRG 72026/
BRG 72154/SBRG 72026/
SBRG 72154/61124
cd: SBK 48267/88697 279872

recorded on 14 may 1974 in the academy of music
philadelphia lp: victor ARL1 1407
orchestra cd: 74321 242082

respighi/**fontane di roma**
recorded on 14 april 1957 in the broadwood hotel
philadelphia   lp: columbia ML 5279/MS 6001/
orchestra   MS 6587/philips A01394L/
                         SABL 113/835 506AY
                         cd: 88697 279872

recorded on 27 february 1968 in the town hall
philadelphia   lp: columbia MG 32308/M 30829/
orchestra   BRG 72154/SBRG 72154/61124
                         cd: SBK 48267

recorded on 4 december 1974 in the academy of music
philadelphia   lp: victor ARL1 1407
orchestra   cd: 74321 242082/disco
                         archivia 749

pini di roma
recorded on 24 january 1946 in the academy of music
philadelphia   78: columbia M 616/swiss columbia
orchestra   LZX 227-229
                         lp: columbia ML 4020

recorded on 28 march 1958 in the broadwood hotel
philadelphia   lp: columbia ML 5279/MS 6001/
orchestra   MS 6587/philips A01394L/
                         SABL 113/835 506AY
                         cd: 88697 279872

recorded on 6 march 1968 in the town hall
philadelphia   lp: columbia MPG 7/BRG 72154/
orchestra   SBRG 72154/78207/61124
                         cd: SBK 48267

recorded between 23-26 april 1973 in the academy of music
philadelphia   lp: victor ARL1 1407
orchestra   cd: 74321 242082

gli uccelli
recorded on 26 january 1966 in the town hall
philadelphia   lp: columbia MS 7242/MG 32308/
orchestra   61082
                         cd: SBK 60311

respighi/**vetrate di chiesa**
recorded on 17 february 1964 in the town hall
philadelphia   lp: columbia MS 7242/MG 32208/
orchestra   61082
                        cd: SBK 60311

FEDERICO RICCI (1809-1877)
io non sono/crispino e la comare
recorded on 24 january 1970 at a concert in the academy of music
philadelphia   lp: private edition MMR 566
orchestra
sutherland

KNUDAAGE RIJSAGER (1897-1974)
concertino for trumpet and orchestra
recorded on 5 april 1962 in the town hall
philadelphia   lp: columbia ML 6191/MS 6791
orchestra
johnson

NIKOLAI RIMSKY-KORSAKOV (1844-1908)
russian easter festival overture
recorded on 13 october 1946 in the academy of music
philadelphia   78: columbia M 276/australian
orchestra   columbia LOX 670-671
                        lp: columbia ML 2035/english
                        columbia 33C 1025/french columbia
                        FC 1007/italian columbia QC 5015

recorded on 1 april 1959 in the broadwood hotel
philadelphia   lp: columbia ML 5414/ML 6275/
orchestra   MS 6092/MS 6875/BRG 72455/
                        SBRG 72455/61586/philips
                        ABL 3306/SABL 110/A01440L/
                        835 539AY
                        cd: SBK 46537

rimsky-korsakov/**capriccio espagnol**
recorded on 1 november 1953 in the town hall
philadelphia   lp: columbia ML 4856/CL 707
orchestra

recorded on 17 february 1965 in the town hall
philadelphia   lp: columbia MS 6917/MG 30947/
orchestra   M 31850/BRG 72527/
                         SBRG 72527/61586
                         cd: SBK 46537

scheherazade, symphonic suite
recorded on 31 october-1 november 1947 in the academy of music
philadelphia   78: columbia M 772
orchestra   lp: columbia ML 4089

recorded on 23 december 1953 in the town hall
philadelphia   lp: columbia ML 4888/CL 850/
orchestra   philips NBL 5013/GBL 5555/
                         N02112L/G03551L

recorded on 11 february 1962 in the town hall
philadelphia   lp: columbia ML 5765/MS 6365/
orchestra   BRG 72075/SBRG 72075/61044
                         cd: SBK 46537/88697 279872

recorded on 29 february 1972 in the academy of music
philadelphia   lp: victor ARL1 0028/ARD1 0028
orchestra   cd: 74321 178992

recorded on 27 october 1974 at a concert in the academy of music
philadelphia   lp: victor DPL1 0094
orchestra   cd: disco archivia 743

televised on 30 june-1 july 1978 at concerts in the academy of music
philadelphia   dvd video: euroarts 207 2278
orchestra

rimsky-korsakov/**le coq d'or, suite from the opera**
recorded on 1 march 1959 in the town hall
philadelphia　　　　　　lp: columbia ML 5414/MS 6092/
orchestra　　　　　　　　philips ABL 3306/SABL 110/
　　　　　　　　　　　　　A01440L/835 539AY
　　　　　　　　　　　　cd: SBK 62647

bridal procession/le coq d'or
recorded betweeen 1-3 may 1965 in the town hall
philadelphia　　　　　　lp: columbia MS 6917/BRG 72527/
orchestra　　　　　　　　SBRG 72527/61586

recorded on 12 april 1973 in the academy of music
philadelphia　　　　　　lp: victor AGL1 4298
orchestea　　　　　　　cd: 09026 612092

polonaise/christmas eve
recorded on 13 april 1966 in the town hall
philadelphia　　　　　　lp: columbia
orchestra

procession of the nobles/mlada
recorded on 15 december 1966 in the town hall
philadelphia　　　　　　lp: columbia MS 6979/61292
orchestra

dance of the tumblers/the snow maiden
recorded on 1 november 1958 in the town hall
philadelphia　　　　　　45: columbia A 1828
orchestra　　　　　　　　lp: columbia ML 4856/CL 707

recorded on 23 march 1965 in the town hall
philadelphia　　　　　　lp: columbia M2X 786
orchestra

rimsky-korsakov/**farewell of the tsar/the tale of tsar sultan**
recorded on 7 december 1964 in the town hall
philadelphia   lp: columbia MS 6979/61292
orchestra

flight of the bumble bee/the tale of tsar sultan
recorded on 1 november 1953 in the town hall
philadelphia   45: columbia A 1828
orchestra   lp: columbia ML 4856/CL 707

recorded on 1 may 1965 in the town hall
philaderlphia   lp: columbia MS 6993/MS 7146
orchestra

recorded on 17 may 1973 in the academy of music
philadelphia   lp: victor
orchestra

glory glory glory!/communion hymn
recorded on 3 november 1958 in the broadwood hotel
philadelphia   lp: columbia MS 6058/philips
orchestra   ABL 3304/A01440L
mormon tabernacle
choir

LEROY ROBERTSON (1898-1971)
the lord's prayer; come ye saints!
recorded on 3 november 1958 in the broadwood hotel
philadelphia   lp: columbia MS 6068/MS 6679/
orchestra   philips A01439L
mormon tabernacle
choir

**old things are done away; how beautiful upon the mountain/
oratorio from the book of mormon**
recorded on 22 may 1962 in the salt lake tabernacle
philadelphia   lp: columbia MS 6367/MS 6679
orchestra
mormon tabernacle
choir

JOAQUIN RODRIGO (1901-1999)
concierto de aranjuez
recorded on 14 december 1965 in the town hall
philadelphia orchestra williams
lp: columbia MS 6834/M3X 31508/ BRG 72439/SBRG 72439/ 77334/77355
cd: SBK 61716

GIOACHINO ROSSINI (1792-1868)
la boutique fantasque, ballet arranged by respighi
recorded on 13 january 1965 in the town hall
philadelphia orchestra
lp: columbia M 30463/61242
cd: SBK 46360

una voce poco fa/il barbiere di siviglia
recorded in 1975 at a concert in the academy of music
philadelphia orchestra verrett
cd: bella voce BLV 107 009

guglielmo tell, overture
recorded on 9 may 1954 in the town hall
philadelphia orchestra
lp: columbia ML 5206/philips ABL 3215/GBL 5626/ A01356L/G03604L

recorded on 27 february 1968 in the town hall
philadelphia orchestra
lp: columbia M 31640/MG 35188/ BRG 72300/SBRG 72300/78207
cd: SBK 62653

recorded on 16 may 1973 in the academy of music
philadelphia orchestra
lp: victor AGL1 3657

rossini/**passo a tre/guglielmo tell**
recorded on 7 december 1964 in the town hall
philadelphia   lp: columbia
orchestra

la danza
recorded on 8 december 1940 at a ford sunday evening concert in the masonic temple detroit
detroit   cd: video artists international
symphony   VAI 1189
björling

CLAUDE-JOSEPH ROUGET DE LISLE (1760-1836)
la marseillaise
recorded on 21 may 1962 in the salt lake tabernacle
philadelphia   lp: columbia MS 6419
orchestra
mormon tabernacle
choir

ALBERT ROUSSEL (1869-1937)
bacchus et ariane, second concert suite from the ballet
recorded on 5 june 1959 at a concert in the herkulessaal munich
sinfonieorchester   cd: orfeo C199 891B
des bayerischen
rundfunks

recorded on 1 may 1960 in the town hall
philadelphia   lp: columbia ML 5667/MS 6267/
orchestra   BRG 72025/SBRG 72025
                           cd: SBK 62644

CAMILLE SAINT-SAENS (1835-1921)
symphony no 3 "organ"
recorded on 17 october 1956 in the town hall
philadelphia orchestra power biggs	lp: columbia ML 5212

recorded on 7 october 1962 in the town hall
philadelphia orchestra power biggs	lp: columbia ML 5869/MS 6469/ BRG 72132/SBRG 72132 cd: SBK 47655

recorded on 5 december 1973 in the academy of music
philadelphia orchestra fox	lp: victor AGL1 5269 cd: disco archivia 751

recorded on 6 february 1980 in the academy of music
philadelphia orchestra murray	cd: telarc CD 80051/DG 10051

piano concerto no 2
recorded on 12 may 1964 in the town hall
philadelphia orchestra entremont	lp: columbia ML 6178/MS 6778/ BRG 72417/SBRG 72417 cd: SBK 48276

recorded on 2 january 1969 in the academy of music
philadelphia orchestra rubinstein	lp: victor LSC 3165/SB 6861/ ARL1 0484/ARD1 0484/ AGL1 3711 cd: RD 85666/09026 618632

piano concerto no 4
recorded in 1952 at a concert in the titania palast berlin
rias-orchester casadesus	cd: audite 95589

recorded on 5 february 1961 in the town hall
philadelphia orchestra entremont	lp: columbia ML 6178/MS 6778/ BRG 72417/SBRG 72417 cd: SBK 48276

saint-saens/**cello concerto no 1**
recorded on 27 march 1967 in the town hall
philadelphia lp: columbia M 30113
orchestra cd: SBK 48276
rose

introduction and rondo capriccioso for violin and orchestra
recorded on 5 november 1950 in the town hall
philadelphia lp: columbia ML 2194/ML 5253/
orchestra english columbia 33C 1029/
francescatti french columbia FC 1017/
 philips SBL 5234/S04643L

recorded on 13 april 1957 in the town hall
philadelphia lp: columbia ML 5208
orchestra cd: SX9K 67194
stern

recorded on 12 december 1980 in the academy of music
philadelphia lp: victor ARC1 4548/ATC1 3972
orchestra cd: RD 84548
jenson

morceau de concert pour cor et orchestre
recorded on 4 december 1961 in the town hall
philadelphia lp: columbia ML 6191/MS 6791
orchestra
jones

danse macabre
recorded on 12 april 1959 in the broadwood hotel
philadelphia lp: columbia ML 5461/ML 5857/
orchestra MS 6241/MS 6457/BPG 62153/
 SBPG 62153
 cd: SBK 47655

recorded on 30 september 1971 in the academy of music
philadelphia lp: victor ARD1 0002/CRL3 0985/
orchestra CRL3 2182
 cd: 09026 612112/disco archivia 741

saint-saens/**marche militaire francaise/suite algerienne**
recorded on 3 february 1963 in the town hall
philadelphia　　　　　lp: columbia MS 6979/M2X 786/
orchestra　　　　　　61292
　　　　　　　　　　cd: SBK 47655

le cygne/le carnaval des animaux
recorded on 18 june 1966 in the town hall
philadelphia　　　　　lp: columbia
orchestra

bacchanale/samson et dalila
recorded on 23 march 1964 in the town hall
philadelphia　　　　　lp: columbia MS 7267
orchestra　　　　　　cd: SBK 47655

recorded on 12 june 1972 in the academy of music
philadelphia　　　　　lp: victor
orchestra

PABLO DE SARASATE (1844-1908)
introduction et tarantelle pour violon et orchestre
recorded on 4 december 1961 in the town hall
philadelphia　　　　　lp: columbia ML 6191/MS 6791
orchestra
brusilow

FLORENT SCHMITT (1870-1958)
psalm 47
recorded in 1976 at a concert in the academy of music
philadelphia　　　　　cd: disco archivia 748
orchestra
and chorus
bouleyn

ARNOLD SCHOENBERG (1874-1951)
orchestral variations
recorded on 23 october 1963 in the town hall
philadelphia orchestra
lp: columbia MS 7041/M2S 767
cd: russ oppenheim ROCD 0059

verklärte nacht/ orchestral version
recorded between 16-24 january 1934 in minneapolis
minneapolis symphony
78: victor M 207/hmv DB 2439-2442
cd: dante LYS 057/membran 205 235/231 058
recorded on 19 march 1950 in the academy of music
philadelphia orchestra
78: columbia M 939
lp: columbia ML 4316
cd: philadelphia orchestra centennial collection

FRANZ ANTON SCHUBERT (1808-1878)
the bee, orchestral arrangement of the song
recorded on 7 december 1966 in the town hall
philadelphia orchestra
lp: columbia MS 7146
cd: russ oppenheim ROCD 0069

FRANZ SCHUBERT (1797-1828)
symphony no 4 "tragic"
recorded on 8 april 1962 in the town hall
philadelphia orchestra
lp: columbia M 31635
cd: SBK 60267

symphony no 8 "unfinished"
recorded on 25 november 1956 in the town hall
philadelphia orchestra
lp: columbia ML 5221/philips ABL 3230/A01379L/G03500L
recorded on 12 november 1967 at a concert in the concertgebouw amsterdam
concertgebouw orkest
cd: q-disc 97019/RCO 05001
recorded on 27 may 1968 in the academy of music
philadelphia orchestra
lp: victor LSC 3056

symphony no 9 "great"
recorded on 28 december 1966 in the town hall
philadelphia orchestra
lp: columbia MS 7272

schubert/**wanderer fantasy, arranged by liszt for piano and orchestra**
recorded on 31 october 1981 in the academy of music
philadelphia   lp: angel 37888/emi ASD 4258/
orchestra   1C065 43199/2C069 43199/
katsaris   3C065 43199
                       cd: piano P21 022A

marche militaire, orchestral arrangement
recorded on 23-24 february 1963 in the town hall
philadelphia   lp: columbia ML 5874/MS 6474
orchestra

recorded on 16 june 1972 in the academy of music
philadelphia   lp: victor AGL1 4298
orchestra

ständchen, orchestral arrangement
recorded on 28 february 1966 in the town hall
philadelphia   lp: columbia MS 7103
orchestra

an die musik, choral arrangement
recorded on 3 november 1958 in the broadwood hotel
philadelphia   lp: columbia MS 6058/philips
orchestra   ABL 3304/A01441L
mormon tabernacle
choir

schubert/**ave maria, choral arrangement**
recorded on 3 november 1958 in the broadwood hotel
philadelphia   lp: columbia MS 6058/philips
orchestra   ABL 3304/A01441L
mormon tabernacle
choir

recorded on 29 march 1962 in the town hall
philadelphia   lp: columbia MS 6993
orchestra
temple university
choir

recorded on 21 may 1962 in the salt lake tabernacle
philadelphia   lp: columbia MS 6367
orchestra
mormon tabernacle
choir

erlkönig/version with orchestra
recorded on 24 september 1939 at a ford sunday evening concert in the masonic temple detroit
detroit symphony   lp: ed smith records UORC 370
tibbett

psalm 23/the lord is my shepherd
recorded on 21 may 1962 in the salt lake tabernacle
philadelphia   lp: columbia MS 6679
orchestra
mormon tabernacle
choir

der wanderer/version with orchestra
recorded on 24 september 1939 at a ford sunday evening concert in the masonic temple detroit
detroit symphony   lp: ed smith records UORC 370
tibbett

WILLIAM SCHUMAN (1910-1992)
symphony no 3
recorded on 11 march 1951 in the town hall
philadelphia orchestra   lp: columbia ML 4413

symphony no 6
recorded on 15 november 1953 in the town hall
philadelphia orchestra
lp: columbia ML 4992
cd: american archives ALB 256

symphony no 9 "the ardentine coves"
recorded on 27 may 1969 in the academy of music
philadelphia orchestra   lp: victor LSC 3212

credendum
recorded on 11 march 1956 in the town hall
philadelphia orchestra
lp: columbia ML 5185/contemporary recordings CRISD 308
cd: american archives ALB 276

new england tryptich
recorded on 28 october 1968 in the academy of music
philadelphia orchestra   lp: victor LSC 3060/SB 6798

ROBERT SCHUMANN (1810-1856)
symphony no 2
recorded on 12 october 1937 in the academy of music
philadelphia orchestra   78: victor M 448

symphony no 4
recorded on 22 january 1934 in minneapolis
minneapolis symphony   78: victor M 201/hmv DB 2231-2233

schumann/**cello concerto**
recorded on 28-29 may 1953 in the eglise saint pierre prades
prades festival   lp: columbia ML 4926/77363/
orchestra   philips A01369L/ABR 4035/
casals   A01617R/G05621R
                           cd: SMK 58993
                           also published on cd by pearl and music and arts

piano concerto
recorded on 21 january 1946 in the academy of music
philadelphia   78: columbia M 734
orchestra   lp: columbia ML 4041
serkin

recorded on 11 march 1956 in the broadwood hotel
philadelphia   lp: columbia ML 5168/philips fontana
orchestra   CFL 1002/EFR 2000/699 000CL/
serkin   664 001ER
                           cd: SBK 46543/SBK 89901/
                           SM3K 47269
                           recording completed on 19 december 1956

recorded on 17 march 1964 in the town hall
philadelphia   lp: columbia MS 6688/MS 7185/
orchestra   D3S 741/73145
serkin   cd: SBK 37256

introduction and allegro appassionato for piano and orchestra
recorded on 16 march 1964 in the town hall
philadelphia   lp: columbia MS 6688/73145
orchestra   cd: SBK 46543/SBK 48166/
serkin   SBK 89901

konzertstück for piano and orchestra
recorded on 17 march 1964 in the town hall
philadelphia   lp: columbia MS 7183/MS 7423/
orchestra   M 32042/73145
serkin   cd: SBK 89901

schumann/**träumerei, orchestral arrangement**
recorded on 19 january 1934 in minneapolis
minneapolis   78: victor M211/hmv DB 2353
symphony
recorded on 14 february 1966 in the town hall
philadelphia   lp: columbia MS 6883/MS 7267
orchestra

ALEXANDER SCRIABIN (1872-1915)
symphony no 4 "poeme de l'extase"
recorded on 3 march 1971 in the academy of music
philadelphia   lp: victor LSC 3214/CRL3 2026/
orchestra   SB 6854
         cd: 09026 380612

symphony no 5 "prometheus"
recorded on 21 april 1971 in the academy of music
philadelphia   lp: victor LSC 3214/SB 6854
orchestra   cd: 09026 380612

DAVID SHAW (born 1814)
columbia gem of the ocean
recorded on 21 may 1962 in the salt lake tabernacle
philadelphia   lp: columbia MS 6419
orchestra   cd: MDK 48295
mormon tabernacle
choir

DIMITRI SHOSTAKOVICH (1906-1975)
symphony no 1
recorded on 8 november 1959 in the broadwood hotel
philadelphia   lp: columbia ML 5452/MS 6124/
orchestra   BRG 72081/SBRG 72081/
         philips ABL 3315/SABL 165/
         A01442L/835 549AY
         cd: SBK 62642/88697 279872

symphony no 4
recorded on 17 february 1963 in the town hall
philadelphia   lp: columbia ML 5859/MS 6459/
orchestra   BRG 72129/SBRG 72129
         cd: SB2K 62409

shostakovich/**symphony no 5**
recorded on 1 april 1965 in the town hall
philadelphia　　　　　lp: columbia MS 7279/BRG 72811/
orchestra　　　　　　SBRG 72811/61643
　　　　　　　　　　cd: SBK 53261

recorded on 5 february 1975 in the academy of music
philadelphia　　　　　lp: victor ARL1 1149/ARD1 1149/
orchestra　　　　　　AGL1 3886

symphony no 6
recorded on 15 may 1969 at a conert in the academy of music
philadelphia　　　　　cd: philadelphia orchestra
orchestra　　　　　　centennial collection

recorded in 1971 at a concert in the academy of music
philadelphia　　　　　cd: disco archivia 724
orchestra

symphony no 10
recorded between 10-18 april 1968 in the town hall
philadelphia　　　　　lp: columbia M 30295/BRG 72886/
orchestra　　　　　　SBRG 72886
　　　　　　　　　　cd: SB2K 62409

symphony no 13 "babi yar"
recorded between 21-23 january 1970 in the academy of music
philadelphia　　　　　lp: victor LSC 3162/SB 6830
orchestra　　　　　　cd: 09026 382982
mendelssohn club
choir
krause

symphony no 14
recorded between 4-6 january 1971 in the academy of music
philadelphia　　　　　lp: victor LSC 3206/LSB 5002
orchestra　　　　　　cd: 09026 382992
curtin, estes

symphony no 15
recorded on 4-5 october 1972 in the scottish rite cathedral philadelphia
philadelphia　　　　　lp: victor ARL1 0014/ARD1 0014
orchestra　　　　　　cd: 09026 635872

shostakovich/**piano concerto no 1**
recorded on 1 december 1945 at a concert in the academy of music
philadelphia   lp: discocorp MLG 71
orchestra   cd: arbiter ARBT 108
kapell

cello concerto no 1
recorded on 8 november 1959 in the broadwood hotel
philadelphia   lp: columbia ML 5452/MS 6124/
orchestra   BRG 72081/SBRG 72081/
rostropovich   philips ABL 3315/SABL 165/
     A01442L/835 549AY
     cd: MHK 63327/MPK 44850/
     88697 279872
recorded on 3 may 1982 in the academy of music
philadelphia   lp: columbia IM 37840/MK 37840
orchestra   cd: SMK 37840
ma

polka/the age of gold
recorded on 13 april 1966 in the town hall
philadelphia   lp: columbia MS 6958
orchestra

JEAN SIBELIUS (1865-1957)
symphony no 1
recorded on 16 january 1935 in minneapolis
minneapolis   78: victor M 290/hmv DB 2709-2713
symphony   cd: dante LYS 057
recorded on 25 october 1941 in the academy of music
philadelphia   78: victor M 881
orchestra   cd: biddulph WHL 062/membran
     205 235/222 343/231 058
recorded on 11 march 1962 in the town hall
philadelphia   lp: columbia ML 5795/MS 6395/
orchestra   BRG 72111/SBRG 72111
     cd: SBK 63060
recorded on 17 april 1978 in the academy of music
philadelphia   lp: victor AGL1 5272
orchestra   cd: 74321 242162/09026 381222

sibelius/**symphony no 2**
recorded on 1 november 1947 in the academy of music
philadelphia   78: columbia M 759/english
orchestra   columbia LX 1175-1179
                         lp: columbia ML 4131

recorded on 17 march 1957 in the town hall
philadelphia   lp: columbia ML 5207/MS 6024/
orchestra   Y 30046/philips ABL 3214/
                         A01353L
                         cd: SBK 53509

recorded on 26 april 1972 in the academy of music
philadelphia   lp: victor ARD1 0018/AGL1 3785
orchestra   cd: 74321 179042

symphony no 4
recorded on 28 november 1954 in the town hall
philadelphia   lp: columbia ML 5045/philips
orchestra   ABL 3084/A01226L

recorded on 4 march 1978 in the academy of music
philadelphia   lp: victor ARL1 3978
orchestra   cd: 09026 381242

symphony no 5
recorded on 19 december 1954 in the town hall
philadelphia   lp: columbia ML 5045/philips
orchestra   ABL 3084/A01226L

recorded on 18 november 1975 in the academy of music
philadelphia   lp: victor ARL1 2906
orchestra   cd: 74321 242162/
                         09026 381232

sibelius/**symphony no 7**
recorded on 1 may 1960 in the town hall
philadelphia lp: columbia ML 5675/MS 6275
orchestra cd: SBK 53509

recorded on 27 november 1969 at a concert in the concertgebouw amsterdam
concertgebouw cd: q-disc 97019/RCO 06004
orkest

recorded on 10 december 1975 in the academy of music
philadelphia lp: victor ARL1 4566
orchestra cd: 09026 381242

violin concerto
recorded between 21-24 december 1959 in the town hall
philadelphia lp: columbia ML 5492/MS 6157/
orchestra Y 30489/61041/60312/philips
oistrakh ABL 3366/SABL 195/A01484L/
 835 570AY/melodiya
 S10 22197-22198
 cd: MPK 44854/SBK 47659/
 SB3K 52516

recorded on 3-4 february 1968 in the town hall
philadelphia lp: columbia M 30068/72885
orchestra cd: SBK 66829
stern

recorded on 12 december 1980 in the academy of music
philadelphia lp: victor ARD1 4548/ATC1 3972
orchestra cd: RD 84548/74321 179042
jenson

sibelius/**en saga**
recorded on 11 march 1955 in the town hall
philadelphia   lp: columbia ML 5249/philips
orchestra   ABL 3227/A01355L
recorded on 20 january 1963 in the town hall
philadelphia   lp: coumbia MS 6732/BRG 72340/
orchestra   SBRG 72340
                             cd: SBK 48271
recorded in 1973 at a concert in the academy of music
philadelphia   cd: disco archivia 740
orchestra
recorded on 10 december 1975 in the academy of music
philadelphia   lp: victor ARL1 2906
orchestra

finlandia
recorded on 20 october 1940 in the academy of music
philadelphia   78: victor 17701/hmv DB 5842
orchestra
recorded on 2 april 1950 in the town hall
philadelphia   78: columbia 13131D
orchestra   lp: columbia ML 2158/
                             philips GL 5678
recorded on 1 november 1959 in the town hall
philadelphia   lp: columbia ML 5596/MS 6196/
orchestra   MS 6732/BRG 72340/SBRG
                             72340/BPG 62907/SBPG
                             62907/61286
recorded on 24 february 1968 in the town hall
philadelphia   lp: columbia MS 7527
orchestra   cd: SBK 48271
recorded on 22 march 1972 in the academy of music
philadelphia   lp: victor LSC 3302/CRL3 0985
orchestra
recorded on 27 october 1974 at a concert in the academy of music
philadelphia   lp: victor DPL1 0094
orchestra

sibelius/**finlandia, choral version**
recorded on 3 november 1958 in the broadwood hotel
philadelphia orchestra
mormon tabernacle choir
lp: columbia MS 6058/philips ABL 3304/A01441L
cd: disco archivia 745

karelia suite
recorded on 24 february 1968 in the town hall
philadelphia orchestra
lp: columbia MS 7674/M 30068/ BRG 72885/SBRG 72885
cd: SBK 48271

recorded on 10 december 1975 in the academy of music
philadelphia orchestra
lp: victor ARL1 2613/RL 12613
recording completed on 2 november 1977; this version includes karelia overture

lemminkainen and the maidens of sari/4 legends
recorded on 16 december 1951 in the town hall
philadelphia orchestra
lp: columbia ML 4672/ philips S06603R

recorded on 20 february 1978 in the old metropolitan opera house philadelphia
philadelphia orchestra
lp: angel 37537/emi ASD 3644/ 1C065 03468/2C069 03468/ 3C065 03468
cd: emi 565 1762

lemminkainen in tuonela/4 legends
recored on 20 february 1978 in the old metropolitan opera house philadelphia
philadelphia orchestra
lp: angel 37537/emi ASD 3644/ 1C065 03468/2C069 03468/ 3C065 03468
cd: emi 565 1762

sibelius/**lemminkainen's return/4 legends**
recorded on 20 october 1940 in the academy of music
philadelphia   78: victor M 750/australian
orchestra   hmv ED 157
                       cd: dante LYS 288/biddulph WHL 062/
                       membran 205 235/231 058

recorded on 20 february 1978 in the old metropolitan opera house
philadelphia
philadelphia   lp: angel 37537/38270/emi ASD 3644/
orchestra   1C065 03468/2C069 03468/
                       3C065 03468
                       cd: emi 565 1762/575 1272

the oceanides
recorded on 24 december 1955 in the town hall
philadelphia   lp: columbia ML 5249/philips
orchestra   ABL 3227/A01355L

recorded on 26 october 1970 in the academy of music
philadelphia   lp: victor ARL1 4566
orchestra

pohjola's daughter
recorded on 11 march 1955 in the town hall
philadelphia   lp: columbia ML 5249/philips
orchestra   ABL 3227/A01355L

recorded on 26 october 1970 in the academy of music
philadelphia   lp: victor ARL1 4566
orchestra

sibelius/**the swan of tuonela/4 legends**
recorded on 20 october 1940 in the academy of music
philadelphia   78: victor 17702/hmv DB 5832
orchestra

recorded on 2 april 1950 in the town hall
philadelphia   78: columbia 13130D
orchestra   lp: columba ML 2158/ML 4672/
                           philips S06603R

recorded on 31 january 1960 in the town hall
philadelphia   lp: columbia ML 5492/MS 6157/
orchestra   MS 6732/MS 7527/Y 30489/
                           BRG 72340/SBRG 72340/
                           philips ABL 3366/SABL 195/
                           A01484L/835 570AY/melodiya
                           S10 22197-22198
                           cd: SBK 48271

recorded on 15 january 1973 in the academy of music
philadelphia   lp: victor AGL1 5272
orchestra

recorded in 1974 at a concert in the academy of music
philadelphia   cd: disco archivia 744/752
orchestra

recorded on 20 february 1978 in the old metropolitan opera house
philadelphia
philadelphia   lp: angel 37537/38270/emi
orchestra   ASD 3644/1C065 03468/
                           2C069 03468/3C065 03468
                           cd: emi 565 1762

sibelius/**tapiola**
recorded on 24 december 1955 in the town hall
philadelphia				lp: columbia ML 5249/MS 6196/
orchestra				MS 6732/philips ABL 3227/
					A01355L
recorded on 26 october 1976 in the academy of music
philadelphia				lp: victor ARL1 3978
orchestra

valse triste
recorded on 25 january 1959 in the broadwood hotel
philadelphia				lp: columbia ML 5492/MS 6157/
orchestra				MS 6196/MS 6732/Y 30489/
					BRG 72167/BRG 72340/
					SBRG 72167/SBRG 72340/
					61286/philips ABL 3366/SABL 195/
					A01484L/835 570AY
					cd: SBK 48271/88697 279872
recorded on 15 january 1973 in the academy of music
philadelphia				lp: victor AGL1 5272
orchestra

BEDRICH SMETANA (1824-1884)
the moldau/ma vlast
recorded on 10 january 1956 in the town hall
philadelphia				lp: columbia ML 5261
orchestra
recorded on 5 february 1970 in the academy of music
philadelphia				lp: victor LSC 3302
orchestra

the bartered bride, overture
recorded on 24 june 1953 in the town hall
philadelphia				lp: columbia ML 5206/BRG 72300/
orchestra				SBRG 72300/philips ABL 3215/
					GBL 5626/A01356L/G03604L
recorded on 11 june 1968 in the academy of music
philadelphia				lp: victor LSC 3085
orchestra				*recording completed on 8 january 1969*
recorded in 1974 at a concert in the academy of music
philadelphia				cd: disco archivia 744
orchestra

smetana/**the bartered bride, suite from the opera**
comprising polka, furiant and dance of the comedians
recorded on 19 january 1934 in minneapolis
minneapolis symphony   78: victor 8694/hmv DB 2862/ australian hmv ED 39

recorded on 24 june 1953 in the town hall
philadelphia orchestra   lp: columbia ML 5206
dance of the comedians only
lp: columbia ML 5223/M2X 786

recorded on 11 june 1968 in the academy of music
philadelphia orchestra   lp: victor LSC 3085
recording completed on 8 january 1969

JOHN STAFFORD SMITH (1750-1836)
the star-spangled banner
recorded on 21 may 1962 in the salt lake tabernacle
philadelphia orchestra
mormon tabernacle choir   lp: columbia MS 6419
cd: MDK 48295

recorded on 15 may 1968 in the town hall
philadelphia orchestra   lp: columbia

LUDWIG SPOHR (1784-1859)
violin concerto no 8 "gesangsszene"
recorded on 5 september 1938 in the academy of music
philadelphia orchestra
spalding   78: victor M 544/hmv DB 3831-3832
cd: biddulph LAB 054/
symposium 1291

sousa/**washington post, march**
recorded on 6 march 1942 in the academy of music
philadelphia   78: columbia
orchestra

recorded on 15 may 1968 in the town hall
philadelphia   lp: columbia
orchestra

LEO SOWERBY (1895-1968)
the irish washerwoman
recorded on 23 january 1934 in minneapolis
minneapolis   78: victor 1761/hmv DA 1554
symphony

JOSEF STRAUSS (1827-1870)
aquarellen, waltz
recorded between 12-14 january 1935 in minneapolis
minneapolis   78: victor 8867
symphony

feuerfest, polka
recorded on 23 december 1951 in the town hall
philadelphia   45: columbia A 1013/A 1543
orchestra   lp: columbia CL 839/ML 4589/
                                     MS 7072/BPG 62079/SBPG 62079/
                                     philips SBR 6214/S06618R

recorded on 8-9 january 1974 in the academy of music
philadelphia   lp: victor ARL1 2266
orchestra

schwert und leyer, waltz
recorded on 13 may 1952 in the town hall
philadelphia   lp: columbia ML 5166
orchestra

sphärenklänge, waltz
recorded on 13 may 1952 in the town hall
philadelphia   lp: columbia ML 5166
orchestra

JOHANN STRAUSS I (1804-1849)
radetzky march
recorded on 13 may 1952 in the town hall
philadelphia orchestra   lp: columbia CL 839/philips GBL 5553/G03547L

recorded on 3 february 1963 in the town hall
philadelphia orchestra   lp: columbia ML 5874/MS 6474/ MG 32314

recorded on 15 june 1972 in the academy of music
philadelphia orchestra   lp: victor AGL1 4298

JOHANN AND JOSEF STRAUSS
pizzicato polka
recorded on 20 january 1934 in minneapolis
minneapolis symphony   78: victor 1757/hmv DA 1509

recorded on 13 may 1952 in the town hall
philadelphia orchestra   lp: columbia CL 839/philips SBR 6214/ GBL 5553/S06618R/G03547L

recorded on 7 december 1966 in the philadelphia hotel
philadelphia orchestra   lp: columbia MS 7146/MS 7502
     cd: SBK 48164

JOHANN STRAUSS II (1825-1899)
die fledermaus/sung in english
recorded on 24 december 1950 in the columbia studios new york city

metropolitan	78: columbia MOP 32
opera orchestra	45: columbia MOP 4-32
and chorus	lp: columbia SL 108/Y2 32666/78245/
welitsch, pons,	philips GBL 5643-5644/
lipton, kullmann,	G03609-03610L
tucker, brownlee	*recording completed on 29 december 1950 and 7 january 1951*

recorded on 20 january 1951 at a performance in the metroploitan opera house new york city

metropolitan   unpublished met broadcast
opera orchestra
and chorus
piazza, munsel,
stevens, kullmann,
tucker, brownlee

recorded on 22 december 1951 at a performance in the metropolitan opera house new york city

metropolitan   unpublished met broadcast
opera orchestra
and chorus
resnik, munsel,
thebom, kullmann,
sullivan, brownlee

die fledermaus, overture
recorded on 10 january 1935 in minneapolis

minneapolis	78: victor M 262/hmv DB 2632/
symphony	australian hmv ED 33

recorded on 22 november 1947 in the academy of music

philadelphia	78: columbia M 311/english
orchestra	columbia LX 1182
	lp: columbia ML 2041

recorded on 13 may 1952 in the town hall

philadelphia	lp: columbia ML 4686
orchestra	

recorded on 8-9 january 1974 in the academy of music

philadelphia	lp: victor ARL1 2266
orchestra	

johann strauss/**accelerationen, waltz**
recorded on 14 january 1935 in minneapolis
minneapolis symphony
78: victor M 262/hmv DB 2624/ australian hmv ED 34

recorded on 23 december 1951 in the town hall
philadelphia orchestra
lp: columbia ML 4589

ägyptischer marsch
recorded on 13 may 1952 in the town hall
philadelphia orchestra
lp: columbia ML 4589/CL 839/ philips SBR 6214/GBL 5553/ S06618R/G03547L

annen polka
recorded on 13 may 1952 in the town hall
philadelphia orchestra
lp: columbia CL 839/philips SBR 6214/GBL 5553/S06618R/ G03547L

recorded on 28 december 1961 in the broadwood hotel
philadelphia orchestra
lp: columbia ML 5752/MS 6352/ BPG 62709/SBPG 62709
cd: SBK 48164

recorded on 8-9 january 1974 in the academy of music
philadelphia orchestra
lp: victor ARL1 2266

auf der jagd, polka
recorded on 28 december 1961 in the broadwood hotel
philadelphia orchestra
lp: columbia ML 5752/MS 6352/ BPG 62709/SBPG 62709
cd: SBK 48164

recorded on 8-9 january 1974 in the academy of music
philadelphia orchestra
lp: victor ARL1 2266

johann strauss/**an der schönen blauen donau, waltz**
recorded between 12-14 january 1935 in minneapolis
minneapolis   78: victor M 262/hmv DB 2621/
symphony   australian hmv ED 32
                              45: victor ERB 6
                              lp: victor (italy) A12R 0093

recorded on 27 august 1947 at a concert in the hollywood bowl
los angeles   cd: melodram MEL 16215/
philharmonic   andromeda ANDRCD 5133

recorded on 4 december 1947 in the academy of music
philadelphia   78: columbia M 315
orchestra   lp: columbia AL 13/ML 2041

recorded on 23 december 1957 in the town hall
philadelphia   lp: columbia ML 5238/philips
orchestra   GBL 5518/G03523L

recorded on 27 december 1959 in the broadwood hotel
philadelphia   lp: columbia ML 5617/MS 6217/
orchestra   MS 6934/MS 7502/D3S 789/
                              BPG 62709/SBPG 62709
                              cd: SBK 48164

recorded on 14 january 1971 in the academy of music
philadelphia   lp: victor LSC 3250
orchestra   cd: VD 60490/74321 242052/
                              74321 740392

expolsionen, polka
recorded on 21 december 1952 in the town hall
philadelphia   lp: columbia CL 839/BPG 62709/
orchestra   SBPG 62709/philips GBL 5553/
                              G03547L

johann strauss/**frühlingsstimmen, waltz**
recorded on 15 march 1941 in the academy of music
philadelphia   78: victor 18060/hmv DB 5963
orchestra

recorded on 27 december 1959 in the broadwood hotel
philadelphia   lp: columbia ML 5617/MS 6217/
orchestra   MS 7502/D3S 789
                            cd: SBK 48164

recorded on 24 november 1971 in the academy of music
philadelphia   lp: victor LSC 3250
orchestra

g'schichten aus dem wienerwald, waltz
recorded on 10 january 1935 in minneapolis
minneapolis   78: victor M 262/hmv DB 2623/
symphony   australian hmv ED 30

recorded on 7 january 1945 at a concert in the nbc studios new york city
nbc symphony   unpublished radio broadcast

recorded on 4 december 1947 in the town hall
philadelphia   78: columbia M 315/english
orchestra   columbia LX 1180
                            lp: columbia AL 13/ML 2041

recorded on 27 december 1959 in the broadwood hotel
philadelphia   lp: columbia ML 5617/MS 6217/
orchestra   MS 7502/D3S 789/MG 35918
                            cd: SBK 48164

recorded on 13 january 1969 in the academy of music
philadelphia   lp: victor LSC 3149/LSC 3250
orchestra   cd: VD 60490/74321 242052/
                            74321 740392

recorded on 27 october 1974 at a concert in the academy of music
philadelphia   lp: victor DPL1 0094
orchestra

johann strauss/**kaiserwalzer**
recorded on 1 august 1941 in the academy of music
philadelphia   78: victor 18220/australian
orchestra   hmv ED 229

recorded on 23 december 1951 in the town hall
philadelphia   45: columbia A 1031
orchestra   lp: columnia AL 13/ML 4589

recorded on 23 december 1957 in the town hall
philadelphia   lp: columbia ML 5238/philips
orchestra   GBL 5518/G03523L

recorded on 27 december 1959 in the broadwood hotel
philadelphia   lp: columbia ML 5617/MS 6217/
orchestra   MS 7502/D3S 789

recorded on 28 may 1969 in the academy of music
philadelphia   lp: victor LSC 3149
orchestra   cd: VD 60490/74321 242052/
                        74321 740392

recorded on 8-9 january 1974 in the academy of music
philadelphia   lp: victor LSC 3250/ARL1 2266
orchestra

künstlerleben, waltz
recorded on 28 may 1969 in the academy of music
philadelphia   lp: victor LSC 3149/ARL1 2266
orchestra   cd: VD 60490/74321 242052/
                        74321 740392

morgenblätter, waltz
recorded on 28 may 1969 in the academy of music
philadelphia   lp: victor LSC 3149
orchestra   cd: VD 60490/74321 242052/
                        74321 740392

johann strauss/**neue pizzicato polka**
recorded on 20 january 1934 in minneapolis
minneapolis   78: victor V-1757
symphony

recorded on 28 december 1961 in the town hall
philadelphia   lp: columbia ML 5752/MS 6352/
orchestra   BPG 62079/SBPG 62079
                       cd: SBK 48164

perpetuum mobile
recorded on 23 december 1951 in the town hall
philadelphia   45: columbia A 1031/A 1543
orchestra   lp: columbia ML 4589

eine nacht in venedig, overture
recorded on 23 december 1951 in the town hall
philadelphia   45: columbia A 1031
orchestra   lp: columbia ML 4589

rosen aus dem süden, waltz
recorded on 23 december 1957 in the town hall
philadelphia   lp: columbia ML 5238/philips
orchestra   GBL 5518/G03523L

recorded on 28 december 1961 in the town hall
philadelphia   lp: columbia ML 5752/MS 6352/
orchestra   D3S 789/MG 35918/BPG 62079/
                       SBPG 62079/63254
                       cd: SBK 48164

recorded on 8-9 january 1974 in the academy of music
philadelphia   lp: victor LSC 3250/ARL1 2266
orchestra

schatzwalzer
recorded on 28 may 1969 in the academy of music
philadelphia   lp: victor LSC 3149
orchestra   cd: VD 60490/74321 242052/
                       74321 740392

johann strauss/**das spitzentuch der königin, overture**
recorded on 21 december 1952 in the town hall
philadelphia　　　　　　lp: columbia ML 4686
orchestra

tausend und eine nacht, waltz
recorded on 9 january 1955 in the town hall
philadelphia　　　　　　lp: columbia
orchestra

recorded on 28 december 1961 in the town hall
philadelphia　　　　　　lp: columbia ML 5752/MS 6352/
orchestra　　　　　　　　MS 7032/D3S 789/MG 35198/
　　　　　　　　　　　　BPG 62079/SBPG 62079/63254
　　　　　　　　　　　　cd: SBK 48164

tritsch tratsch polka
recorded on 13 may 1952 in the town hall
philadelphia　　　　　　lp: columbia CL 839/ML 4589/
orchestra　　　　　　　　philips GBL 5553/G03547L

recorded on 28 december 1961 in the town hall
philadelphia　　　　　　lp: columbia ML 5752/MS 6352/
orchestra　　　　　　　　MS 6739/MS 6993/MS 7502/
　　　　　　　　　　　　BPG 62079/SBPG 62079
　　　　　　　　　　　　cd: SBK 48164

unter donner und blitz, polka
recorded on 21 december 1952 in the town hall
philadelphia　　　　　　lp: columbia CL 839/philips
orchestra　　　　　　　　GBL 5553/G03547L

recorded on 28 december 1961 in the town hall
philadelphia　　　　　　lp: columbia ML 5752/MS 6352/
orchestra　　　　　　　　BPG 62079/SBPG 62079
　　　　　　　　　　　　cd: SBK 48164

recorded on 8-9 january 1974 in the academy of music
philadelphia　　　　　　lp: victor LSC 3250/ARL1 2266
orchestra

johann strauss/**waldmeister, overture**
recorded on 26 april 1953 in the town hall
philadelphia   lp: columbia CL 839/philips
orchestra   SBR 6214/GBL 5553/
     S06618R/G03547L

wein weib und gesang, waltz
recorded on 2 june 1945 in the academy of music
philadelphia   78: columbia M 588
orchestra   lp: columbia ML 2017

recorded on 23 december 1951 in the town hall
philadelphia   45: columbia A 1031/A 1543
orchestra   lp: columbia AL 13/ML 4589

recorded on 28 december 1961 in the town hall
philadelphia   lp: columbia ML 5752/MS 6352/
orchestra   MS 7032/BPG 62079/SBPG
     62079/MG 35918/63254
     cd: SBK 48164

wiener blut, waltz
recorded on 15 march 1941 in the academy of music
philadelphia   78: victor 18060/hmv DB 5963/
orchestra   australian hmv ED 255

recorded on 27 december 1959 in the broadwood hotel
philadelphia   lp: columbia ML 5617/
orchestra   MS 6217/D3S 789
     cd: SBK 48164

recorded on 28 september 1971 in the academy of music
philadelphia   lp: victor LSC 3250
orchestra   cd: VD 60490/74321 740392/
     disco archivia 741

johann strauss/**wo die zitronen blüh'n, waltz**
recorded on 13 january 1969 in the academy of music
philadelphia orchestra
    lp: victor LSC 3149
    cd: VD 60490/74321 242052/
    74321 740392

der zigeunerbaron, overture
recorded on 12 january 1935 in minneapolis
minneapolis symphony
    78: victor M 262/hmv DB 2625/
    australian hmv ED 35
    45: victor ERB 6
    lp victor (italy) A12R 0093

recorded on 22 november 1947 in the town hall
philadelphia orchestra
    lp: columbia ML 2041

EDUARD STRAUSS (1835-1916)
bahn frei, galop
recorded on 23 december 1951 in the town hall
philadelphia orchestra
    lp: columbia ML 4589

RICHARD STRAUSS (1864-1949)
serenade for wind instruments
recorded on 28 may 1955 in the town hall
philadelphia orchestra
    lp: columbia ML 5129

horn concerto no 1
recorded on 18 june 1966 in the town hall
philadelphia orchestra
jones
    lp: columbia M 32233

338

strauss/**burleske for piano and orchestra**
recorded on 11 march 1955 in the broadwood hotel
philadelphia   lp: columbia ML 5168
orchestra   cd: SM2K 47269
serkin

recorded on 3 february 1966 in the town hall
philadelphia   lp: columbia MS 7183/MS 7423/
orchestra   MP 39056
serkin   cd: MK 42261/SBK 53262

also sprach zarathustra
recorded on 3 february 1963 in the town hall
philadelphia   lp: columbia ML 5947/MS 6547/
orchestra   M 31829/77359
                          cd: SBK 46457/SBK 47656

recorded on 26 february 1975 in the academy of music
philadelphia   lp: victor ARL1 1220/AW 26 41370
orchestra   cd: VD 60793/74321 292502

recorded on 24 november 1979 in the academy of music
philadelphia   lp: angel 37744/38270/emi
orchestra   ASD 3897/EG 29 0615/
                          1C065 03810/2C069 03810/
                          3C065 03810
                          cd: emi 764 1062

der bürger als edelmann, suite from the incidental music
recorded on 13 february 1965 in the town hall
philadelphia   lp: columbia M 32233
orchestra   cd: SBK 62659

love scene/feuersnot
recorded on 6 april 1952 in the town hall
philadelphia   lp: columbia ML 5177
orchestra

strauss/**die frau ohne schatten, orchestral suite from the opera**
recorded on 14 april 1957 in the town hall
philadelphia   lp: columbia ML 5333/
orchestra   philips A01421L

don juan
recorded on 23 october 1955 in the town hall
philadelphia   lp: columbia ML 5177
orchestra

recorded on 12 june 1959 at a concert in the deutsches museum munich
sinfonieorchester   cd: emi 575 1272
des bayerischen
rundfunks

recorded on 31 january 1960 in the town hall
philadelphia   lp: columbia ML 5724/MS 6324/
orchestra   BRG 72029/SBRG 72029/77359

recorded on 6 june 1963 at a concert in the musikhalle hamburg
sinfonieorchester   cd: originals
des norddeutschen
rundfunks

recorded on 17 january 1974 in the academy of music
philadelphia   lp: victor ARL1 1408
orchestra   *recording completed on 28 march 1974*

recorded in 1974 at a concert in the academy of music
philadelphia   cd: disco archivia 750
orchestra

metamorphosen
recorded on 8 february 1978 in the academy of music
philadelphia   lp: victor AGL1 4291
orchestra   cd: RCD 17076

strauss/**don quixote**
recorded on 24 february 1940 in the academy of music
philadelphia   78: victor M 720/australian
orchestra   hmv ED 269-273
feuermann   lp: victor CAL 202
                      cd: biddulph LAB 042/membran
                      205 235/231 058

recorded on 4 december 1955 in the town hall
philadelphia   lp: columbia ML 5292/
orchestra   philips A01419L
munroe

recorded on 26 february 1961 in the town hall
philadelphia   lp: columbia ML 5915/MS 6515/
orchestra   BRG 72161/SBRG 72161/77359
munroe   cd: SBK 46457/SBK 47656

recorded on 19 january 1972 in the academy of music
philadelphia   lp: victor ARL1 2287
orchestra   cd: disco archivia 741
mayes

ein heldenleben
recorded on 30 april 1939 in the academy of music
philadelphia   78: victor M 610/australian
orchestra   hmv ED 334-338

recorded on 14 march 1954 in the town hall
philadelphia   lp: columbia ML 4887/philips
orchestra   ABL 3061/A01148L

recorded on 15 december 1960 in the manhattan centre new york city
philadelphia   lp: columbia ML 5649/MS 6249/
orchestra   Y 31922/77359
                      cd: SBK 48272

recorded on 15 february 1978 in the academy of music
philadelphia   lp: victor ARL1 3581
orchestra

strauss/**der rosenkavalier, orchestral suite from the opera**
recorded on 1 november 1947 in the academy of music
philadelphia   78: columbia M 742/english
orchestra   columbia LX 1183-1185
                        lp: columbia ML 4044

recorded on 23 december 1957 in the town hall
philadelphia   lp: columbia ML 5333/
orchestra   philips A01421L

recorded on 12 february 1964 in the town hall
philadelphia   lp: columbia MS 6678/MGP 17/
orchestra   BRG 72342/SBRG 72342
                        cd: SBK 62650

recorded on 28 march 1974 in the academy of music
philadelphia   lp: victor ARL1 1408/AGL1 4291
orchestra

televised on 30 june-1 july 1978 at concerts in the academy of music
philadelphia   dvd video: euroarts 207 2278
orchestra

der rosenkavalier, waltz sequence from the opera
recorded on 10 january 1935 in minneapolis
minneapolis   78: victor 1758-1759/
symphony   hmv DA 1507-1508

recorded on 25 october 1941 in the academy of music
philadelphia   78: victor 18390
orchestra

recorded on 6 april 1952 in the town hall
philadelphia   lp: columbia ML 5177/philips
orchestra   SBR 6211/S06623R

dance of the seven veils/salome
recorded on 20 march 1947 in the academy of music
philadelphia   78: english columbia LX 1172/
orchestra   french columbia LFX 891/italian
                        columbia GQX 11288

recorded on 15 november 1962 in the town hall
philadelphia   lp: columbia MS 6678/BRG
orchestra   72342/SBRG 72342
                        cd: SBK 53511

strauss/**sinfonia domestica**
recorded on 9 may 1938 in the academy of music
philadelphia   78: victor M 520/hmv DB 3763-3767
orchestra   cd: biddulph WHL 064-065/membran
                    205 235/231 058

till eulenspiegels lustige streiche
recorded on 23 november 1952 in the town hall
philadelphia   lp: columbia ML 5177/philips
orchestra   SBR 6211/S06623R

recorded on 13 november 1963 in the town hall
philadelphia   lp: columbia MS 6678/BRG 72342/
orchestra   SBRG 72342/77359
                    cd: SBK 46457

recorded in 1970 at a concert in the academy of music
philadelphia   cd: disco archivia 747
orchestra

recorded on 28 march 1974 in the academy of music
philadelphia   lp: victor ARL1 1408
orchestra   cd: VD 60793

tod und verklärung
recorded on 19 november 1945 in the academy of music
philadelphia   78: columbia M 613/australian
orchestra   columbia LOX 663-665
                    lp: columbia ML 4044
                    recording completed in january and april 1946

recorded on 21 december 1959 in the town hall
philadelphia   lp: columbia ML 5724/MS 6324/
orchestra   BRG 72029/SBRG 72029/77359
                    cd: SBK 46457

recorded on 8 february 1978 in the academy of music
philadelphia   lp: victor AGL1 4291
orchestra   cd: RCD 17076

strauss/**meine seele gibt reinen ton, song with orchestra**
recorded on 27 august 1947 at a concert in the hollywood bowl
los angeles cd: melodram MEL 16215/
philharmonic andromeda ANDRCD 5133
yeend *also issued on cd by gala*

songs with orchestra: allerseelen; traum durch die dämmerung; morgen; zueignung
recorded on 5 august 1948 at a concert in the hollywood bowl
los angeles cd: video artists international
philharmonic VAI 1247/archipel ARPCD 0037
lehmann

IGOR STRAVINSKY (1882-1971)
l'oiseau de feu, suite from the ballet
recorded on 25 december 1944 at a concert in the nbc studios new york city
nbc symphony unpublished radio broadcast
recorded on 1 march 1953 in the town hall
philadelphia lp: columbia ML 4700/philips
orchestra NBL 5032/GBL 5508/A01187L/
 N01232L/G03509L
recorded on 11 july 1954 at a concert in recklinghausen
sinfonieorchester unpublished radio broadast
des westdeutschen
rundfunks
recorded on 18 october 1967 in the town hall
philadelphia lp: columbia M 31632
orchestra
recorded on 18-19 december 1973 in the academy of music
philadelphia lp: victor CRL3 2026
orchestra

petrushka
recorded on 22 june 1954 at a concert in the funkhaus cologne
sinfonieorchester unpublished radio broadcast
des westdeutschen
rundfunks
recorded on 7 november 1954 in the town hall
philadelphia lp: columbia ML 5030
orchestra
recorded on 23 march 1964 in the town hall
philadelphia lp: columbia MS 6746/M 31632
orchestra cd: SBK 47664

stravinsky/**le sacre du printemps**
recorded on 24 april 1955 in the town hall
philadelphia orchestra   lp: columbia ML 5030/philips NBL 5032/N01232L
recording completed on 14 may 1955

FRANZ VON SUPPE (1819-1895)
dichter und bauer, overture
recorded on 2 april 1950 in the town hall
philadelphia orchestra   78: columbia 13155D/english columbia LX 1396
lp: philips SBL 5234/S04643L

recorded on 12 january 1972 in the academy of music
philadelphia orchestra   lp: victor AGL1 3657

leichte kavallerie, overture
recorded on 12 april 1973 in the academy of music
philadelphia orchestra   lp: victor AGL1 3657

die schöne galathea, overture
recorded on 9 may 1954 in the town hall
philadelphia orchestra   lp: columbia ML 5206/BRG 72300/SBRG 72300/philips ABL 3215/GBL 5626/A01356L/G03604L

PIOTR TCHAIKOVSKY (1840-1893)
symphony no 1 "winter dreams"
recorded on 11 october 1976 in the academy of music
philadelphia orchestra   lp: victor ARL1 3063/RL 13063
cd: 09026 382882

symphony no 2 "little russian"
recorded on 7 january 1976 in the academy of music
philadelphia orchestra   lp: victor ARL1 3352
cd: 09026 382882

tchaikovsky/**symphony no 3 "polish"**
recorded on 24 october 1974 in the academy of music
philadelphia   lp: victor ARL1 4121
orchestra   cd: 09026 382882

symphony no 4
recorded on 3-4 december 1947 in the town hall
philadelphia   78: columbia M 736
orchestra   lp: columbia ML 4050

recorded on 23 december 1953 in the town hall
philadelphia   lp: columbia ML 5074/philips
orchestra   GBL 5630/G03612L

recorded on 22 june 1954 at a concert in the funkhsus cologne
sinfonieorchester   lp: movimento musica 01.037
des westdeutschen
rundfunks

recorded in 1954 at a concert in the titania palast berlin
rias-orchester   cd: audite 95589

recorded on 13 november 1963 in the town hall
philadelphia   lp: columbia MS 6756/D3S 727/
orchestra   M7X 30830/61092
                      cd: SBK 46334

recorded on 9 may 1973 in the academy of music
philadelphia   lp: victor ARL1 0665/CRL3 1838
orchestra   cd: 74321 292522

tchaikovsky/**symphony no 5**
recorded on 15 march 1941 in the academy of music
philadelphia   78: columbia M 828
orchestra

recorded on 19 november 1950 in the town hall
philadelphia   lp: columbia ML 4400
orchestra

recorded on 25 january 1959 in the broadwood hotel
philadelphia   lp: columbia ML 5435/MS 6109/
orchestra   M7X 30830/D3S 727/M 31842
                                cd: SBK 46538/88697 279872

recorded on 1 june 1959 at a concert in the funkhaus cologne
sinfonieorchester   unpublished radio broadcast
des westdeutschen
rundfunks

recorded on 21 march 1974 in the academy of music
philadelphia   lp: victor ARL1 0664/CRL3 1838
orchestra   cd: 74321 212912

recorded on 25 april 1981 in the academy of music
philadelphia   cd: delos DMS 3015
orchestra

tchaikovsky/**symphony no 6 "pathetique"**
recorded on 13 december 1936 in the academy of music
philadelphia 78: victor M 337/hmv DB 3309-3313/
orchestra DB 6070-6074
 cd: biddulph WHL 046/membran
 205 235/231 058
 recording completed on 9 january 1937

recorded on 6 april 1952 in the town hall
philadelphia lp: columbia ML 4544/philips
orchestra SBL 5214/S04637L

recorded on 10 april 1960 in the town hall
philadelphia lp: columbia ML 5495/MS 6160/
orchestra MS 7169/M7X 30830/D3S 727/
 M 31833/BRG 72004/SBRG
 72004/61077
 cd: SBK 47657

recorded on 22 june 1963 at a concert in the kurzaal scheveningen
residentie unpublished radio broadcast
orkest

recorded on 27-28 may 1968 in the academy of music
philadelphia lp: victor LSC 3058/SB 6828/
orchestra CRL3 1838
 cd: VD 60908/74321 242102

recorded on 26 september 1981 in the academy of music
philadelphia cd: delos DMS 3016
orchestra

symphony no 7, sketches arranged by bogateyrev
recorded on 11 march 1962 in the town hall
philadelphia lp: columbia ML 5749/MS 6349/
orchestra BRG 72042/SBRG 72042

manfred symphony
recorded on 27 october 1976 in the academy of music
philadelphia lp: victor ARL1 2945/RL 12945
orchestra cd: 09026 382912

tchaikovsky/**piano concerto no 1**
recorded on 8-10 december 1949 in the town hall
philadelphia   78: columbia M 785
orchestra   lp: columbia ML 4096
levant   cd: dante HPC 085/membran
                     205 235/222 343/231 058

recorded on 19 april 1959 in the town hall
philadelphia   lp: columbia MS 6079/Y 34606/
orchestra   77357/philips GBL 5522/
istomin   G03538L

recorded on 2 october 1974 in the academy of music
philadelphia   lp: victor ARL1 0751
orchestra
joselson

piano concerto no 2
recorded on 17 february 1965 in the town hall
philadelphia   lp: columbia MS 6755/BRG
orchestra   72385/SBRG 72385/77357
graffman   cd: S2K 94737

piano concerto no 3
recorded on 17 february 1965 in the town hall
philadelphia   lp: columbia MS 6755/BRG
orchestra   72385/SBRG 72385/77357
graffman   cd: S2K 94737

tchaikovsky/**violin concerto**
recorded in march 1946 at a concert in the academy of music
philadelphia cd: music and arts CD 299/CD 4299
orchestra
huberman
recorded in 1947 at a concert in the hollywood bowl
los angeles cd: doremi DHR 7736
philharmonic
elman
recorded on 23 march 1958 in the broadwood hotel
philadelphia lp: columbia ML 5379/MS 6062/
orchestra D3S 721/BRG 72083/SBRG
stern 72083/77418/61029/philips
fontana 699 017CL/876 004CY
cd: SMK 66827/SX11K 67193/
88697 279872
recorded on 24 december 1959 in the town hall
philadelphia lp: columbia ML 5696/MS 6298/
orchestra Y 30313/BRG 72064/SBRG 72064/
oistrakh 77357/60312/philips 610 305VR/
836 402VZ/melodiya 110 0217/
supraphon SUA 10934/SUAST 50934
cd: MPK 44854/M2K 46450/
SBK 46339
recorded in 1974 at a concert in the academy of music
philadelphia cd: disco archivia 751
orchestra
markovici
recorded on 13 november 1978 in the academy of music
philadelphia lp: angel 37640/emi ASD 3726/
orchestra SLS 5280/1C065 03509/2C069 03509/
perlman 3C065 03509/1C153 54347-54348
cd: 747 1062/562 5912/585 0832
televised in june 1979 at a concert in the academy of music
philadelphia vhs video: victor CSMV 0036
orchestra laserdisc: polygram 070 2101
perlman dvd video: euroarts 207 2128

serenade melancholique pour violon et orchestre
recorded on 13 november 1978 in the academy of music
philadelphia lp: angel 37640/emi ASD 3726/
orchestra 1C065 03509/2C069 03509/
perlman 3C065 03509
cd: 747 1062/562 5912/585 0832

tchaikovsky/**rococo variations for cello and orchestra**
recorded on 15 november 1962 in the town hall
philadelphia   lp: columbia MS 6714/BRG 72296/
orchestra   SBRG 72296/77357/61036
rose   cd: SBK 48278

andante cantabile, arrangement from the first string quartet
recorded on 20 january 1934 in minneapolis
minneapolis   78: victor 1719/hmv DA 1461
symphony

recorded on 15 november 1953 in the town hall
philadelphia   45: columbia A 1828/philips NBE 11011/
orchestra   409 011NE
                    lp: columbia ML 4856/CL 707/philips
                    SBL 5229/S04642L/GL 5678

recorded on 14 february 1966 in the town hall
philadelphia   lp: columbia MS 7146
orchestra   cd: 88697 279872

capriccio italien
recorded on 1 november 1953 in the town hall
philadelphia   lp: columbia CL 707/philips GBL
orchestra   5522/GBL 5555/G03538L/
                    G03551L

recorded on 24 june 1957 at a concert in the funkhaus cologne
sinfonieorchester   lp: movimento musica 01.055
des westdeutschen   cd: frequenz 041.017
rundfunks

recorded on 22 february 1966 in the town hall
philadelphia   lp: columbia MS 6917/M7X 30830/
orchestra   MG 30947/MG 31190/M 31850/
                    MGP 7/BRG 72527/SBRG 72527/
                    SPR 43/77343
                    cd: SBK 47657/SB2K 63281

recorded on 15-16 february 1972 in the academy of music
philadelphia   lp: victor LSC 3301/CRL3 2026
orchestra   cd: VD 60492

tchaikovsky/**casse noisette, selections from the ballet**
recorded on 20 december 1941 in the academy of music
philadelphia			78: victor M 915/M 1020/M 1063
orchestra			45: victor ERB 8
				lp: victor LM 8

recorded on 21 december 1952 in the town hall
philadelphia			lp: columbia A 1059/ML 4729/
orchestra			ML 5257/philips GBL 5642/
				G03620L
				standard suite only
				lp: columbia ML 5238/philips
				SBL 5229/SBL 5234/GBL 5518/
				S04642L/S04643L/G03523L
				recording completed on 1 november 1953

recorded on 16 december 1963 in the town hall
philadelphia			lp: columbia MS 6621/MS 6807/
orchestra			D3S 706/M7X 30830/
				77343/77373
				cd: SBK 89284
				standard suite only
				lp: columbia M3L 306/M3S 706
				cd: SBK 46550

recorded between 23-26 september 1972 in the academy of music
philadelphia			lp: victor LMDS 61008/RL 10027
orchestra			*standard suite only*
				cd: GD 60878/74321 292532

waltz and polonaise/evgeny onegin
recorded on 14 january 1965 in the town hall
philadelphia			lp: columbia MS 6917/BRG 72527/
orchestra			SBRG 72527/77343
				cd: SBK 47657

recorded on 24 january 1973 in the academy of music
philadelphia			lp: victor
orchestra

tchaikovsky/**francesca da rimini**
recorded on 9 january 1955 in the town hall
philadelphia orchestra   lp: columbia ML 5242/philips ABL 3228/A01368L

recorded between 23-29 december 1976 in the academy of music
philadelphia orchestra   lp: victor ARL1 2490
cd: VD 60492

marche slave
recorded on 16 december 1951 in the town hall
philadelphia orchestra   lp: columbia AL 24/ML 4997/philips SBL 5229/S04642L

recorded on 27 april 1964 in the town hall
philadelphia orchestra   lp: columbia ML 6275/MS 6875/M7X 30830/MG 30947/BRG 72455/SBRG 72455/77343
cd: SBK 46334/SB2K 63281

recorded on 17 february 1972 in the academy of music
philadelphia orchestra   lp: victor LSC 3301/CRL3 2026
cd: VD 60492/74321 212912

1812, ouverture solennelle
recorded on 16 december 1951 in the town hall
philadelphia orchestra   lp: columbia ML 4997/philips SBL 5229/S04642L

recorded on 12 april 1959 in the town hall
philadelphia orchestra
mormon tabernacle choir   lp: columbia ML 5392/MS 6073/M7X 30830/M 30447/M 31831/77343/61441
cd: SBK 46334/SB2K 63281

recorded on 16 november 1970 in the academy of music
philadelphia orchestra
temple university choir   lp: victor LSC 3204/LSC 3301/LSB 4031
cd: VD 60492/VD 87731/74321 212912/disco archivia 745

tchaikovsky/**romeo and juliet**
recorded on 23 december 1953 in the town hall
philadelphia   lp: columbia ML 4997/ML 5242/
orchestra   philips ABL 3228/A01368L

recorded on 14 april 1964 in the town hall
philadelphia   lp: columbia MS 6942/M2S 738/
orchestra   M7X 30830/MG 30947/
                         M 31831/BRG 72561/
                         SBRG 72561
                         cd: SB2K 63281

recorded between 23-30 december 1976 in the academy of music
philadelphia   lp: victor ARL1 2490/CRL3 2026
orchestra   cd: VD 60908/74321 292522

televised in june 1979 at a concert in the academy of music
philadelphia   vhs video: victor CSMV 0036
orchestra   dvd video: euroarts 207 2128

serenade for strings
recorded on 19 april 1946 in the academy of music
philadelphia   78: columbia M 677
orchestra   lp: columbia ML 4121

recorded on 21 december 1952 in the town hall
philadelphia   45: philips ABE 10039/409 074AE
orchestra   lp: columbia ML 5187/philips
                         ABL 3200/SBL 5229/A01332L/
                         S04642L
                         waltz only
                         lp: philips GL 5518/GL 5678

recorded on 22 june 1954 at a concert in the funkhaus cologne
sinfonieorchester   lp: movimento musica 01.055
des westdeutschen
rundfunks

recorded on 10 april 1960 in the broadwood hotel
philadelphia   lp: columbia ML 5624/MS 6224/
orchestra   M7X 30830/M 30447/
                         77343/61441
                         cd: SBK 46538/88697 279872

tchaikovsky/**the sleeping beauty, selections from the ballet**
recorded on 21 december 1952 in the town hall
philadelphia orchestra
lp: columbia ML 4729/philips GBL 5642/G03620L
standard suite only
lp: columbia ML 5238/philips SBL 5229/SBL 5234/GBL 5518/S04642L/S04643L/G03523L

recorded on 12 february 1961 in the town hall
philadelphia orchestra
lp: columbia ML 5679/MS 6279/MS 6942/D3S 706/M7X 30830/MG 30297/M 31838/BRG 72561/SBRG 72561/77343/77373
cd: SBK 46340/SBK 89284
standard suite only
lp: columbia M3L 306/M3S 706

recorded between 15-23 january 1973 in the academy of music
philadelphia orchestra
lp: victor LMDS 61008/ARL1 0169/CRL3 1261/RL 10169
standard suite only
cd: 74321 292532

june, orchestral arrangement from the seasons
recorded on 8 may 1968 in the town hall
philadelphia orchestra
lp: columbia

none but the lonely heart, orchestral arrangement
recorded on 28 february 1966 in the town hall
philadelphia orchestra
lp: columbia

tchaikovsky/**swan lake, selections from the ballet**
recorded on 17 october 1956 in the town hall
philadelphia   lp: columbia ML 5201/philips
orchestra   ABL 3209/A01332L
standard suite only
lp: columbia ML 5238/philips
GBL 5518/G03620L

recorded on 19 february 1961 in the town hall
philadelphia   lp: columbia ML 5708/ML 5837/
orchestra   MS 6437/MS 6807/M7X 30830/
M 31838/KS 6308/MG 30297/
BRG 72049/SBRG 72049
cd: SBK 46341/SBK 89284
standard suite only
lp: columbia M3L 306/M3S 706

recorded on 26-27 september 1972 in the academy of music
philadelphia   lp: victor LMDS 61008/ARL1 0030/
orchestra   CRL3 1261/RL 10030
standard suite only
cd: 74321 292532

GEORG PHILIPP TELEMANN (1681-1767)
4 concerti for various instruments
recorded on 10-11 june 1968 in the academy of music
philadelphia   lp: victor LSC 3057
orchestra

suite for flute and strings
recorded on 15 march 1941 in the academy of music
philadelphia   78: victor M 890/australian
orchestra   hmv ED 288-289
kincaid

AMBROISE THOMAS (1811-1896)
mignon, overture
recorded on 24 june 1953 in the town hall
philadelphia orchestra   lp: columbia ML 5206/BRG 72300/ philips ABL 3215/GBL 5626/ A01356L/G03604L

gavotte/mignon
recorded on 8 may 1968 in the town hall
philadelphia orchestra   lp: columbia 61301

VIRGIL THOMSON (1896-1989)
four blake songs
philadelphia orchestra   cd: composers' recordings SD 398

JOHANN BAPTIST VANHAL (1739-1813)
concerto for double bass and orchestra
recorded on 5 april 1962 in the town hall
philadelphia orchestra scott   lp: columbia ML 6191/MS 6791

RALPH VAUGHAN WILLIAMS (1872-1958)
fantasia on greensleeves
recorded on 14 april 1957 in the broadwood hotel
philadelphia orchestra   45: philips ABE 10039/409 074AE
lp: columbia ML 5187/ML 5975/ MS 6224/MS 6575/MS 6934/ MS 7103/philips ABL 3200/ GL 5678/A01332L
cd: SBK 62645/88697 279872

recorded on 12 january 1972 in the academy of music
philadelphia orchestra   lp: victor ARL1 2744
cd: 74321 179052/disco archivia 745

fantasia on a theme of thomas tallis
recorded on 13 october 1963 in the town hall
philadelphia orchestra   lp: columbia M 31074/BRG 72982/ SBRG 72982
cd: SBK 62645/88697 279872

recorded on 6 may 1970 in the academy of music
philadelphia orchestra   lp: victor ARL1 2744
cd: 74321 179052

GIUSEPPE VERDI (1813-1901)
messa da requiem
recorded on 6 april 1957 at a concert in the academy of music
philadelphia   cd: standing room only
orchestra
and chorus
price, merriman,
tucker, tozzi

recorded on 14-15 may 1964 in the manhattan centre new york city
philadelphia   lp: columbia M2L 307/M2S 707/
orchestra   Y2 35230/BRG 72997-72998/
westminster choir   SBRG 72997-72998
amara, forrester,   cd: M2K 77231/SB2K 53252
tucker, london

celeste aida/aida
recorded on 12 december 1937 at a ford sunday evening concert in the masonic temple detroit
detroit symphony   lp: ed smith records EJS 425
masini

grand march/aida
recorded on 3 february 1963 in the town hall
philadelphia   lp: columbia MS 7072/61301
orchestra

recorded on 9 june 1967 in the salt lake tabernacle
philadelphia   lp: columbia MS 7061
orchestra
mormon tabernacle
choir

recorded on 12 june 1972 in the academy of music
philadelphia   lp: victor AGL1 4298
orchestra

per me giunto/don carlo
recorded on 12 november 1939 at a ford sunday evening concert in the masonic temple detroit
detroit symphony   lp: ed smith records EJS 214/
thomas   EJS 531

verdi/**quando le sere/luisa miller**
recorded in 1975 at a concert in the academy of music
philadelphia orchestra
pavarotti
cd: bella voce BLV 107 009

questa o quella/rigoletto
recorded on 12 december 1937 at a ford sunday evening concert in the masonic temple detroit
detroit symphony
masini
lp: ed smith records EJS 425

recorded on 2 october 1938 at a ford sunday evening concert in the masonic temple detroit
detroit symphony
gigli
lp: ed smith records EJS 414

la traviata, act one prelude
recorded on 20 december 1967 in the town hall
philadelphia orchestra
lp: columbia 61301

parigi o cara/la traviata
recorded on 28 august 1947 at a concert in the hollywood bowl
los angeles philharmonic
yeend, lanza
lp: ed smith records EJS 457
cd: melodram MEL 16215/
andromeda ANDRCD 5133
also issued on cd by gala

anvil chorus/il trovatore
recorded on 9 june 1967 in the mormon tabernacle salt lake city
philadelphia orchestra
mormon tabernacle choir
lp: columbia MS 7061

HENRI VIEUXTEMPS (1820-1881)
violin concerto no 4
recorded on 14 april 1957 in the town hall
philadelphia   lp: columbia ML 5184/MP 39125/
orchestra   BRG 72351/SBRG 72351
francescatti

HEITOR VILLA LOBOS (1887-1959)
bachianas brasileiras no 1
recorded on 7 january 1945 at a concert in the nbc studios new york city
nbc symphony   unpublished radio broadcast

JOHN VINCENT (born 1902)
symphony in d
recorded on 14 april 1957 in the town hall
philadelphia   lp: columbia ML 5263/ML 5579/
orchestra   MS 6179
                        cd: american archives ALB 250

symphonic poem after descartes
recorded on 1 april 1959 in the town hall
philadelphia   lp: columbia ML 5579/MS 6179
orchestra   cd: american archives ALB 250

GIOVANNI BATTISTA VIOTTI (1755-1824)
violin concerto no 22
recorded on 26 march 1961 in the town hall
philadelphia   lp: columbia ML 5677/MS 6277/
orchestra   Y 35225/BRG 72009/SBRG 72009
stern

ANTONIO VIVALDI (1678-1741)
le 4 stagioni
recorded on 1 may 1960 in the town hall
philadelphia lp: columbia ML 5595/MS 6195/
orchestra philips fontana EFL 2522/
brusilow 697 208EL

concerto for 2 violins op 3 no 8
recorded on 24 december 1955 in the town hall
philadelphia 45: philips 409 020AE
orchestra lp: columbia ML 5087/M4 42003/
oistrakh, stern MG 33328/philips ABL 3138/
A01239L/G05650R/melodiya
M10 46429-46430/eterna 825 612
cd: MHK 42003/SM3K 45952/
SM2K 66472

4 concerti for 2 violins
recorded on 31 december 1959 in the town hall
philadelphia lp: columbia ML 5604/MS 6204/
orchestra BRG 72082/SBRG 72082/
oistrakh, stern philips fontana CFL 1070/SCFL 136/
699 061CL/876 008CY/supraphon
SUA 10932/SUAST 10932
cd: SM2K 66472/SX11K 67193
2 concerti only
45: philips 494 100AE

RICHARD WAGNER (1813-1883)
der fliegende holländer, overture
recorded on 4 february 1970 in the academy of music
philadelphia lp: victor ARL1 2528
orchestra

dawn and rhine journey/götterdämmerung
recorded on 15 march 1971 in the academy of music
philadelphia lp: victor LSC 3264/LSB 4062
orchestra cd: 74321 178932

wagner/**siegfried's funeral march/götterdämmerung**
recorded on 23 november 1952 in the town hall
philadelphia   lp: columbia ML 4742
orchestra

recorded on 15 march 1971 in the academy of music
philadelphia   lp: victor LSC 3264/LSB 4062
orchestra

brünnhilde's immolation/götterdämmerung
recorded on 17 october 1937 in the academy of music
philadelphia   lp: victor VIC 1517/PVM1 9068/
orchestra   AG26 41399/ed smith
flagstad   records EJS 432
                       cd: preiser 89141
                       unpublished victor 78rpm recording

recorded on 23 november 1952 in the town hall
philadelphia   lp: columbia ML 4742
orchestra
harshaw

brünnhilde's immolation, orchestral version
recorded on 16 march 1971 in the academy of music
philadelphia   lp: victor LSC 3264/LSB 4062
orchestra

lohengrin, act 3 prelude
recorded on 1 march 1953 in the town hall
philadelphia   lp: columbia ML 4865/
orchestra   philips GBL 5625

recorded on 30 december 1959 in the town hall
philadelphia   lp: columbia ML 5842/MS 6442/
orchestra   MS 6624/MS 6701/MS 7511/
                       M2X 786/MG 30300

recorded on 25 april 1972 in the academy of music
philadelphia   lp: victor
orchestra

wagner/**mein lieber schwan/lohengrin**
recorded on 17 april 1938 in the academy of music
philadelphia   78: victor M 516/hmv DA 1664
orchestra   cd: GD 87914/testament
melchior   SBT 1005
                           also published by danacord

euch lüften die mein klagen/lohengrin
recorded on 17 october 1937 in the academy of music
philadelphia   78: victor 1901/hmv DA 1623
orchestra   lp: victor LM 20144/VIC 1517/
flagstad   CAL 462/PVM1 9068/AG26 41399/
                           preiser LV 1372/top classic TC 9046
                           cd: GD 87915/nimbus NI 7847/
                           pickwick GLRS 105/simax PSC 1821/
                           preiser 89141

bridal chorus/lohengrin
recorded on 9-10 june 1967 in the salt lake tabernacle
philadelphia   lp: columbia MS 6701/MG 30300
orchestra
mormon tabernacle
choir

das süsse lied verhallt/lohengrin
recorded on 26 august 1948 at a concert in the hollywood bowl
los angeles   lp: voce VOCE 94
philharmonic
traubel, melchior

in fernem land/lohengrin
recorded on 30 april 1939 in the academy of music
philadelphia   78: victor M 749/M 979/hmv
orchestra   DB 3936/australian hmv ED 232
melchior   cd: GD 87914
                           also published by danacord
recorded on 26 august 1948 at a concert in the hollywood bowl
los angeles   lp: voce VOCE 94
philharmonic
melchior

die meistersinger von nürnberg, overture
recorded on 30 december 1959 in the town hall
philadelphia   lp: columbia ML 5842/MS 6442/
orchestra   MG 30300
recorded on 8 february 1973 in the academy of music
philadelphia   lp: victor ARL1 1868
orchestra   cd: VD 60493/74321 178932/
                           disco archivia 745

wagner/**am stillen herd; morgenlich leuchtend/die meistersinger von nürnberg**
recorded on 30 april 1939 in the academy of music
philadelphia   78: victor M 749/hmv DB 3951
orchestra   *also published by danacord*
melchior

die meistersinger von nürnberg, orchestral suite
comprising act 3 prelude, dance of the apprentices and entry of the masters
recorded on 1 march 1953 in the town hall
philadelphia   lp: columbia ML 4865/
orchestra   philips GBL 5625
recorded on 30 december 1959 in the town hall
philadelphia   lp: columbia ML 5842/MS 6442/
orchestra   MGP 7/MG 30300
recorded on 25 april 1972 in the academy of music
philadelphia   lp: victor ARL1 1868
orchestra   cd: VD 60493

parsifal, prelude and good friday music
recorded on 24 april 1955 in the town hall
philadelphia   lp: columbia ML 5080
orchestra   *recording completed on 23 october 1955*
recorded on 2 april 1970 in the academy of music
philadelphia   lp: victor ARL1 2528
orchestra   *recording completed on 6 may 1970*

amfortas die wunde!/parsifal
recorded on 17 april 1938 in the academy of music
philadelphia   78: victor M 516/M 755/
orchestra   hmv DB 3781
melchior   lp: victor VIC 1455/VL 47217
         cd: musica MM 30285
         also published by danacord

nur eine waffe taugt/parsifal
recorded on 17 april 1938 in the academy of music
philadelphia   78: victor M 516/hmv DB 3664
orchestra   lp: victor VIC 1500/VL 47217
melchior   cd: GD 87914/musica MM 30285
         also published by danacord

wagner/**alberich's curse and entry of the gods, orchestral version/das rheingold**
recorded on 16 march 1971 in the academy of music
philadelphia lp: victor LSC 3264/LSB 4062
orchestra cd: 74321 178932

nothung neidliches schwert!/siegfried
recorded on 17 april 1938 in the academy of music
philadelphia 78: victor 2035/hmv DA 1664
orchestra *also published by danacord*
melchior

forest murmurs/siegfried
recorded on 30 december 1959 in the town hall
philadelphia lp: columbia ML 5842/MS 6442
orchestra cd: SBK 60847
recorded on 16 march 1971 in the academy of music
philadelphia lp: victor LSC 3264/LSB 4062
orchestra cd: 74321 178932

siegfried idyll
recorded on 13 october 1963 in the town hall
philadelphia lp: columbia MS 6701/MG 30300
orchestra

tannhäuser, overture and venusberg music
recorded on 1 march 1953 in the town hall
philadelphia lp: columbia ML 4865/
orchestra philips GBL 5625
recording completed on 1 november 1953
recorded on 7 december 1964 in the town hall
philadelphia lp: columbia ML 5842/MS 6442
orchestra
recorded on 17 may 1973 in the academy of music
philadelphia lp: victor ARL1 1868
orchestra cd: VD 60493
overture only
cd: 74321 178932

dich teure halle/tannhäuser, choral arrangement
recorded on 9-10 june 1967 in the salt lake tabernacle
philadelphia lp: columbia MS 6701
orchestra
mormon tabernacle
choir

wagner/**entry of the guests/tannhäuser**
recorded on 9-10 june 1967 in the salt lake tabernacle
philadelphia lp: columbia MS 6701/MS 6979/
orchestra MG 30300/61292
mormon tabernacle
choir

recorded on 16 june 1972 in the academy of music
philadelphia lp: victor ARL1 1868
orchestra

tristan und isolde, prelude and liebestod
recorded on 17 february 1952 in the town hall
philadelphia lp: columbia ML 4742
orchestra

recorded on 30 december 1959 in the town hall
philadelphia lp: columbia MS 6701/M2L 338/
orchestra M2S 738/MG 30300/71028
  cd: MBK 38914
  liebestod only
  lp: columbia MS 7511

recorded on 16 february 1972 in the academy of music
philadelphia lp: victor ARL1 2528
orchestra cd: GD 89293/VD 60493/
  74321 178932
  liebestod only
  lp: victor LSC 5007

isolde's narration and curse/tristan und isolde
recorded on 26 august 1948 at a concert in the hollywood bowl
los angeles lp: voce VOCE 94
philharmonic cd: eklipse EKRCD 27/EKRCD 56
traubel

liebesnacht/tristan und isolde
recorded on 26 august 1948 at a concert in the hollywood bowl
los angeles lp: voce VOCE 94
philharmonic cd: eklipse EKRCD 27
traubel, melchior

366

wagner/**du bist der lenz/die walküre**
recorded on 17 october 1937 in the avademy of music
philadelphia   78: victor 1901/hmv DA 1623
orchestra   lp: victor LM 20144/CAL 462/VIC 1208/
flagstad   VIC 1517/PVM1 9068/AG26 41399/
                preiser LV 1372/top classic TC 9046/
                emi EX 29 01693
                cd: GD 87915/nimbus NI 7847/
                pearl GEMMCD 9049/simax PSC 1821/
                pickwick GLRS 105/preiser 89141/
                testament SBT 0132

winterstürme wichen dem wonnemond/die walküre
recorded on 17 april 1938 in the academy of music
philadelphia   78: victor 2035/hmv DA 1664
orchestra   lp: hmv CSLP 503
melchior   *also published by danacord*

ride of the valkyries/die walküre
recorded on 1 march 1953 in the town hall
philadelphia   lp: columbia ML 4865/philips
orchestra   GBL 5625/GL 5678

recorded on 13 october 1963 in the town hall
philadelphia   lp: columbia ML 6624/MS 6993/
orchestra   MS 6701/MG 30300

recorded on 15-16 march 1971 in the academy of music
philadelphia   lp: victor LSC 3264/LSB 4062
orchestra   cd: 74321 178932
                recording completed on 8 february 1973

recorded on 27 october 1974 at a concert in the academy of music
philadelphia   lp: victor DPL1 0094
orchestra

wagner/**magic fire music/die walküre**
recorded on 1 march 1953 in the town hall
philadelphia lp: columbia ML 4865/philips
orchestra GBL 5625/GL 5678

recorded on 13 october 1963 in the town hall
philadelphia lp: columbia MS 6701/MG 30300
orchestra

recorded on 16 march 1971 in the academy of music
philadelphia lp; victor LSC 3264/LSB 4062
orchestra

schmerzen; träume/wesendonk-lieder
recorded on 30 april 1939 in the academy of music
philadelphia 78: hmv DB 3936
orchestra *also published by danacord*
melchior

EMIL WALDTEUFEL (1837-1915)
espana, waltz
recorded on 26 june 1953 in the town hall
philadelphia lp: columbia CL 849/philips
orchestra SBR 6205/S06612R

estudianita, waltz
recorded on 26 june 1953 in the town hall
philadelphia lp: columbia CL 849/philips
orchestra SBR 6205/S06612R

recorded on 20 april 1967 in the town hall
philadelphia lp: columbia MS 7032/D3S 789/
orchestra BPG 63254/SBPG 63254

waldteufel/**les patineurs, waltz**
recorded on 26 june 1953 in the town hall
philadelphia orchestra   lp: columbia CL 849/philips SBR 6205/S06612R

recorded on 20 april 1967 in the town hall
phiadelphia orchestra   lp: columbia MS 7032/BPG 63254/SBPG 63254

pluie de diamante, waltz
recorded on 26 june 1953 in the town hall
philadelphia orchestra   lp: columbia CL 849/philips SBR 6205/S06612R

WILLIAM WALTON (1902-1983)
violin concerto
recorded between 1-14 march 1959 in the town hall
philadelphia orchestra
francescatti   lp: columbia ML 5601/MS 6201/ philips ABL 3296/SABL 191
cd: SMK 58931

façade
recorded on 19 february 1961 in the town hall
philadelphia orchestra
zorina   lp: columbia ML 5849/MS 6449/ BRG 72123/SBRG 72123
cd: SBK 62400/SBK 87833

partita for orchestra
recorded in 1972 at a concert in the academy of music
philadelphia orchestra   cd: disco archivia 749

belshazzar's feast
recorded on 16 april 1961 in the broadwood hotel
philadelphia orchestra
rutgers university choir
cassel   lp: columbia ML 6167/MS 6267/ BRG 72025/SBRG 72025/61264
cd: SB2K 89934

SAMUEL AUGUSTUS WARD (1848-1903)
america the beautiful, patriotic song
recorded between 20-22 may 1962 in the salt lake tabernacle
philadelphia orchestra
mormon tabernacle choir
lp: columbia MS 6419
cd: MDK 48295

PETER WARLOCK (1894-1930)
yarmouth fair/norfolk songs
recorded on 12 november 1939 at a ford sunday evening concert in the masonic temple detroit
detroit symphony
thomas
lp: ed smith records EJS 214

CARL MARIA VON WEBER (1786-1826)
adagio and rondo for cello and orchestra
recorded on 5-6 april 1952 in the town hall
philadelphia orchestra
munroe
lp: columbia ML 4629

andante and rondo ungarese for bassoon and orchestra
recorded on 5 april 1962 in the town hall
philadelphia orchestra
garfield
lp: columbia MS 6977
cd: SBK 62652

concertino for clarinet and orchestra
recorded on 5-6 april 1952 in the town hall
philadelphia orchestra
gigliotti
lp: columbia ML 4629

aufforderung zum tanz, arranged by berlioz
recorded on 4 december 1947 in the academy of music
philadelphia orchestra
78: columbia 12750D/english
columbia LX 1247

recorded on 23 december 1957 in the town hall
philadelphia orchestra
lp: columbia ML 5261/ML 5359/ MS 5641/MS 6241

weber/**euryanthe, overture**
recorded on 24 june 1957 at a concert in the funkhaus cologne
sinfonieorchester unpublished radio broadcast
des westdeutschen
rundfunks

recorded on 10 december 1961 in the town hall
philadelphia   lp: columbia MG 31190
orchestra

der freischütz, overture
recorded on 12 january 1946 in the academy of music
philadelphia   78: columbia 12265D
orchestra   lp: columbia ML 2043/philips
         SBL 5234/S04643L

leise leise/der freischütz
recorded on 27 august 1947 at a concert in the hollywood bowl
los angeles   cd: melodram MEL 16215/
philharmonic   andromeda ANDRCD 5133
yeend   *also published on cd by gala*

huntsmens' chorus/der freischütz
recorded on 10 june 1967 in the salt lake tabernacle
philadelphia   lp: columbia MS 7061
orchestra
mormon tabernacle
choir

ozean du ungeheuer/oberon
recorded on 17 october 1937 in the academy of music
philadelphia   78: victor 15224/hmv DB 3440
orchestra   lp: victor LM 6701/LM 20144/
flagstad   LCT 6705/CAL 462/VIC 1208/
         VIC 1517/PVM1 9068/AG26 41399/
         preiser LV 1372/top classic TC 9046
         cd: nimbus NI 7847/simax PSC 1821/
         pickwick GLRS 105/preiser 89141

ANTON VON WEBERN (1883-1945)
3 pieces for orchestra
recorded on 20 april 1967 in the town hall
philadelphia   lp: columbia MS 7041
orchestra   cd: russ oppenheim ROCD 0059

im sommerwind
recorded on 17 february 1963 in the town hall
philadelphia   lp: columbia MS 7041
orchestra   cd: emi 575 1272/russ
     oppenheim ROCD 0059

JAROMIR WEINBERGER (1896-1967)
polka and fugue/schwanda the bagpiper
recorded on 20 january 1934 in minneapolis
minneapolis   78: victor 7958/M 1062/
symphony   hmv DB 2223

recorded on 18 december 1944 in the academy of music
philadelphia   78: columbia 12372D/english
orchestra   columbia LX 1005
     lp: columbia ML 2043

recorded on 24 december 1955 in the town hall
philadelphia   lp: columbia ML 5289
orchestra

recorded on 17 january 1962 in the town hall
philadelphia   lp: columbia MG 31190
orchestra

HENRYK WIENIAWSKI (1835-1880)
violin concerto no 2
recorded on 31 december 1944 at a concert in the nbc studios
new york city
nbc symphony   cd: doremi DHR 7762
morini

recorded on 14 march 1957 in the town hall
philadelphia   lp: columbia ML 5208/Y 35225
orchestra   cd: SMK 66830/SX11K 67193
stern

ERMANNO WOLF-FERRARI (1876-1948)
i gioielli della madonna, act 2 intermezzo
recorded on 8 january 1935 in minneapolis
minneapolis   78: victor 1743/hmv DA 1493
symphony

i gioielli della madonna, act 3 intermezzo
rcorded on 8 january 1935 in minneapolis
minneapolis   78: victor 1742/hmv DA 1492
symphony
recorded on 27 february 1968 in the town hall
philadelphia   lp: columbia 61301
orchestra   cd: SBK 63053

il segreto di susanna, overture
televised on 30 june-1 july 1978 at concerts in the academy of music
philadelphia   dvd video: euroarts 207 2088
orchestra

RICHARD YARDUMIAN (born 1917)
symphony no 1
philadelphia   lp: columbia ML 5862/MS 6462/
orchestra   MS 6859
                           cd: russ oppenheim ROCD 0072

symphony no 2
philadelphia   lp: columbia MS 6859
orchestra   cd: russ oppenheim ROCD 0072
chookasian

violin concerto
recorded on 15 april 1954 in the town hall
philadelphia   lp: columbia ML 4991/ML 5862/
orchestra   MS 6462
brusilow   cd: russ oppenheim ROCD 0072

armenian suite
recorded on 14 march 1954 in the town hall
philadelphia   lp: columbia ML 4991
orchestra

yardumian/**cantus animae et cordis**
recorded on 19 april 1959 in the town hall
philadelphia   lp: columbia ML 5629/MS 6229
orchestra   cd: russ oppenheim ROCD 0093

chorale prelude
recorded on 12 april 1959 in the town hall
philadelphia   lp: columbia ML 5629/MS 6229
orchestra

desolate city
recorded on 15 march 1954 in the town hall
philadelphia   lp: columbia ML 4991
orchestra

passacaglia recitative and fugue for piano and orchestra
recorded on 30 december 1959 in the town hall
philadelphia   lp: columbia ML 5629/MS 6229
orchestra   cd: russ oppenheim ROCD 0093
pennink

psalm 130
recorded on 15 march 1954 in the town hall
philadelphia   lp: columbia ML 4991
orchestra
zulick, temor

EUGENE ZADOR (1894-1977)
hungarian caprice
recorded on 14 january 1935 in minneapolis
minneapolis   78: victor 14031
symphony   cd: biddulph WHL 064-065

ARNOLD ZAMACHSON (1892-1956)
chorale and fugue
recorded on 14 january 1935 in minneapolis
minneapolis   78: victor 8294-8295
symphony   cd: biddulph WHL 064-065

THE GLORIOUS SOUND OF CHRISTMAS
with music by adam, beethoven, gruber, mason, mendelssohn, schubert, wade and walford davies
recorded between 13-24 august 1964 in philharmonic hall new york city
philadelphia orchestra
temple university choir
lp: columbia MS 6369
cd: MK 46369

JOY TO THE WORLD
with music by anderson, bach, handel, gruber, livingston, mason, niles, mendelssohn, tchaikovsky and wade
philadelphia orchestra and chorus
lp: columbia MS 6430
cd: MK 46430

A CONCERT OF BALLADS AND ARIAS WITH JOHN CHARLES THOMAS
recorded on 13 july 1948 at a concert in the hollywood bowl
los angeles philharmonic
thomas
lp: ed smith records EJS 564

MOVIE LOVE SONGS
with music by bernstein, grusin, lai, legrand, lennon and mccartney, mozart, rota, richard strauss, tchaikovsky and wagner
recorded between 12-18 january 1971 in the academy of music
philadelphia orchestra
wild, piano
lp: victor
cd: 09026 609652

YELLOW RIVER CONCERTO
piano concerto based on chinese folk tunes
recorded on 10 october 1973 in the academy of music
philadelphia orchestra
epstein, piano
lp: victor
cd: 09026 892732

recorded in 1974 at a concert in the academy of music
philadelphia orchestra
epstein, piano
cd: disco archivia 744/750

LONDONDERRY AIR; SAILORS' HORNPIPE
recorded on 1 may 1965 in the town hall
philadelphia orchestra
lp: columbia M 30066
cd: 88697 279872

HOW GREAT THE WISDOM AND THE LOVE
recorded on 5 november 1958 in the broadwood hotel
philadelphia orchestra
mormon tabernacle choir
lp: columbia MS 6068/MS 6679/ philips A01439L

WAS IT A DREAM?
recorded on 16 july 1928 in new york
dorsey brothers' concert orchestra
78: okeh 41083/parlophone R 226/ A 2567/harmony 6000-H
cd: biddulph WHL 064-065

RECORDINGS WITH THE MAJOR BOWES CAPITOL THEATRE TRIO
also known as major bowes string trio

indian love call
recorded on 23 august 1927 in new york
                        78: okeh 40930/parlophone R 2542

by the waters of minnetonka
recorded on 23 august 1927 in new york
                        78: okeh 40930/parlophone
                        R 3542/A 2416

the rosary; kiss me again
recorded on 23 august 1927 in new york
                        78: okeh 40963/parlophone
                        R 316/A 2429

ah sweet mystery of life; a kiss in the dark
recorded on 26 january 1928 in new york
                        78: okeh 40999/parlophone
                        R 190/A 2473

from the land of the sky; barcarolle
recorded on 26 january 1929 in new york
                        78: okeh 41156/parlophone R 2542

RECORDINGS WITH THE ORMANDY SALON ORCHESTRA
sometimes also known as eddie gordon band, ed loyd orchestra, edward kennedy orchestra, will perry orchestra and capitol players

southern rhapsody
recorded in 1927 in new york
        78: judson 487
        cd: biddulph WHL 064-065

deep night
recorded on 1 march 1929 in new york
        okeh unpublished

a kiss to remember
recorded on 1 march 1929 in new york
        78: parlophone E 6202

she's funny that way; the song i love
recorded on 1 march 1929 in new york
        78: okeh 41217

go to bed; dance away the night
recorded on 17 september 1929 in new york
        78: okeh 41300/parlophone R 518/
        A 2902/odeon ONY 41300

a little breath of springtime
recorded on 17 september 1929 in new york
        78: okeh 41319/parlophone R 586

the verdict is life
recorded on 21 march 1930 in new york
        78: okeh 41408/parlophone R 675/
        E 5150/E 6331/odeon ONY 36003

i never dreamt you'd fall in love
recorded on 21 march 1930 in new york
        78: okeh 41401/parlophone E 6331/
        odeon ONY 36063

only a rose
recorded on 21 march 1930 in new york
        78: okeh 41401/parlophone R 675/
        odeon ONY 36064/U 126
see also in the composer section under brahms hungarian dance no 2

RECORDINGS AS SOLO VIOLINIST

hymn to the sun; song of the indian guest
recorded between 8-10 november 1923 in new york
axt, piano   78: cameo 465/lincoln 2225/
                              tremont 474
                              cd: biddulph WHL 064-065
recorded on 26 april 1929 in new york
                              78: parlophone A 3213

kiss me again
recorded between 24-26 may 1925 in new york
axt, piano   78: cameo 746
                              cd: biddulph WHL 064-065

in shadowland
recorded between 24-26 may 1925 in new york
axt, piano   78: cameo 746

the prisoner's song; home sweet home
recorded between 7-9 february 1926 in new york
                              78: cameo 889/lincoln 2484

humoresque; souvenir
recorded on 30 august 1928 in new york
goldner, harp   78: okeh 41147/parlophone A 2627
                              these items were re-recorded on
                              2 october 1928

holy holy holy!; rock of ages
recorded on 30 august 1928 in new york
goldner, harp   78: okeh 45282/parlophone A 2616
                              these items were re-recorded on
                              2 october 1928

abide with me; lead kindly light!
Recorded on 30 august 1928 in new york
goldner, harp   78: okeh 45282/parlophone A 2616
for further recordings of ormandy as solo violinist see in composer section under d'ambrosio, drdla, drigo, dvorak and liszt

Discographies by Travis & Emery:

Discographies by John Hunt.

1987: From Adam to Webern: the Recordings of von Karajan.

1991: 3 Italian Conductors and 7 Viennese Sopranos: 10 Discographies: Arturo Toscanini, Guido Cantelli, Carlo Maria Giulini, Elisabeth Schwarzkopf, Irmgard Seefried, Elisabeth Gruemmer, Sena Jurinac, Hilde Gueden, Lisa Della Casa, Rita Streich.

1992: Mid-Century Conductors and More Viennese Singers: 10 Discographies: Karl Boehm, Victor De Sabata, Hans Knappertsbusch, Tullio Serafin, Clemens Krauss, Anton Dermota, Leonie Rysanek, Eberhard Waechter, Maria Reining, Erich Kunz.

1993: More 20th Century Conductors: 7 Discographies: Eugen Jochum, Ferenc Fricsay, Carl Schuricht, Felix Weingartner, Josef Krips, Otto Klemperer, Erich Kleiber.

1994: Giants of the Keyboard: 6 Discographies: Wilhelm Kempff, Walter Gieseking, Edwin Fischer, Clara Haskil, Wilhelm Backhaus, Artur Schnabel.

1994: Six Wagnerian Sopranos: 6 Discographies: Frieda Leider, Kirsten Flagstad, Astrid Varnay, Martha Moedl, Birgit Nilsson, Gwyneth Jones.

1995: Musical Knights: 6 Discographies: Henry Wood, Thomas Beecham, Adrian Boult, John Barbirolli, Reginald Goodall, Malcolm Sargent.

1995: A Notable Quartet: 4 Discographies: Gundula Janowitz, Christa Ludwig, Nicolai Gedda, Dietrich Fischer-Dieskau.

1996: The Post-War German Tradition: 5 Discographies: Rudolf Kempe, Joseph Keilberth, Wolfgang Sawallisch, Rafael Kubelik, Andre Cluytens.

1996: Teachers and Pupils: 7 Discographies: Elisabeth Schwarzkopf, Maria Ivoguen, Maria Cebotari, Meta Seinemeyer, Ljuba Welitsch, Rita Streich, Erna Berger.

1996: Tenors in a Lyric Tradition: 3 Discographies: Peter Anders, Walther Ludwig, Fritz Wunderlich.

1997: The Lyric Baritone: 5 Discographies: Hans Reinmar, Gerhard Hüsch, Josef Metternich, Hermann Uhde, Eberhard Wächter.

1997: Hungarians in Exile: 3 Discographies: Fritz Reiner, Antal Dorati, George Szell.

1997: The Art of the Diva: 3 Discographies: Claudia Muzio, Maria Callas, Magda Olivero.

1997: Metropolitan Sopranos: 4 Discographies: Rosa Ponselle, Eleanor Steber, Zinka Milanov, Leontyne Price.

1997: Back From The Shadows: 4 Discographies: Willem Mengelberg, Dimitri Mitropoulos, Hermann Abendroth, Eduard Van Beinum.

1997: More Musical Knights: 4 Discographies: Hamilton Harty, Charles Mackerras, Simon Rattle, John Pritchard.

1998: Conductors On The Yellow Label: 8 Discographies: Fritz Lehmann, Ferdinand Leitner, Ferenc Fricsay, Eugen Jochum, Leopold Ludwig, Artur Rother, Franz Konwitschny, Igor Markevitch.

1998: More Giants of the Keyboard: 5 Discographies: Claudio Arrau, Gyorgy Cziffra, Vladimir Horowitz, Dinu Lipatti, Artur Rubinstein.

1998: Mezzos and Contraltos: 5 Discographies: Janet Baker, Margarete Klose, Kathleen Ferrier, Giulietta Simionato, Elisabeth Höngen.
1999: The Furtwängler Sound Sixth Edition: Discography and Concert Listing.
1999: The Great Dictators: 3 Discographies: Evgeny Mravinsky, Artur Rodzinski, Sergiu Celibidache.
1999: Sviatoslav Richter: Pianist of the Century: Discography.
2000: Philharmonic Autocrat 1: Discography of: Herbert Von Karajan [Third Edition].
2000: Wiener Philharmoniker 1 - Vienna Philharmonic & Vienna State Opera Orchestras: Disc. Part 1 1905-1954.
2000: Wiener Philharmoniker 2 - Vienna Philharmonic & Vienna State Opera Orchestras: Disc. Part 2 1954-1989.
2001: Gramophone Stalwarts: 3 Separate Discographies: Bruno Walter, Erich Leinsdorf, Georg Solti.
2001: Singers of the Third Reich: 5 Discographies: Helge Roswaenge, Tiana Lemnitz, Franz Völker, Maria Müller, Max Lorenz.
2001: Philharmonic Autocrat 2: Concert Register of Herbert Von Karajan Second Edition.
2002: Sächsische Staatskapelle Dresden: Complete Discography.
2002: Carlo Maria Giulini: Discography and Concert Register.
2002: Pianists For The Connoisseur: 6 Discographies: Arturo Benedetti Michelangeli, Alfred Cortot, Alexis Weissenberg, Clifford Curzon, Solomon, Elly Ney.
2003: Singers on the Yellow Label: 7 Discographies: Maria Stader, Elfriede Trötschel, Annelies Kupper, Wolfgang Windgassen, Ernst Häfliger, Josef Greindl, Kim Borg.
2003: A Gallic Trio: 3 Discographies: Charles Münch, Paul Paray, Pierre Monteux.
2004: Antal Dorati 1906-1988: Discography and Concert Register.
2004: Columbia 33CX Label Discography.
2004: Great Violinists: 3 Discographies: David Oistrakh, Wolfgang Schneiderhan, Arthur Grumiaux.
2006: Leopold Stokowski: Second Edition of the Discography.
2006: Wagner Im Festspielhaus: Discography of the Bayreuth Festival.
2006: Her Master's Voice: Concert Register and Discography of Dame Elisabeth Schwarzkopf [Third Edition].
2007: Hans Knappertsbusch: Kna: Concert Register and Discography of Hans Knappertsbusch, 1888-1965. Second Edition.
2008: Philips Minigroove: Second Extended Version of the European Discography.
2009: American Classics: The Discographies of Leonard Bernstein and Eugene Ormandy.

Discography by Stephen J. Pettitt, edited by John Hunt:
1987: Philharmonia Orchestra: Complete Discography 1945-1987

Available from: Travis & Emery at 17 Cecil Court, London, UK.
(+44) 20 7 240 2129. email on sales@travis-and-emery.com .

© Travis & Emery 2009

Music and Books published by Travis & Emery Music Bookshop:

Anon.: Hymnarium Sarisburense, cum Rubris et Notis Musicus
Agricola, Johann Friedrich from Tosi: Anleitung zur Singkunst. (Faksimile 1757)
Bach, C.P.E.: edited W. Emery: Nekrolog or Obituary Notice of J.S. Bach.
Bateson, Naomi Judith: Alcock of Salisbury
Bathe, William: A Briefe Introduction to the Skill of Song
Bax, Arnold: Symphony #5, Arranged for Piano Four Hands by Walter Emery
Burney, Charles: The Present State of Music in France and Italy
Burney, Charles: The Present State of Music in Germany, The Netherlands …
Burney, Charles: An Account of the Musical Performances … Handel
Burney, Karl: Nachricht von Georg Friedrich Handel's Lebensumstanden.
Burns, Robert (jnr): The Caledonian Musical Museum (1810 volume)
Cobbett, W.W.: Cobbett's Cyclopedic Survey of Chamber Music. (2 vols.)
Corrette, Michel: Le Maitre de Clavecin
Crimp, Bryan: Dear Mr. Rosenthal … Dear Mr. Gaisberg …
Crimp, Bryan: Solo: The Biography of Solomon
D'Indy, Vincent: Beethoven: Biographie Critique
D'Indy, Vincent: Beethoven: A Critical Biography
D'Indy, Vincent: César Franck (in French)
Fischhof, Joseph: Versuch einer Geschichte des Clavierbaues
Frescobaldi, Girolamo: D'Arie Musicali per Cantarsi. Primo Libro & Secondo Libro.
Geminiani, Francesco: The Art of Playing the Violin.
Handel; Purcell; Boyce; Green et al: Calliope or English Harmony: Volume First.
Hawkins, John: A General History of the Science and Practice of Music (5 vols.)
Herbert-Caesari, Edgar: The Science and Sensations of Vocal Tone
Herbert-Caesari, Edgar: Vocal Truth
Hopkins and Rimboult: The Organ. Its History and Construction.
Hunt, John: some 40 discographies – see list of discographies
Isaacs, Lewis: Hänsel and Gretel. A Guide to Humperdinck's Opera.
Isaacs, Lewis: Königskinder (Royal Children) A Guide to Humperdinck's Opera.
Lacassagne, M. l'Abbé Joseph : Traité Général des élémens du Chant.
Lascelles (née Catley), Anne: The Life of Miss Anne Catley.
Mainwaring, John: Memoirs of the Life of the Late George Frederic Handel
Malcolm, Alexander: A Treaty of Music: Speculative, Practical and Historical
Marx, Adolph Bernhard: Die Kunst des Gesanges, Theoretisch-Practisch
May, Florence: The Life of Brahms
Mellers, Wilfrid: Angels of the Night: Popular Female Singers of Our Time
Mellers, Wilfrid: Bach and the Dance of God

Travis & Emery Music Bookshop
17 Cecil Court, London, WC2N 4EZ, United Kingdom.
Tel. (+44) 20 7240 2129

Music and Books published by Travis & Emery Music Bookshop:

Mellers, Wilfrid: Beethoven and the Voice of God
Mellers, Wilfrid: Caliban Reborn - Renewal in Twentieth Century Music
Mellers, Wilfrid: François Couperin and the French Classical Tradition
Mellers, Wilfrid: Harmonious Meeting
Mellers, Wilfrid: Le Jardin Retrouvé, The Music of Frederic Mompou
Mellers, Wilfrid: Music and Society, England and the European Tradition
Mellers, Wilfrid: Music in a New Found Land: ... ... American Music
Mellers, Wilfrid: Romanticism and the Twentieth Century (from 1800)
Mellers, Wilfrid: The Masks of Orpheus: ...... the Story of European Music.
Mellers, Wilfrid: The Sonata Principle (from c. 1750)
Mellers, Wilfrid: Vaughan Williams and the Vision of Albion
Panchianio, Cattuffio: Rutzvanscad Il Giovine.
Pearce, Charles: Sims Reeves, Fifty Years of Music in England.
Pettitt, Stephen: Philharmonia Orchestra: Complete Discography 1945-1987
Playford, John: An Introduction to the Skill of Musick.
Purcell, Henry et al: Harmonia Sacra ... The First Book, (1726)
Purcell, Henry et al: Harmonia Sacra ... Book II (1726)
Quantz, Johann: Versuch einer Anweisung die Flöte traversiere zu spielen.
Rameau, Jean-Philippe: Code de Musique Pratique, ou Methodes.
Rastall, Richard: The Notation of Western Music.
Rimbault, Edward: The Pianoforte, Its Origins, Progress, and Construction.
Rousseau, Jean Jacques: Dictionnaire de Musique
Rubinstein, Anton : Guide to the proper use of the Pianoforte Pedals.
Sainsbury, John S.: Dictionary of Musicians. Vol. 1. (1825). 2 vols.
Simpson, Christopher: A Compendium of Practical Musick in Five Parts
Spohr, Louis: Autobiography
Spohr, Louis: Grand Violin School
Tans'ur, William: A New Musical Grammar; or The Harmonical Spectator
Terry, Charles Sanford: Four-Part Chorals of J.S. Bach. (German & English)
Terry, Charles Sanford: Joh. Seb. Bach, Cantata Texts, Sacred and Secular.
Terry, Charles Sanford: The Origins of the Family of Bach Musicians.
Tosi, Pierfrancesco: Opinioni de' Cantori Antichi, e Moderni
Van der Straeten, Edmund: History of the Violoncello, The Viol da Gamba ...
Van der Straeten, Edmund: History of the Violin, Its Ancestors... (2 vols.)
Walther, J. G.: Musicalisches Lexikon ober Musicalische Bibliothec (1732)

Travis & Emery Music Bookshop
17 Cecil Court, London, WC2N 4EZ, United Kingdom.
Tel. (+44) 20 7240 2129

© Travis & Emery 2009

www.ingramcontent.com/pod-product-compliance
Lightning Source LLC
Chambersburg PA
CBHW052048230426
43671CB00011B/1833